WRITING.COM

Creative Internet Strategies
to Advance Your Writing Career

MOIRA ANDERSON ALLEN

ALLWORTH PRESS
NEW YORK

04   03   02   01   00   5   4   3   2

Published by Allworth Press
An imprint of Allworth Communications
10 East 23rd Street, New York, NY 10010

Cover design by Douglas Design Associates, New York, NY

Page composition/typography by Sharp Des!gns, Lansing, MI

ISBN: 1-58115-029-6

Library of Congress Catalog Card Number: 98-74529

Printed in Canada

Contents

Section Two: Communicating Online

Section Three: Publishing Online

The Future of Information
The Future of Markets
The Future of Electronic Rights
The Future of Communication
The Future of Promotion
The Future of Electronic Books
The Future of Creativity

Resources

Another Book on
the Internet? Why?

Finding a title for this book was not easy, because every possible variation on "Writer's Guide" and "Internet" has already been taken. With so many guides to the Internet, do writers really need another?

Obviously, I believe the answer is yes, or the book you hold in your hand wouldn't exist. So the real question is, "What makes this book different from all the others?"

The difference, I believe, is that while most Internet books aimed at writers talk primarily about the Internet, this book talks about writing. It will not tell you what the Internet is. It will not tell you how to select an ISP or connect to AOL. It will not tell you what search engines are or what a URL is or how to use e-mail. It will not tell you how to create a Web site (in the generic sense); it assumes that you already know all these things and more. It also will not simply present a list of the best Web sites for writers and leave it at that (although the resource appendix lists more than five hundred excellent writing sites).

What this book *will* tell you is how to use all that information—and how to apply it specifically to the business of writing. You know how to use e-mail; this book will tell you how to use it to query editors at home and abroad, how to submit manuscripts, and how to conduct interviews. You know how to find a search engine; this book will explain some of the intricacies of advanced search techniques to help you find the information that you need most for your research (and how to find information that isn't indexed by search engines). You know how to create a Web site; this book will tell you how to design a Web site that specifically addresses your professional goals as a writer (and how to promote that Web site through search engines and other sources).

In short, this book discusses the many ways in which the Internet is changing the business of writing—and how it can make you more effective, more productive, more successful.

I've divided the material in this book into three main sections that parallel the way many writers approach the Internet:

- Section One: **Researching online**—including research strategies and market information, plus a special chapter on electronic rights
- Section Two: **Communicating online**—using e-mail, joining groups, and finding places to learn more about writing
- Section Three: **Publishing online**—building a writer's Web site, promoting your book online, and exploring e-books and e-zines

This book also differs from other writing/Internet guides in the way resources are listed. Most Internet guides list URLs right in the middle of the text, wherever a site is mentioned. This can make it difficult to relocate those URLs when you need them. In this book, sites and URLs are listed either in the resource guide at the end of each chapter or in the master resource appendix at the end of the book. This enables you to easily locate the URLs for the sites you need, without having to comb through an entire chapter to find them.

Obviously, by the time this book is printed, some of those URLs will have disappeared or changed and new sites will have gone online. I welcome information on new sites for future updates to this book—and I also welcome information on how the Internet has changed the way *you* do business as a writer. If you have a story to share or a site to recommend, don't hesitate to contact me at:

Moira Allen
Mountain View, California
mkallen@best.com

RESEARCHING
ONLINE

1

Writing and the Internet: A World of Possibilities

In 1997, I made the decision to become a full-time freelance writer. (Before anyone applauds such daring, let me add that this decision was made with the blessing of a spouse with a full-time income.) My writing efforts in the previous twenty years had produced a host of magazine articles, three books (two still in print), and a stint as a magazine editor. With the exception of the editorship, however, these were the results of writing "when I had time." Could I make a career of writing?

The answer, so far, seems to be "yes." Without access to the Internet, however, I am convinced it would have been "no."

Don't worry—this book isn't about me. My experience, however, seems a reasonable point of departure from which to introduce what this book is about: the myriad ways in which the Internet can enhance, advance, and accelerate *your* writing career. If you're not "connected," this book will give you some excellent reasons to get online. If you're already using the Internet, it will (I hope) give you some new ideas on how to exploit the resources that are literally at your fingertips.

Advantages for the Writer Online

The chapters that follow list specific advantages, resources, and techniques that you can find (or use) via the Internet. Following, however, are five general advantages that apply to almost everything a writer can do online:

The Internet makes it possible to be a successful freelancer no matter where you live.

Our local library is half an hour away and not worth the trip. Its collections are limited, outdated, and definitely not designed with research deadlines in mind. A magazine ordered through interlibrary loan, for example, took four weeks to arrive—from a branch twenty minutes away. In short, if I'd had to rely on the library for background research, answers to quick but bizarre questions, or access to experts, my writing career would have been doomed from the start.

Thanks to the Internet, however, I have access to libraries (and bookstores) from around the world. I have only to ask a question and, within minutes, I usually have dozens of resources at my fingertips. Moreover, many of those resources wouldn't be available to me even if I lived next door to the most sophisticated library in the world. The miracle of the information age isn't so much access as the amazing willingness of thousands of individuals and organizations to make their information available to the world for absolutely nothing.

Universities have dumped thousands of materials online, including a host of primary documents such as journals, diaries, historical documents, original texts, and more. Want to find a list of the British crews that sailed against the Spanish Armada? It's online. Need the text of a recent state or federal bill, plus the arguments and testimonies for and against it? It's online. Care to learn how to speak Klingon? That's online too.

The Internet also provides access to experts around the world. There's no such thing as "living in a backwater" anymore; the same search that brings me information can also bring me the names and e-mail addresses of the authors or sponsors of that information. Another search can fill me in on the background of potential interviewees. A simple e-mail can set up an interview with just about anyone, anywhere in the world—and to save my phone bill, I may even be able to conduct some or all of the interview by e-mail as well.

No matter where I live, I can be in instant contact with the editor of any of thousands of publications—print or electronic. Often, I can do business with that editor without ever licking a stamp. It doesn't matter whether the editor is in the same country as I am; no matter where I travel, my writing business no longer depends on stamps and post office lines. It's even possible to conduct my business banking electronically, if necessary.

The Internet saves writers money.

One of the first things I always did with a new *Writer's Market* was to comb the pages for new magazines and send for sample copies. Lately, however, those copies have been running around $5 apiece—a hefty sum if you're ordering a dozen or more. The price seems even heftier when many of those magazines turn out to be inappropriate markets.

The Internet offers another, much less expensive option: the opportunity to check out a magazine online. Many magazines post samples of current articles and extensive archives of back issues. While browsing online isn't the same as flipping through the real thing (you don't get the ads, the illustrations, the layout, or the "feel" of the magazine), you can often determine what type of material the magazine accepts and whether a sample is worth ordering. Similarly, more and more magazines are now posting their guidelines online, saving writers the cost of an SASE and the endless wait for those guidelines to arrive.

Editors are becoming increasingly willing to accept queries and assigned manuscripts by e-mail, which translates into significant savings on postage, envelopes, computer disks, and disk mailers. When you start tapping international markets, those savings increase dramatically—and you'll never have to wait in a post office line to buy International Reply Coupons (IRCs). You may, indeed, be able to conduct an entire manuscript sale, from query to payment, without ever leaving your modem.

E-mail can also save a host of telephone charges. When I locate an expert I'd like to interview, I always make initial contact by e-mail. Depending on the subject of the article, I then ask whether the individual would prefer to be interviewed by telephone or by e-mail. Many prefer the latter, as it gives them a chance to compose answers to my questions on their own time, which may result in more information than I would have obtained the traditional way. Recently, a well-known author sent me ten pages of material in response to my questions. Trying to exchange that much information by telephone would have exhausted us both!

The Internet saves time.

Perhaps even more important than the savings in postage and telephone charges are the savings in time. To a writer, time is money, and the Internet can not only save us time, but enable us to use time more efficiently.

Granted, I spend more time online today than I've spent inside a library since I graduated from high school. However, the question is not necessarily how much time one spends, but how productive that time is. Seeking the answer to a question at the library might take hours, days, or weeks; finding that same answer online could take minutes. What's the currency in Ghana?[1] How do you say "glass" in French?[2] How many angels can dance on the head of a pin?[3]

The Internet is the first resource to virtually guarantee a writer the ability to track down information, sources, and experts on almost any imaginable topic within a single day. If you need further information, such as a book on

---

[1] The "cedi" (which is divided into 100 pesewas).

[2] "Vair." Not to be confused with "verre," which is a heraldic term for a type of fur—and a source of some confusion as to the exact nature of Cinderella's slipper.

[3] Answers vary. It is rumored that OSHA regulations now restrict the number to four, however, and require the angels to wear safety helmets and glasses. The pin must also be inspected for structural defects twice a year. (See "Angels Dancing," *www.groupz.net/~david/7-13-98.htm* or "FAQs About Christmas," *www.alharris.com/holidays/faqxmas.htm*.)

the topic, chances are that your online research will not only turn up the reference you need, but give you the chance to order the most obscure of titles for delivery within days.

To translate this into money, simply add up the hours you spend on every aspect of an article—research, interviews, and actual writing—and divide those hours by your fee. Another approach is to consider how many articles can be written in the time it once took you to research a single piece. How many articles could you write in a single month if you knew it would take only a day or two apiece to find the bulk of your background material and track down four or five experts for interviews?

Thanks to e-mail, questions can now be asked and answered at the speed of light. To get clarification from an editor or a source, you no longer have to play "telephone tag," and most editors are far happier communicating with writers by e-mail than in person. More significantly, editors seem to respond far more quickly to e-mail queries than to snail mail. Even when I send a "cold" query to an editor who has never heard of me, I am still more likely to see a response within a week or two, rather than in the standard four to six weeks for a traditional query. This means I spend less time waiting to hear from editors and more time producing articles.

The ability to submit a manuscript by e-mail automatically extends any deadline by at least a week. You can literally send your piece the morning it is due. (Believe me, I know.) This also beats running to the post office or Federal Express office to pay for last-minute express shipping.

E-mail also reduces the time required to negotiate an assignment or contract. For example, both the preliminary stages of proposing this book and the final stages of negotiating the contract took place via e-mail. A publisher can simply e-mail a sample contract and then discuss specific clauses by e-mail until an agreement is reached. Then, the final contract can be delivered by snail mail (or even by fax).

The Internet keeps writers connected.

Writing is often described as a lonely, isolated profession. Now, however, it is only as lonely as you want it to be. A thriving writing community flourishes online, welcoming both the "newbie" and the established professional with open arms (or at least open mailboxes).

I confess, I've never been much of a "joiner." Too many real-time writing groups seem to contain a high percentage of "wannabe" writers and a correspondingly low percentage of people who actually write. On the Internet, however, one is no longer limited to the pool of writers available in one's local community. Geography is immaterial; groups form on the basis of shared interests and skills. Some groups are open to members of any skill level; others prefer their members to share a comparable level of expertise.

Through an online discussion group, a critique group, and the feedback generated by my Internet articles and columns, I am in touch with writers around the world on a daily basis. In a single week, I might discuss pet loss with a correspondent in Australia, fax an article to a fellow writer in Singapore, and chat about fantasy fiction and religion with another writer in Indonesia. I may share my own expertise one day and learn from a more experienced writer the next. I've also built genuine friendships with writers I've never met—people who can be relied upon to give me honest feedback on my work, and who expect me to do the same. Plus, there's something especially magical about discovering that the author of one of your favorite books is actually a member of your writing group!

Several newsgroups also serve as hangouts for big-name authors and editors. No longer are these people remote, untouchable, or unapproachable. If you want to find out how an editor thinks or what a magazine wants, participate in a newsgroup and find out! It's also possible to learn from an experienced writer or editor in just about any field, through online classes that bring together instructors and students from all over the world.

The Internet brings writers worldwide exposure.

Toward the end of 1998, I had a special thrill: A writers' group in South Africa reprinted (with permission) one of my online articles in their newsletter. At about the same time, an organization in Russia requested a copy of my pet loss brochure, and a week later, I received another such request from a monastery in Switzerland!

When I write for print publications, I rarely hear from my readers. Whenever I publish something online, however, readers respond. Online, readers feel that they can interact with the writer, which turns writing into a dialogue instead of a one-way transaction. This dialogue—whether it starts with a reader asking a question, expressing appreciation, or pointing out grammatical errors—is a wonderful assurance that one's work isn't simply disappearing into the ether.

And those readers include editors. Though online publication rarely brings the big bucks, it does bring a degree of name recognition that can be priceless when it comes to winning assignments in more lucrative publications. I don't recall ever contacting an editor who mentioned seeing my previous work in print, but I've contacted several who remember seeing my articles or columns online. I'm also contacted regularly by editors of small publications (such as writing newsletters) who want to reprint my online articles.

Once, people exchanged calling cards as a way to get to know one another. Now, they exchange URLs. Your Web site can be one of your most valuable introductions into the publishing community. Post your clips online, and let editors and potential interviewees "check you out." You could become world-famous overnight.

Five Myths and a Hit

Numerous rumors and predictions have circulated regarding the "threat" (or threats) the Internet poses for writers: It would replace books and put novelists out of business. It would replace magazines and put the rest of us out of business. Writing, we were warned, would never be able to compete with the seduction of multimedia Web sites. Good writing would never be able to compete in an environment where anyone could publish anything. Our works would be stolen, and copyright would become meaningless.

Let's take a look at what has really happened in each of these areas:

Myth One: The Internet will replace books.

So far, books are still alive and well—they may even find new ways to flourish now that online bookstores can make more obscure, hard-to-find books readily available. Novelists face a number of threats today, but most of these relate to mergers, bookstore buying practices, and miserable contracts—not to the Internet. Nor are print books threatened as yet by the emergence of "e-books" (books published electronically—see chapter 11) or even the development of handheld book readers (such as SoftBooks or RocketBooks).

Myth Two: The Internet will replace magazines and newspapers.

Around 1997, a host of major magazines and newspapers began to jump to the Net. Some even talked of discontinuing their print editions and tailoring online editions to the needs of individual readers. Pundits wondered whether this meant that print journalism was about to go the way of the dinosaur.

Such concerns were premature. Most publications found that it was very difficult to earn a profit online, either through advertising or by selling subscriptions. Consequently, most print publications that maintain an online presence view their site as complementary to their print editions—either as a "mirror" of the print edition, an expansion of that edition, an archive for back issues, or just a "click here to subscribe" site. (The only major magazine to completely abandon its print edition was *Omni*.) Nor are e-zines—publications that exist only online—considered a serious threat to the existence of print periodicals.

Myth Three: "Real" writing will be replaced by multimedia.

One of the lures of the Internet is the ability to produce sites that offer not only words, but graphics, audio clips, animation, even video. It was predicted that users would flock to these high-tech, interactive sites, abandoning those that offered more boring, traditional material. It was the age of the short attention span, we were told; Web surfers are impatient, "clicking" from one experience to the next, unwilling to linger over text or absorb difficult information.

The truth has proven just the opposite. While plenty of hyperclicking Web surfers no doubt exist, today's Internet pundits now tell us that "content is king." In other words, the vast majority of users surf the Internet for information, not for thrills. While many online publications seek hyperlinked texts that enable readers to pick and choose what elements of an article to read (sort of like those "choose your own adventure" books), a great many others are publishing very traditional articles that have a beginning, a middle, and an end. Online publishers of fiction and poetry still seek the same thing that print publishers have always sought: quality.

Myth Four: Good writing can't compete on the Internet.

Today, just about anyone can put up a Web site and put just about anything on it. Many writers, or would-be writers, seized this opportunity to post their unpublished (and often unpublishable) stories, poems, novels, and articles online, no doubt expecting an eager audience to beat an electronic path to their pages.

It hasn't happened. Bad writing hasn't glutted the market, because the market for writing hasn't changed: Readers want quality material and seek the sites that provide it. The end result is that the Internet has actually created far more opportunities for good writers than formerly existed in print.

Myth Five: Any work put online will be stolen.

Piracy has been of great concern to authors online, but so far that concern has proven ill-founded. Outright theft of material has occurred less frequently than anyone anticipated. One reason may be that such theft is so easy to discover: All you have to do is enter a distinctive phrase from one of your online writings into a search engine to determine whether it appears on another site or under another name. If it does, it is usually fairly easy to track down the owner of the infringing site.

E-mail has proven more of a problem. When stories, excerpts from Web sites and newsletters, and other materials (including excerpts from printed books) are forwarded from one person to another, the accompanying author attribution is frequently lost. It becomes easy for recipients to assume that a piece is either anonymous or public domain and to continue to pass it along without giving credit to the author. While such transmissions are certainly a form of copyright infringement, the jury is still out as to whether e-mail is actually a form of "publication," and therefore damaging to the original author.

. . . And the Hit: You'll lose your rights and copyright.

While copyright still exists (and electronic materials are protected as thoroughly from the moment of creation as print materials), the question of loss of rights is very real. Perhaps the greatest threat the Internet has created for writers is the risk of losing the rights to one's work—even if one submits only to print publications.

This issue applies to every writer, even if you're still tapping out material on a manual Remington in an unlighted attic. You don't have to publish online, post material to a Web site, or even own a modem to be affected. All you have to do is offer your work to a publication that wants to secure the ability to publish that material in some electronic form—online, on a CD-ROM, or perhaps on a Klingon data crystal—at some time, in the present or in the future.

Thanks to the Tasini decision (see chapter 4), many publishers have begun grabbing not only electronic rights to material they purchase, but often all rights as well. Some have begun to claim that electronic rights are automatically included in a transfer of First North American Serial Rights (FNASR). Others are imposing work-for-hire contracts on simple magazine articles. Some do so even if they have no immediate intention of using the material electronically; they argue that it is a "safety precaution," in case they can't locate the writer later for another transfer of rights. In short, the biggest threat of electronic "piracy" comes not from copyists filching material from writers' Web sites, but from the publishers who are writers' only source of revenue. (For more information, see chapter 4.)

The Bottom Line

Writing is a risky business. At times, it can be a scary business. Amazingly, however, the Internet has added very little to the risks and a great deal to the benefits. In the chapters that follow, you'll find a host of opportunities, resources, techniques, and suggestions that will, I hope, help you take *your* writing career to new heights. Happy surfing!

●

RESOURCES

Getting Started: Launch Sites for Writers

Authorlink *www.authorlink.com/*

Links to publishers' guidelines; articles on writing; writers' organizations; and "The Writer's Store," where authors can post material available for sale.

The Eclectic Writer *www.eclectics.com/writing/writing.html*

A number of resources, including many useful articles on various aspects of writing.

Forwriters.com *www.forwriters.com*

Though this site tends to emphasize resources for writers of speculative fiction, it has something for everyone, including an excellent research section.

Inkspot *www.inkspot.com*

Widely regarded as one of the best sites for writers, Inkspot offers links to writing, publishing, marketing, and research information; columns and feature articles; a chat room and bulletin boards; and the free e-mail newsletter *Inklings*. (My monthly "Freelancing 101" column can be found at *www.inkspot.com/columns/moira*).

Preditors and Editors *www.sfwa.org/prededitors/*

Categorized links to a wide range of resources, including agents, publishers, articles, associations, and more.

Pure Fiction *www.purefiction.com/menus/writing.htm*

Among other resources, this site has good lists of editors, publishers, and agents.

Resources for Writers *www.execpc.com/~dboals/write.html*

Browsing this site (part of the History/Social Studies Web Site for K–12 Teachers) is like exploring a used bookstore: You never know what treasures you'll find in the way of fascinating, useful, and unusual links. For research, be sure to check its history and sociology links, which include a range of primary resources, such as journals and original documents.

Tips for Writers *www.tipsforwriters.com/*

My own writing site, offering articles on various aspects of writing and freelancing, plus links, a bookstore, and a special section of resources for fantasy writers.

WriteLinks *www.writelinks.com*

This site offers one of the largest collections of links for writers on the Web. It also hosts critique groups, editing and tutorial services through "The Friendly Pencil," and a free newsletter.

Writers on the Net *www.writers.com*

Classes, workshops, a message forum, fun quizzes, a monthly newsletter, and other resources.

Writer's Toolbox: Internet Resources for Writers *www.geocities.com/Athens/6346/*

Links, chat, and articles.

Writers Write *www.writerswrite.com/*

Links, critique groups, a writing "university," contests, job listings, book promotion services, classifieds, a guidelines directory, and *The Internet Writing Journal*.

Zuzu's Petals Literary Resources *www.zuzu.com*

A particularly useful site if you're looking for lists (such as magazines, newspapers, libraries, associations, etc.). Unfortunately, many lists are text-only (no hotlinks).

Online Publications for Writers

Global Writers' Ink *www.inkspot.com/global/*

A biweekly newsletter from Inkspot offering information on international writing and markets.

Inklings *www.inkspot.com/inklings/*

This free biweekly newsletter is rated one of the best on the Web. It offers articles, "ask the expert" columns, market information, and links to sites of interest to writers.

Inscriptions *come.to/Inscriptions.com*

Also free, Inscriptions is a weekly e-mail newsletter that covers market lists, contests, and job listings for writers, along with excellent articles.

NovelAdvice www.noveladvice.com

A monthly e-zine on fiction writing.

RestStop Writer's Newsletter www.geocities.com/SoHo/Village/2115/index.html

A high-quality e-zine offering author interviews and articles on important trends and issues, such as e-publishing and "book doctoring."

The Write Markets Report www.writersmarkets.com

Listing dozens of markets each month, this newsletter costs $9.95 for a monthly e-mail subscription or $19.95 for the print edition. Check the sample onsite. Also offers a free e-mail publication, *National Writer's Monthly,* with tips and marketing information.

Writer On Line www.novalearn.com/wol/

This monthly e-zine covers many different types of writing, including playwriting, public relations, business writing, and a monthly column on "writing for international markets" by Michael Sedge.

Writing for DOLLARS! www.awoc.com

A monthly newsletter offering tips and markets.

② Conducting Research on the Internet

Research has always been one of a writer's most time-consuming tasks. One could spend hours, days, even weeks tracking down an elusive bit of information or locating an expert to interview on an obscure topic. Today's shrinking library budgets, dwindling collections, and (in many areas) diminishing hours compound the problem.

Enter the Internet—and a solution to many writers' research needs. While the Internet is no substitute for a library in some cases (just as there is often no substitute for a good book), in others, it offers unparalleled access to material that has never before been easily available to writers. Plus, location is no longer an issue: You can conduct the same research whether you live in New York or New Guinea.

On the Internet, no topic is too obscure. You don't have to know much (if anything) about a subject to go online and find enough information to build a coherent query, gather the basic facts and figures to fill in the background of your article, and locate an expert to interview for the substance of the piece. This means you can cover a broader range of topics, pitch to a wider range of markets, and sell more articles.

Virtual Libraries versus Real Libraries

What can you find on the Internet that you can't find in that venerable library building down the street? The differences begin with the way information is organized online and the ease with which you can find material that might not be available at your local library. For example:

- **The Internet offers up-to-the-minute information and research results.** Scholarly papers may appear online as soon as they are published or approved. It could take months for that material to appear in book form in a regular library.
- **The Internet offers older material that traditional libraries can't afford to archive.** Since electrons are inexpensive, it is easy for universities, publications, and other sources to archive huge amounts of older (and positively ancient) material online.
- **The Internet makes it possible to find information without knowing exactly what you're looking for.** While you can search a card catalog by subject, you have to have an author name or catalog number to actually locate the materials themselves. Online, you don't have to know what has been written on a topic, or by whom. Simply type in a keyword, and you'll be taken directly to the information you're looking for. And it won't be checked out by someone else when you find it!
- **The Internet enables you to search on details as well as subjects.** Searching for details in a traditional library involves a "top-down" approach: First you must define the general subject, then the books on that subject that are most likely to contain the details you want. Then, you must search the indexes of those books and hope that your details were considered worthy of indexing by the author. Online, you can start your search at the detail level (e.g., Was Cinderella's slipper made of glass or fur?) and have the answer in minutes.
- **On the Internet, information leads to more information.** Once you've found a site that addresses your topic, it will usually lead you to other sites (and other experts).
- **The Internet puts you in instant contact with authors, experts, and other interview sources.** Most material on the Internet includes a contact address, which gives you a chance to speak directly to the person who provided the information or conducted the study. This makes finding an expert far easier than combing through directories or telephone books.

By far, the most significant advantage of the Internet, however, is its ability to connect you with information that you couldn't possibly find anywhere else—even through interlibrary loan—including:
- **Government documents.** Bills, proposals, legal documents, legislation—and the official arguments and testimonies for and against such legislation—can now be found online, not only for the federal government, but also for most states and a number of towns and counties. Many of these are "mirrored" on other sites. Several universities, for example, maintain extensive collections of legal materials, while institutions like **The Association of Research Libraries** (ARL) post just about every imaginable legal document related to changes in copyright law.
- **Government studies.** Besides posting contemporary legal documents,

many government sites also post the results of studies, projects, and other types of research. **The Library of Congress**, for example, offers more than two thousand oral histories from the 1940s that were gathered by the WPA project. NASA offers a wealth of information and photos on astronomy, space technology, and space exploration.

- **Primary source documents.** Due to the efforts of universities and private individuals, thousands of primary materials are now online—historical journals, diaries, records, letters, texts, and other documents that were formerly nearly impossible to find—because many have never been published or collected in book form. Try **The History/Social Studies Web Site for K–12 Teachers** for links to such materials.

- **Original texts.** Medieval manuscripts, ancient texts, sagas, classics, historical records, and other hard-to-find documents—translated and untranslated—are posted on various sites. Check **The On-line Books Page** for a list of more than seven thousand e-texts on the Web.

- **Current research studies.** Find the latest discoveries and developments in science, medicine, history, astronomy, and any other topic through journal articles, research reports, and conference proceedings. Most of these are posted through university Web sites and professional databases.

- **Clearinghouses and directories.** Several sites have attempted to collect links to all sites on the Web relating to a particular topic—such as **U.C. Riverside's Horus World Wide Web Links to History Resources**. Such clearinghouses are far often more effective than search engines in tracking down information on a specific subject. For more information, see Directories and Clearinghouses.

- **Databases.** Much of the information on the Internet is stored in databases, which cannot be searched by search engines. For more information, see Databases.

- **Journals.** Once, professional, technical, and scholarly journals were available only to subscribers. Now, many post their contents online.

- **Newspapers.** The latest news is available online from a variety of sources, including newsfeeds such as Reuters. Older stories are usually archived in fee-based databases. Smaller papers, however, often provide free access to back issues. You can also access newspapers around the world for an international perspective—including English-language and non-English papers. For a local slant, try one of the hundreds of regional papers online. Start your search for newspapers through an online newsstand such as **NewsDirectory.com** or **Enews**.

- **Magazines.** Looking up an older article from a consumer magazine has become much easier, as hundreds of publications now provide complete archives of back issues online. You can also find archives of semischolarly publications like *Military History Quarterly* and *British Archaeology*.

- **Books.** Thousands of free, classic, and public-domain books are now available as e-texts. **Project Gutenberg** focuses primarily, but not exclusively, on literature and fiction. This is the place to go for the books you remember from childhood, plus hundreds of novels, short stories, and other materials. The On-line Books Page offers links not only to literary e-texts, but to hundreds of scholarly, technical, professional, and historical documents (such as studies, conference proceedings, and public-domain government documents).

- **Private organizations.** Thousands of groups, agencies, organizations, associations, medical institutions, research centers, and benevolent associations that formerly offered free literature by mail now post that information online. This provides the researcher with a wealth of tips, background basics, statistics, and current research news on an incredible range of topics.

- **International governments.** To find out basic facts about any country in the world, just look for that country's Web site. Some focus primarily on tourism. Others offer statistics, historical data, information on currency, weather, and language, and more. International information can also be found through a host of travel and tourism sites.

- **Educational materials.** Instructors, teaching organizations, and many other agencies have provided huge quantities of teaching materials, often consisting of links to informational sites that might be of benefit to instructors or students. These often provide a good starting point for researchers as well.

- **Commercial organizations and businesses.** While some commercial sites are little more than electronic catalogs or storefronts, you can also find useful information from commercial sources. Just be sure to filter fact from hype.

- **Individual experts.** Personal and personal/professional sites are often excellent sources of information. For example, members of the Society for Creative Anachronisms have posted vast quantities of obscure, hard-to-find historical information (such as lists of "historical period" names and genealogies) online. Personal experts also include hobbyists, fans, activists, and authors. Some provide useful information onsite; others develop link sites that will take you to the best sources of information on a particular topic.

Searching for Data

Knowing what is available on the Internet is one thing; actually locating it can be something else. Search engines still offer the primary means of locating material online, but that method is far from ideal. Not all search engines are alike, which means that different engines may produce very different results on the same search.

While there is no single "best" search engine, **AltaVista** and **Infoseek** consistently receive the highest ratings in independent evaluations. AltaVista generally wins on the basis of having the largest index (several million entries), while Infoseek comes in second for being easy to use.

Your criteria for choosing a search engine should include two considerations: number of hits per query and ease of use. For example, if one search engine offers three hundred results on a query and another offers only three, you're ahead even if two hundred of those three hundred results prove worthless. "Ease of use" can mean different things to different people. For example, I prefer Infoseek's ability to progressively refine a search-within-a-search. Other researchers may prefer the ability to use Boolean operators (e.g., AND, NOT, NEAR) to specify all of the search terms at once.

Knowing how different engines work can also help in your quest for the best. The following questions can be helpful when researching search engines:

- **What are the indexing criteria?** Some search engines index a site's META tags, which are chosen by the owner of the site. If no META tags are present, the engine will choose, by default, the first 250 characters of the first page. Other engines ignore META tags and use only the first 250 characters. Some engines rank sites by how close to the top of the page a keyword appears; others rank them by the frequency with which the keyword appears on a page.
- **Does the engine index every word on a page?** Most search engines index every "meaningful" word (excluding common words such as articles and conjunctions, or words like "Web"), up to 1 MB of text.
- **Does the engine offer a directory of "best sites"?** Most search engines offer mini-directories of "preferred sites" on popular subjects. In some cases, these directories can be an excellent place to start your search—far easier than wading through a morass of query results. (Someone else has done that work for you!) However, the criteria used to build a directory may not always match the criteria needed for your research, so it's not wise to rely solely on lists of favorites. If you don't find what you're looking for in the directory, you may still find it through a search query.
- **How does one specify search criteria?** Most search engines employ some form of Boolean operators to enable a researcher to specify multiple words within a query or to exclude unwanted terms. For example, one can usually conduct a search for "Term 1 AND Term 2," or specify that Term 1 should be NEAR Term 2, or exclude unwanted results by specifying "Term 1 NOT Term 2." For example, when looking for information on limericks, it's a good idea to exclude "Ireland," or you'll be bombarded with tour information. Unfortunately, not all engines accept the same operators or use the same words or symbols. Infoseek, for example, uses + and | for "AND." Be sure to check the help pages before launching a complicated search.
- **Can you use wild cards?** If you don't know exactly how a word is spelled, some search engines will allow you to insert wild cards (usually asterisks) in place of the missing letters or sections.

- **What are your options for displaying results?** Most engines allow you to choose between short descriptions (100 characters), longer descriptions (250 characters), or no description at all (just the site title and URL). You may also be able to choose whether the engine displays ten, twenty-five, or fifty results at a time.
- **Can you "group" results?** One of the early frustrations in searching was the redundancy of hits from a site with multiple pages. Now several search engines "group" results from a single site, so that, for example, you don't have to wade through every university course offering on your search topic.
- **Can you search newsgroups?** Many search engines retrieve material archived on a newsgroup's Web site. A better way to search newsgroups, however, is to use a service specifically designed for that type of search, such as **DejaNews** or **Reference.com.**
- **Can you specify advanced search options?** Different search engines offer specific search parameters, such as:
  - **A date or range of dates. HotBot**, for example, enables you to search for material posted in the last week, the last month, or even the last two years. It also allows you to specify a month and/or year of publication. AltaVista enables you to search within a range of dates (e.g., "From 01/Jan/95 to 01/Jan/96"). This enables you to find the most recent information on a topic or to exclude outdated materials.
  - **A specific domain**, enabling you to search for materials posted by a government organization (.gov), a university (.edu), a nonprofit group (.org), etc.
  - **A specific country or region**, either by specifying the country code (e.g., ".ca" for Canada, ".jp" for Japan) or the name of the region (Asia, South America, etc.).
  - **A specific type of file**, such as image files, audio files, video files, VRML, Shockwave, and so forth.
  - **A specific language**, to be included or excluded in your search.
  - **By keyword ranking**, giving one keyword a higher priority than another.

Every search engine handles advanced searching differently and offers different options, so it's important to read the instructions carefully.

Choosing Effective Keywords

Perhaps the greatest challenge in using search engines is choosing the keywords that will bring the best results. The difficulty lies in the fact that search engines use indexes rather than topical guides. Thus, while you could look up "cats" in a library card catalog and find a selection of subject-specific entries, searching on the word "cats" online will give you thousands of irrelevant results. Your goal should be to find a keyword (or set of keywords) inclusive enough to produce a range of useful results, yet exclusive enough to filter out the chaff. The following techniques can help:

- **Choose the term most likely to be used by your preferred source.** If you want veterinary tips on cat care, for example, keep in mind that most animal care professionals will use the word "feline" rather than the word "cat," which means that a search on "feline care" will produce better results. If you're looking for tips from (or for) average cat owners, however, a search on "cat care" may work better.
- **Use specific or unusual terms.** If you want to find information on "cancer in cats," searching for "feline oncology" will pull up veterinary pages and exclude most personal "cat memorial" pages. A search on "feline lymphosarcoma" will narrow the results even further.
- **Consider how your topic might be indexed in a book.** If you bought a book on cat care, topics such as "how to feed a cat" would be listed under such keywords as "nutrition," "diet," etc. Combine those keywords with your primary subject (e.g., "feline nutrition," "feline diet") to refine your search.
- **Think like the author of the site you're seeking.** If you were writing an article on feline nutrition, what words or phrases would you use? How would you title your site? If you'd call your site "Ten Tips on Feline Nutrition" or "How to Feed Your Cat," try running searches on those phrases.
- **Brainstorm variations on keywords and phrases.** Rather than just searching for "feline nutrition," try searching under "diet," "care," "feeding," "food," or any other variation you can imagine. Use phrase and Boolean operators, e.g., "feline nutrition" (in quotes) and "cats AND nutrition" (not in quotes).
- **Use phrases instead of single words.** Searching on words that are likely to be paired, and on complete phrases, can get you to a specific site more quickly. Most search engines consider any word combination placed in quotes to be a phrase.
- **Use multiple keywords, with the appropriate operator.** A search for Cinderella's slipper, for example, will work better if you search for "Cinderella AND slipper AND glass." By specifying AND, you exclude sites that have only one of your chosen keywords. Most search engines assume OR unless otherwise specified.
- **Use NOT to exclude unwanted results.** A search on "limericks," for example, will bring better results if you specify "NOT Ireland."
- **Use the most obvious keywords first.** It's possible to overspecify a search word or phrase and exclude useful results. Often, what you want can be found under the most obvious terms. When I wanted an Anglo-Saxon name for a character, for example, a simple search for "Anglo-Saxon names" brought immediate results.
- **Check the META tags of your results for other keyword options.** If you've located one or two useful sites, check the source code of those sites

for META tags (located at the top of the document). Those tags can give you hints on other keywords that can be used to find related materials.

Searching without Engines

Search engines are wonderful, but there are many things they cannot do. They cannot, for example, retrieve information from directories or databases that require a secondary, onsite search function. Thus, a search engine won't retrieve book titles from an online bookstore database, or terms and phrases from a reference guide or dictionary. They can't locate information embedded within download-only files, such as zip files, Adobe Acrobat documents, and pdf files. Nor do they always provide access to the most recent documents on the Web: Search engines may be as much as two to three months behind in indexing sites, so they may not provide access to materials posted within the past few weeks.

Fortunately, other tools can help you dig further into the Web for information that search engines miss. These include:

Meta-Search Engines

How do you know if your search engine is giving you the best results? That question plagues us all from time to time. One way to find an answer is to run your search query through a meta-search engine, a service that submits your request to several different search engines at once and then compiles the results. To test the results of different search engines, you could run a query through a meta-search engine such as **Dogpile** and specify that it provide the results by engine. That way, you can determine which regular search engine provided the best answers to your query.

Some researchers swear by meta-search engines; others find them less satisfactory. In general, meta-search engines allow you to determine the sources you want searched (i.e., which regular engines), the maximum number of desired results, how the results should be sorted (i.e., by keyword or by search engine), and an upper limit on search time. Some also allow complex searches or the use of Boolean operators, but not all. Most don't provide the option of tailoring a more advanced search. For a more detailed discussion of how such engines work, see **Finding Information on the Internet: Meta-Search Engines** (a U.C. Berkeley tutorial) or **Internet Tools for the Advanced Searcher: Multi-Search Engines Comparison**.

Directories

On the surface, directories like **Yahoo!** look much like search engines: You enter a keyword and get a list of results. Underneath, however, there is a difference: While search engines build indexes automatically, directories are compiled through human selection.

This can be both an advantage and a disadvantage. The advantage is that human selection filters out irrelevant and inappropriate entries that might pop up under a normal search query. When you search Yahoo! for "writing," for example, you won't be flooded with dozens of "read my writing" sites, or lists of writing classes from twenty different universities.

On the other hand, you have no guarantee that this selection process uses the same criteria you would have chosen. You can't be sure that a directory will include every worthwhile site on a topic, or even those sites that you consider worthwhile. It may also include many sites that you'd choose to omit. In addition, many directories rely on sites being submitted to them, so if they aren't informed of a worthwhile site, it won't be included in the directory.

Nevertheless, directories can be an excellent place to start a search. Besides search directories, you can find a number of excellent online directories and subject-specific directories such as **Handilinks**, **My Virtual Reference Desk**, the **Internet Sleuth**, and the **All-in-One Search Page** (which operates as a sort of directory of directories).

Databases

Huge quantities of information—including statistics, records, research results, figures, lists, compilations, and data of every description—can be found through online databases. Databases fall roughly into three categories (with respect to how they are accessed):

- Databases that can be accessed by the public for a fee, such as archives of magazine and newspaper articles
- Databases that can be accessed only by members of a particular profession or association, such as certain medical or technical databases
- Databases that are free to the public

This final category includes dictionaries, encyclopedias, directories (such as telephone and address directories), compilations of articles or texts, reference utilities (such as stock quotes, currency converters, and weather guides), and many other resources. Such databases can often be a quick and easy way to answer a complex question—and they contain a wealth of information for researchers.

The problem is, you can't locate this information through a search engine, as database entries can't be accessed for indexing by search-engine spiders. Start your search for a database, therefore, by visiting one of the many university "reference desk" sites, or check **Direct Search** (its primary list of databases is thirty pages long), Internet Sleuth (a database of databases and directories), My Virtual Reference Desk (a megasite of information, with new resources added each week), or the All-in-One Search Page.

Clearinghouses

While some directories call themselves "clearinghouses," I prefer to use this term for subject-specific sites that offer extensive resource links. **Inkspot**, for example, could be described as a clearinghouse of writing information, while U.C. Riverside's Horus project is a clearinghouse for history-related links.

Clearinghouse sites range from major directories sponsored by university departments to sites handled by private individuals with a passion for a particular topic. They usually offer better sources of links than more generic directories or search engine "recommended sites," because they are compiled by people with a knowledge of and interest in the site's subject. Such sites offer a number of advantages, including:

- **Comprehensive coverage.** A good clearinghouse will usually offer the best and most complete set of links on a subject. You'll find links that search engines miss, and you're also likely to find that further searching keeps bringing you back to the same links listed on the clearinghouse site.
- **Screening.** A good clearinghouse won't offer a link that hasn't been checked for content and accuracy. You can be confident, in most cases, that irrelevant, inaccurate, or inappropriate sites have been excluded.
- **Timeliness.** Clearinghouses offer links to resources too recent to be indexed by search engines. Good clearinghouses also check old links regularly, removing dead links and updating those that have moved.

Not all clearinghouses are perfect, of course. Many offer only limited collections of links, don't seek out new resources, and never clean outdated URLs from their files. Once you find a good site, however, you'll find that it takes you places that even the best search engine might have missed. Therefore, when you hit a clearinghouse, it's usually wise to explore that site's resources before going back to your regular search.

Evaluating Information

Once you find a site, how do you know if it's any good? After all, anyone with a modem can post absolutely anything online, with no regard for accuracy—so do you dare trust the material you find on the Web?

This argument has been raised by a number of naysayers, as if the accuracy standards (or pitfalls) on the Internet were somehow different from those in traditional media. In reality, it is possible to find inaccurate, misleading, biased, and just plain false information anywhere—online or off. The same criteria for judging material, testing claims, and weighing opinions apply to the Internet as to any other medium. Before accepting anything online at face value, ask the following questions:

- **Who is the author?** What are the author's credentials? Are any credentials listed on the site? Does the author provide a name and a contact address, or is the information posted anonymously or under a pseudonym?
- **Who is the host?** Is the material posted on a reliable site? Does it come from a university? (The ".edu" domain is not a complete guarantee of accuracy. Remember that students and student organizations can also use this domain to post material that has not been screened by a depart-

ment.) Does it come from a reliable organization, agency, association, or institution? Don't summarily dismiss material that comes from a private source, however. Many highly qualified experts and quite a few dedicated amateurs post excellent material on personal Web sites.

- **How current is the information?** Does it have a copyright date or an indication of when it was posted or updated? Some sites don't offer any update information, but even worse are sites that were "last updated on December 3, 1993"—a clear indication that the author hasn't revisited this information in quite some time! (In Netscape Communicator, you can choose "Page Info" in the View menu to find out more about a specific page or URL, including when it was placed online.)
- **What is the purpose of the information?** Can you determine why the author (or compiler) of the information has posted this material online? Is it to educate or inform, or to promote a particular agenda or viewpoint?
- **How objective is the information?** Does it present all sides of a controversial argument, or does it take a particular position? Does it seem balanced or biased? Does it seem rational or designed to push emotional buttons? Does it "shout" at the reader through excess use of boldface, italics, caps, or exclamation points?
- **How detailed and/or comprehensive is the information?** Does it provide concrete, specific facts and figures, or vague comments and opinions?
- **Is the material designed to sell or promote a product?** Many sites appear to be informational at first glance—until you get to the bottom of the page and find out that all the warnings or advice are leading to a pitch for a commercial product.
- **Does the material match or contradict other information on the same topic?** If the information seems significantly out of line with other material, is the author simply taking a controversial stand or out on a limb?
- **Does the site offer links to other resources?** A biased informant may not offer links to other sites that enable you to check out counterarguments. If links are provided, are they balanced or do they lead to only one side of the story? How current are the links? If the majority of a site's links are outdated, this is an indication that the author isn't maintaining the site and/or isn't keeping up to date with new developments.
- **Do you have to pay for the information?** Some sites appear to offer free advice—but these "tips" turn out to be promos for reports or articles that you must pay to read.

Above all, use your common sense. Information that appears in the most reputable of domains may not be free from bias or inaccuracies; conversely, information located on an intensely personal Web site may prove highly valuable. Where lists of criteria fail, good judgment can prevail.

Pulling It All Together

Once you've found what you're looking for, what do you do with it? Here are some tips on managing the information you locate online.

Bookmark useful sites.

Add a bookmark to any site you're using for a current project, that you expect to visit in the future, or that you want to be able to return to easily after exploring other links. Don't rely on your "Back" button to take you back to a useful site; it's too easy to lose that type of navigational information. If, for example, you use the "Go" function to jump back several sites, you may lose subsequent site information—and you'll lose all your navigation information if your browser crashes.

Organize, file, and purge your bookmarks periodically. Rename bookmarks that don't describe their destination. Bookmarks pick up the name that the site owner has given to the site. If no name is given, you'll get the first characters of the site by default, and these may not be useful in helping you re-locate important sites. File bookmarks by project or category, and update them if the URLs change.

Print important material.

Forget the myth of the paperless office. The Internet is an unreliable, ephemeral medium: A site may be here today, gone tomorrow. Don't count on being able to go back a month later, or even a day later, to do more research on an important site. Get what you need now.

Include the page location on your printouts.

You'll find this option under "Page Setup" on most browsers. Some also offer the option of printing the date the site was accessed, which can also be important when referencing a site. By printing out the page location, you'll always be able to relocate a site even if you haven't bookmarked it, and you'll be able to reference it properly.

If you lose a site, or can't find a site as listed, try truncating the URL to relocate it.

Sometimes site owners move pages within a site, and sometimes a link may be misprinted. If you can't find your destination page, peel back the URL section by section (starting at the end and moving back toward the domain name), until you reach a home page or index that can redirect you to the page's new location. You'll be amazed at how often this works.

Note e-mail contacts for possible interview follow-ups.

If you find a good source of material online, the author of that material might be the perfect interview candidate for your article. E-mail makes it easy to ask authors if they would be willing to be interviewed—and in some cases you may even be able to conduct that interview via e-mail as well (see chapter 5).

Know when to quit.

When conducting research online, you may find the lure of "just one more site" hard to resist. It's tempting to check just one more link, visit one more database, do one more variation on your search. How do you know when enough is enough? Some possible stopping points include:

- When you've scanned twenty or thirty search results without finding a useful site; this indicates that you should redefine your keyword search—or conclude that the information may not be available
- When you've found the answer to your question, and further research is unnecessary, even though it might be interesting
- When information becomes redundant—every page you find tells you the same thing
- When links start taking you back to sites you've already visited
- When you find less than one good hit per ten search results
- When you reach an arbitrary limit on search results (e.g., "I will screen no more than one hundred hits")
- When your printer runs out of paper—or when your browser crashes and you don't care

Research online can be addictive. It can also be seductive: It feels like working, but you may find that you're spending more time looking for information (including information that you don't really need) than actually writing. Sometimes, knowing how to stop researching can be more important than knowing how to start.

Citing Electronic References

by Moira Allen

The ability to conduct research online has brought a corresponding confusion about how to cite that research. A number of conflicting instructions have been offered as to how to cite online resources. While there may be no single right way to handle this task, the following tips should help.

Citing Online References in Text

The increasingly accepted method for citing online references in text is to place the URL within angle brackets to distinguish its contents from the surrounding text and punctuation.

Example:

> You can find more useful tips on writing and selling your work in the "Tips for Writers" Web site, hosted by Moira Allen, at <http://www .tipsforwriters.com/index.shtml>.

Use the following guidelines for splitting a URL:
- Always break the URL after the starting protocol.
- Break URLs before punctuation rather than after.

Examples:

> <http://
> www.tipsforwriters.com/index.shtml>
> <http://www
> .tipsforwriters.com /index.shtml>
> <http://www.tipsforwriters.com
> /index.shtml>

- If you must break a URL in the middle of the word, break the word where it would normally be hyphenated, but do not insert a hyphen!

Example:

> <http://www.tipsfor
> writers.com/index.shtml>

Citing a Web Site in a Bibliography or Reference Section

The general rule is to approximate a print citation as closely as possible by including the following information in the order listed. (When information is unavailable, such as the author's name, move to the next item on the list.)
- Author's name if available (last name, first name, middle initial), e.g., Allen, Moira K.
- Name of authoring organization if material does not have an individual author, e.g., Onelook Dictionaries, Inkspot
- Title of document (in quotes), e.g., "How to Cite Internet Resources"
- "In" or "lkd" ("linked") information if document is part of a larger site, with the title of the primary site underlined or italicized, e.g., in *Inkspot*, lkd. *Tips for Writers*
- Address (URL) (in angle brackets), e.g., <http://www.inkspot.com>
- Date of document (such as copyright date, "last updated," or counter date)
- Date document was accessed (in parentheses), e.g., (accessed 5/15/98)

Examples:

Allen, Moira, "FAQs on E-Publishing," in *Inkspot,* <http://www
.inkspot.com/epublish/>, May 1999 (accessed 5/15/99).
Inkspot, "Resources for Young Writers," <http://www.inkspot.com/young/
> (accessed 10/15/98)

Citing E-mail

- Author's name (last, first, middle initial)
- E-mail address (in angle brackets), e.g., <Moira.Allen@inkspot.com>
- Subject line of e-mail (in quotes), e.g., "Re: Citing URLs"
- Date of e-mail
- Nature of e-mail, e.g., personal, business
- Date e-mail was received (in parentheses), e.g., (Received 5/15/98.)

Examples:

Allen, Moira. <Moira.Allen@inkspot.com> "RE: Your question on citations."
15 May 1998. Personal e-mail. (Received 5/16/98.)
Allen, Moira. <Moira.Allen@inkspot.com> "Updated e-mail regulations."
15 May 1998. Office communication. (Received 5/15/98.)

Citing Listserv and Newsgroup Messages

- Author's name if available
- Author's e-mail address (in angle brackets), e.g., <Moira.Allen@olywa.net>
- Subject line of e-mail or posting
- Date of e-mail or posting
- Name and e-mail address of listserv, address of newsgroup, and/or Internet archive address of listserv or newsgroup. Each of these items should be in angle brackets.
- Date you received or viewed message (in parentheses)

Examples:

Allen, Moira. <Moira.Allen@inkspot.com> "On Internet Citations." May
15, 1998. Rec.arts.sf.Imadethisup: <madeup@somewhere.com> (Received
5/28/98.)
Allen, Moira. <Moira.Allen@inkspot.com> "Market News." May 15, 1998.
Writer's e-mail List: <e-mail.list@somewhere.com> or <http://www
.somewhere.com/e-mail list/archives.html> (Accessed 5/28/98.)

For Further Reference

- **Citing Internet Sources** *www.tui.edu/Research/Resources/ResearchHelp/ Cites.html*
- **Citing Internet Sources** (links to education resources on the Web) *www.umass.edu/education/links/cite.html*
- **Evaluating and Citing Internet Sources** *www.albion.edu/fac/libr/ citing.htm*
- **How Students Should Reference Online Sources in Their Bibliographies** *www.classroom.com/resource/citingnetresources.asp*

RESOURCES

Search Engines

AltaVista *www.altavista.com, altavista.digital.com*
Excite *www.excite.com*
HotBot *www.hotbot.com*
InfoSeek *www.infoseek.com*
Looksmart *www.looksmart.com*
Lycos *www.lycos.com*
SearchUK *www.searchuk.com*
    Produces best results for British sites and topics.
WebCrawler *www.webcrawler.com*
Yahoo! *www.yahoo.com*

Meta-Search Engines

Dogpile *www.dogpile.com*
Easysearcher *www.easysearcher.com*
HuskySearch *huskysearch.cs.washington.edu*
Inference Find *www.infind.com/infind*
MetaCrawler *www.metacrawler.com*
Metafind *www.metafind.com*
OneSeek *www.oneseek.com*
SavvySearch *savvy.cs.colostate.edu*

Other Search Tools

All-in-One Search Page *www.allonesearch.com*
    Enables direct keyword searches of hundreds of sites and databases.
Easysearcher *www.easysearcher.com*
    Links to more than three hundred search engines and tools.
Reference.COM *www.reference.com*
    Enables you to submit a search query by e-mail and receive e-mailed results.
Search.com *www.search.com*
    A wide selection of directories, databases, and subject-specific search tools and engines that provide access information not retrievable by regular search engines.
Web Search Tools *www.moorhead.msus.edu/~gunarat/ijr/tools.html*
    A listing of search engines, databases, and other search and research tools.

Directories and Databases

Calculators On-Line Center *www-sci.lib.uci.edu/HSG/RefCalculators.html*
    Calculators on just about every imaginable subject. Besides the basics of numbers and slide rules, this site also offers calculators on such topics as "galaxies and black holes" (coordinates and radiation), pets, religious topics (calculate the date of Easter for any year), sailing, music, navigation, and hundreds of others.
Direct Search *gwis2.circ.gwu.edu/~gprice/direct.htm*
    A huge compendium of directories and databases, including library catalogs, government directories, scientific and medical databases, and research databases in a range of fields. Definitely the place to start searching for database material that can't be retrieved by search engines.
Handilinks *www.handilinks.com*
    Links to a wide range of topics, organized by subject.
History/Social Studies Web Site for K–12 Teachers *www.execpc.com/~dboals/*
    An excellent compendium of links, including many primary sources.
Internet Sleuth *www.isleuth.com*
    Another place to find material that can't be retrieved by search engines and a good "first stop" when looking for topical directories and databases.

Librarians' Index to the Internet *sunsite.berkeley.edu/InternetIndex/*
A directory of topical sites, references, directories and databases. (To find information on how to use search engines, for example, try a search on "searching.")

Library of Congress *www.loc.gov*

LibrarySpot *www.libraryspot.com/*
Links to a wide range of research tools and sites.

Multnomah County Library Electronic Resources *www.multnomah.lib.or.us/lib/ref/quick.html*
An excellent selection of online databases and other reference sites of particular value to writers (such as quotes, authors, associations, statistics, and more).

My Virtual Reference Desk/My Virtual Encyclopedia *www.refdesk.com*
A huge directory of databases, encyclopedias, fact books, databases, and resource sites. Updated regularly; check "new listings" for fascinating sites.

Needle in a CyberStack: The InfoFinder *home.revealed.net/albee/*
Links to a wide range of topics, directories, and research sites.

The On-line Books Page *www.cs.cmu.edu/books.html*
Links to more than 7,000 books and text online.

Search.com *www.search.com*
An index of searchable databases, specialized search engines, and other specialized Web-search tools and indexes.

SunSITE Collection Index *www.sunsite.unc.edu/collection/*
Links to a huge range of directories, databases, resources, information pages, etc. Their list of collections is organized here.

Union Institute Research Engine *www.tui.edu/Research/Research.html*
Reference desk, electronic databases, and research help.

Experts Online

Pitsco's Ask an Expert *www.askanexpert.com*
A source of free advice from experts on a wide range of topics—search the experts' Web sites or submit a query.

ProfNet *www.profnet.com*
"Your direct link to news officers at colleges and universities, corporations, think tanks, national labs, medical centers, nonprofits, and PR agencies." Allows you to send information queries directly to the experts.

Sources and Experts *metalab.unc.edu/slanews/internet/experts.html*
Links to guides, directories, universities, institutions, and other clearinghouses of expert sources.

Searching Newsgroups

The following sites allow you to enter a keyword to search all groups for messages on a particular topic, or to search for newsgroups covering a specified subject area. Results vary from site to site (e.g., a search for newsgroups on "writing" will bring very different responses from each site), so check several sites when looking for a specific type of group or list. (For more information, see chapter 6.)

CataList, the Official Catalog of LISTSERV Lists *www.lsoft.com/lists/listref.html*

DejaNews *www.dejanews.com*

Liszt, The Mailing List Directory *www.liszt.com*

Reference.COM *www.reference.com*

Information on Search Engines and Internet Research

Evaluating Information Found on the Internet *milton.mse.jhu.edu:8001/research/education/net.html*

Evaluating Web Sites *servercc.oakton.edu/~wittman/find/eval.htm*

Finding Information on the Internet: A Tutorial *www.lib.berkeley.edu/TeachingLib/Guides/Internet/Findinfo.html*
A multipart tutorial covering nearly every aspect of Internet research and search techniques (plus loads of links). Topics include "Beyond General WWW Searching" (*/BeyondWeb.html*), "Meta Search

Engines" (/MetaSearch.html), and "Searching the World Wide Web: Strategies, Analyzing Your Topic, Choosing Search Tools" (/Strategies.html).

Finding That Needle in a Haystack: Internet Search Engines www.editors-service.com/articlearchive/search.html

An article by Tim Maloy describing how search engines work and comparing the major engines.

Internet Tools for the Advanced Searcher www.philb.com/adint.htm

An overview of advanced search strategies and tips, plus excellent links. This site also offers comparison tables of the functions, features, and performance of major search engines (/compare.htm) and meta (multi) search engines (/msengine.htm).

The Major Search Engines searchenginewatch.internet.com/facts/major.html

The Search Engine Watch site offers a wealth of information on how search engines work; overviews of search engines, directories, and hybrids; comparison tables of major search engine features; and information on how to design your site for better indexing by search engines (including the use of META tags and other features).

THOR: The Online Resource thorplus.lib.purdue.edu/vlibrary/inet_resources

Links to search engines, search tools, and servers.

Using the Internet for Research www.purefiction.com/pages/res1.htm

A thorough discussion of research techniques and sources.

3

Finding
Markets
Online

Tired of spending money on sample copies of magazines that turn out to be inappropriate markets for your work? Tired of waiting forever for a set of guidelines to arrive by SASE? The Internet provides some wonderful alternatives to traditional methods of searching out new markets—and some equally wonderful opportunities for writers to expand their sales.

You can now explore many traditional markets—such as magazines and newspapers—through nontraditional means, by researching a publication's Web site or locating its guidelines through an online database. The Internet also brings a wealth of formerly hard-to-find, hard-to-reach international markets to your modem. Contacting an editor on the opposite end of the world is now as easy as tapping the "send" button. The Internet also opens doors to a host of new and nontraditional markets: e-zines, e-mail newsletters, online content sites for print publications, Web guides, and online classes.

Even when the markets are new, however, the rule for breaking in remains the same: Study the publication! While terms like "online journalism" and "hypertext writing" may lead one to believe that writing for the Web is somehow different from "traditional" writing, the reality is that online publications feature a wide range of approaches and styles. The only way to determine what will sell is to look at each market individually. Fortunately, the Internet makes that easy. Here's where to start your search:

Print Markets

To find out more about a print magazine or newspaper, or to find new markets that aren't listed in traditional print directories (such as *The Writer's Market*), try these sources:

Electronic Newsstands

Although these are compiled primarily as a means of attracting subscribers, electronic newsstands like **NewsDirectory.com** and **Enews** are gold mines for writers. Search by subject area, and you're guaranteed to find magazines you never heard of before (and probably couldn't find anywhere else). For example, a search under "pets" reveals that Fancy Publications offers nearly thirty pet magazines, rather than just the half-dozen listed in *The Writer's Market*.

You can search a newsstand for a particular title, by subject area, or by country—most newsstands offer links to English-language magazines in other countries. The newsstand will usually give you a direct link to the magazine's Web site and, in some cases, to an e-mail link as well. Often, however, that e-mail link will be to the subscription department. To find the editor's e-mail address, it's usually better to visit the site.

Newsstands also provide links to newspapers throughout the country and English-language papers throughout the world. These may not only turn into new markets for your work, but can also serve as useful sources of information and article ideas. For example, you could scan regional papers for items that could be worked into features for larger publications, such as profiles of interesting people or accounts of unusual events. Some newsstands also provide links to broadcast media.

Publication Web Sites

Rare is the magazine or newspaper today that does not offer some form of online presence. Though some periodical sites are still little more than electronic subscription ads, many offer elaborate mirrors of their print editions. Some sites post articles or excerpts from their current issue; others archive the entire contents of their back issues online. Some larger publications also offer material online that doesn't appear in their print editions at all or expanded coverage of print articles, creating a unique electronic market.

Such Web sites provide a handy, inexpensive way to study the market. While an article archive won't give you the "feel" of the magazine (you won't see most of the illustrations, the advertising, or the quality of the layout and production), you will be able to determine what type of content the publication prefers. Full-length features will give you a chance to study the publication's style, slant, and depth of reporting. If a magazine publishes only a selection of its features online, this offers a hint of what the editor considers the best articles, which in turn can give you an idea of how to catch that editor's attention. And if the publication offers nothing more than an index of back-issue article titles, this will still give you an opportunity to determine whether your topic has recently been covered by the magazine.

Many publications are also including their writers' and photographers' guidelines online. If you don't find an obvious menu option (e.g., "submission guidelines" or "how to write for us"), look under the "contact us" or "for more information" options. These are also good places to search for the e-mail address of a specific editor or to find out which editors handle which departments or types of material.

Guideline Databases

The Internet now offers several general and topical guideline databases. Some link directly to the guidelines on a magazine's Web site; others copy the publication's guidelines to their own site or ask publishers to fill out a detailed form. Guideline databases can usually be searched by subject, magazine title, region, or pay range.

Since such databases aren't constrained by the limitations of a print directory, you'll find much more detailed guidelines online. Some offer three to four pages of tips on what the editor wants (and doesn't want), how to break in, who to contact, and how to prepare and submit a manuscript. However, you're also likely to find just as many obsolete listings and dead links as in a print directory. Though an electronic database should, theoretically, be easier to keep up-to-date, many still have listings of publications that have closed or moved. Of course, if a publication closes, informing an online database that it is no longer in business is probably the least of its concerns!

International Markets

Remember when submitting material to overseas publications meant standing in line at the post office to weigh your package and then trying to figure out how many IRCs (International Reply Coupons) would be needed for return postage? Remember when you had to wait months for a reply, always wondering if your manuscript had even arrived—or if it arrived in one piece? Well, thanks to the Internet, those days are over.

Once, it was nearly impossible to even locate an international market; there was no print directory of such publications.[1] Now, you can find extensive listings of international English-language publications on any of the major electronic newsstands. You can also find newsstands and other sites (such as **EuroWEB**) that are devoted specifically to international publications and that list non-English as well as English periodicals. These sites frequently offer links to international newspapers and broadcast media as well.

---

[1] Fortunately, this has also changed, with the publication of Michael Sedge's *The Writer's and Photographer's Guide to Global Markets*, from Allworth Press (ISBN 1-58115-002-4). This book offers hundreds of addresses, Web sites, and e-mail addresses for English-language publications around the world, along with expert tips on how to pitch to those markets.

Many overseas editors are more than happy to do business with U.S. writers via the Internet. Handling queries and submissions by e-mail is easier for everyone. You can often conduct an entire transaction—from the initial query to depositing your check—without ever leaving your computer. The publication can often deposit your payment electronically, directly from the overseas bank to yours. The fee for such a transaction ranges from $15 to $20, which may be somewhat higher than a currency exchange fee, but this method speeds up the process of payment and ensures that your check doesn't get lost in the mail.

If an international magazine's Web site doesn't offer writing guidelines or indicate whether it accepts e-mail queries, send a polite e-mail to the editor asking whether, as an overseas author, you may submit your query by e-mail. If you don't receive a response, assume the answer is no. If the answer is yes, the publication will often accept the article itself by e-mail as well. Always include the article in the text of your e-mail, even if you send it as an attachment. This ensures that your material reaches the editor in a readable format. If your article includes photos, you'll have to send those by snail mail, but you may be able to submit preliminary samples by scanning your photos and posting them on a Web site or transmitting them as JPEG files. The former approach usually works best, as image files take considerable time to download and many overseas publications pay for connect-time by the minute.

E-mail also provides a quick and easy way to negotiate terms. Many international markets are far less formal about contracts than the United States. Most likely, you'll receive a letter outlining when the material will run, how much you'll be paid, and when. If you don't feel comfortable without a signed contract in hand, ask the editor to fax or snail-mail an agreement for signature. (As yet, electronic signature technologies aren't readily available for writers or editors.) Keep in mind that payment will be made in the currency of the publisher's country; use an online currency converter to find out what you'll be paid in dollars.

Some writers worry about collecting payment if an editor in another country reneges on a contract. While this could certainly prove difficult, it is equally difficult to collect from domestic editors who renege! This, therefore, should not be a deciding factor in approaching new markets.

International publications can be an excellent market for reprints. If you've sold one-time rights or FNASR to your material, you can still offer "First European Rights," "First International Rights," first rights in the language of the publication, and a host of other rights subdivided by regional and other definitions. Some publications pay less for reprints, but others treat them as new material. If you are adept at another language (or know a good translator), this opens up still more markets for your reprints. Do not, however, attempt to run your article through an online translation program—the results may prove humorous, but certainly not saleable!

Book Publishers

While many of the rules for submitting books or book proposals to publishers haven't changed, you can still learn a great deal more about your prospective market online than you could have learned through print directories. Most major book publishers have Web sites that offer detailed information on submission policies, manuscript preparation guidelines, and editorial contacts. Such Web sites usually offer a catalog of recent titles, which can help you determine what types of books the company is looking for or whether they've recently published a book on your topic.

Some publishers also offer free e-mail newsletters that can give you an even better idea of what is in style at a particular house. Subscribing to a publisher's newsletter in your genre can also help keep you up-to-date on the latest publications of other authors in your field, as well as the titles being accepted from newcomers.

A Web site is also the place to find the latest information on house policies and changes. You may find, for example, that a publisher has recently closed its doors to unagented or unsolicited submissions, or that it is no longer accepting a particular type of manuscript.

Some nonfiction publishers are willing to discuss the preliminary stages of a book proposal online. For example, it's sometimes possible to pitch a handful of proposal ideas by e-mail. After determining which topics actually interest the publisher, you can then submit a more detailed proposal by snail mail. This helps ensure that you don't waste time submitting proposals that won't be of interest to the publisher and that your proposal doesn't languish in the slush pile. Be sure, however, that you have the credentials to back up an e-mail pitch, such as a site where an editor can "check you out," before trying to get a publisher's attention in this way.

E-mail can also be used to negotiate a book contract. The publisher simply e-mails a copy of the contract, and then the writer (or agent) can select the clauses that require further negotiation and discuss terms online. Once the contract is finalized, a hardcopy can be mailed for signature.

Electronic Markets

Thousands of electronic publications have appeared on the Internet over the past few years. While the majority still offer no pay, a few high-quality paying markets are emerging. These include e-zines, e-mail newsletters, and the online editions of print publications (or of other media, such as the Discovery Channel). Even those that don't pay much (or at all) can still offer excellent visibility for writers. Such markets likewise include e-zines, e-mail newsletters, and the online editions of print publications or other media.

E-zines

"Electronic magazines" are simply periodicals posted on a Web site and are available on nearly any subject you can imagine (plus a few you probably would never have imagined). An e-zine's editorial content may take one of several forms:

- **Traditional.** Many Web publications still offer traditional, linear material—that is, stories or articles that proceed from beginning to end. Such material is usually presented in a straightforward fashion, on a single page (unless it is exceedingly long), perhaps with graphics, sidebars, or hyperlinks to related materials.
- **Interactive.** An "interactive" text is divided into several stand-alone, hyperlinked sections that enable the reader to "choose a path" through the material. The reader chooses which sections to read and which to ignore. While the text may have an introduction, subsequent sections don't depend on one another or necessarily follow one another in a linear fashion. A hypertext may also offer links to other sources of information outside the e-zine.
- **Multimedia.** A multimedia feature incorporates elements that can't be included in a print publication, such as sound clips, video, or animation. For example, a written interview might include a sound clip of the actual spoken interview; an article on Peruvian music might include a clip of that music. While multimedia has been touted as the future of Internet publishing, it has been slower to catch on than many had expected. Impatient users, or users with slower browsers, don't want to wait for multimedia elements to download. Multimedia elements can also pose challenging copyright issues.

No matter which approach an e-zine uses, solid writing and worthwhile information are still key to breaking in. As with print publications, the more an e-zine pays, the more it insists on quality material.

E-mail Newsletters

Since e-mail newsletters are far less expensive to produce and distribute than their print counterparts, they are proliferating on a wide range of topics. Many private, organizational, and commercial Web sites offer informational news-letters. Most are free, some are offered simply to promote a site or a subject area, and others earn an income from sponsors and classified ads.

E-mail newsletters are a strictly text-only medium. Consequently, they use only traditional, linear articles. Most (but not all) prefer shorter material, seeking articles that do not exceed one thousand words. As well, most don't pay a great deal—rates range from $10 to $50 per article. Some also accept reprints of material that has appeared in print, online, or in another (noncompeting) newsletter.

While you won't get rich writing for e-mail newsletters, you can achieve a high level of visibility, especially if you write for one of the more respected publications. Since such newsletters are often more current than print publications in the same field, they are widely read by the editors of those print publications—who may then recognize your name from the newsletter when you drop by with a query.

Editors may also contact you. E-mail newsletters are distributed worldwide. Don't be surprised if an editor from New Zealand or South Africa contacts you for permission to reprint one of your articles—or even to offer you an assignment.

"Online" Editions

Many newspapers and some magazines host a separate online edition that features articles and other materials that aren't included in the print edition. You may also find online editions of broadcast media, such as the Discovery Channel's Web site. Some online editions provide expanded versions of print articles or supporting materials and links to outside sources. For example, *British Heritage*'s Web site offers temporary links that correspond to feature articles in the print edition, such as a set of links to "Sherlock Holmes" sites to accompany an article on the great detective. The site also offers permanent links that don't change from issue to issue.

Most paying electronic markets request exclusive electronic rights for a specific period of time (e.g., one month, six months, one year). They may also request nonexclusive rights to archive your material online after publication. Once your material is archived, you are usually free to sell or post it elsewhere online. Many electronic markets make no claim to print rights, leaving you free to market the same material to a print publication at any time.

Online Journalism

Not long ago, "nexperts" predicted that the Internet would prove the death of print journalism. Paper was costly, ink stains the hands, and who wants to read a bulky print paper when one could easily surf the headlines online, picking and choosing articles of interest and skipping the rest?

In anticipation of such a future, thousands of newspapers added online editions. Some of these offered little more than electronic "mirrors" of the papers' print editions; others, however, offered expanded versions of print articles that provided more coverage and background information, interactive features, and links to other sources of information.

As with e-zines, no single description can be applied to the wide range of online newspapers. Some offer traditional, linear articles that are no different from articles that appear in print; others provide interactive texts; others offer a multimedia experience. Nevertheless, the phrase "online journalism" has evolved to describe the process of writing for the electronic news media. Doug Millison, host of the **Online Journalist** Web site, defines "online journalism" as follows:

Q. What is online journalism?

The simple answer is, of course, journalism as it is practiced online.

Journalism is any non-fiction or documentary narrative that reports or analyzes facts and events firmly rooted in time (either topical or historical) that are selected and arranged by reporters, writers, and editors to tell a story from a particular point of view. Journalism has traditionally been published in print, presented on film, and broadcast on television and radio. "Online" includes many venues. Most prominent is the World Wide Web, plus commercial online information services like America Online. Simple Internet e-mail also plays a big role. Also important are CD-ROMs (often included with a book) linked to a Web site or other online venue, plus intranets and private dial-up bulletin board systems.

Q. What are the distinguishing characteristics of online journalism as compared to traditional journalism?

- **Online = real time.** Online journalism can be published in real time, updating breaking news and events as they happen. Nothing new here—we've had this ability with telegraph, teletype, radio, and TV. Just as we gather around the TV or radio, so we can gather and attend real-time events online in chat rooms and auditorium facilities.

- **Online = shifted time.** Online journalism also takes advantage of shifted time. Online publications can publish and archive articles for viewing now or later, just as print, film, or broadcast publications can. WWW articles can be infinitely easier to access, of course.

- **Online = multimedia.** Online journalism can include multimedia elements: text and graphics (newspapers and books), plus sound, music, motion video, and animation (broadcast radio, TV, film), plus 3-D (VRML).

- **Online = interactive.** Online journalism is interactive. Hyperlinks represent the primary mechanism for this interactivity on the Web, linking the various elements of a lengthy, complex work, introducing multiple points of view, and adding depth and detail. A work of online journalism can consist of a hyperlinked set of Web pages; these pages can themselves include hyperlinks to other Web sites.

Traditional journalism guides the reader through a linear narrative. The online journalist lets readers become participants, as they click their way through a hyperlinked set of pages. Narrative momentum and a strong editorial voice pull a reader through a linear narrative. With interactivity, the online journalist can predetermine, to a certain extent, the reader/participant's progress through the material, but manifold navigation pathways, branching options, and hyperlinks encourage the reader/participant to continue to explore various narrative threads assembled by the reporter/writer/editor. A Web of interlinked pages is also an ideal mechanism to give reader/participants access to a library of source documents and background information that form the foundation of an extensive journalistic investigation.

Readers/participants can respond instantly to material presented by the online journalist; this response can take several forms. E-mail to the reporter or editor resembles the traditional letter to the editor of print publications, but e-mail letters can be published much sooner online than in print. Online journalists can also take advantage of threaded discussions that let readers respond immediately to an article, and to the comments of other readers, in a bulletin board–style discussion that can be accessed at any time. Readers can become participants in the ongoing cocreation of an editorial environment that evolves from the online journalist's original reporting and the initial article.

Much of the journalism published on the Web and elsewhere online amounts to nothing more than traditional magazine or newspaper articles and graphics, perhaps with some added links to related Web sites. By providing an instant, ubiquitous, cheap distribution medium, the Internet adds tremendous value to such articles. Journalists are still experimenting and discovering how best to take advantage of interactivity and hyperlinking to create distinctive works that take advantage of the benefits of the online medium.[2]

For more information about entering this market, see the sidebar, "Breaking into Online Journalism."

Web Guides and Columns

If you have a passion for a certain subject and would like to share your knowledge with the world while earning a few dollars on the side, a job as a "Web guide" might be perfect for you. The best-known "guide" sites are: **The Mining Co.**, which describes itself as "an online leader of a community of people with common interests and the desire to gain knowledge and share ideas,"[3] and **Suite101**, which calls itself ". . . a Web guide designed to help [visitors] find the best sites on the Web as quickly as possible."[4]

Both sites seek "guides" (also known as hosts or editors) who take responsibility for maintaining a site on a particular subject. You can either select from a site's list of available topics or propose one of your own. A guide is expected to write original material for the site and provide annotated links to "the best sites on the Web" relating to the topic. As The Mining Co. puts it, guides "do all the digging . . . providing the human judgment . . . that you just can't get from a search engine or directory."[5] The workload can be stiff: Mining Co. guides are expected to add new links and features to their sites

---

[2] "Online Journalism FAQ," © 1998 by Doug Millison, from *www.online-journalist.com/faq.html*, last updated November 1997. Reprinted with permission; all rights reserved.

[3] "Be a Guide," *The Mining Co.*, online, <beaguide.miningco.com>, accessed 11/21/98.

[4] "About Suite101.com," online, <www.suite101.com/about.ctm>, copyright 1998, accessed 11/21/98.

[5] *The Mining Co.*, op cit.

each week, while Suite101 editors can choose between writing weekly, bi-weekly, and monthly updates (including five new URLs with each update). Hosts may also be expected to participate with discussions, chats, and forums.

To become a guide, you'll be asked to submit a proposal describing your chosen topic, your expertise, and the type of information you'd provide on your site. If accepted, you'll receive training and site templates (which belong to the host site and cannot be transferred to a personal site). Your host site will also provide editing services and other assistance.

One of the key questions about acting as a guide is that of rights. The Mining Co.'s FAQ page states, rather vaguely, that, "You own the copyrights to all the content and materials created and used by you on the feature and newsletter areas of your Mining Co. site. We own other areas and you give us license to use your copyrighted material on the Internet. We share equally (50/50) in the rights to the commercialization of those sections in other media."[6]

Simply put, this means that you license all electronic rights—or at least all Internet rights—to the host, which precludes you from using that material in any other online venue (such as your personal Web site). It may also mean that any other rights that are actually sold will be treated as subsidiary rights, requiring you to split the proceeds with The Mining Co.

Suite101 demands a similar transfer. A sample of their editorial agreement states, "All original text submitted to Suite101 becomes its exclusive property and the company reserves the right to use the text as it sees fit. . . . We have no objections, though, of the original authors using and printing that same work in their off-line endeavors or personal Web pages."[7]

In exchange, The Mining Co. offers a percentage of revenues to its guides, while Suite101 pays a flat fee based on the number of articles posted to the site: $25 per month for weekly articles, $20 for biweekly, and $15 for a monthly feature.[8]

Opinions on the benefits of such an arrangement are mixed (see the sidebar, "Net Guides: Good for Your Career?"). Such sites can often provide good exposure, especially for a beginning writer or someone who seeks to spotlight her expertise in a particular field. They are certainly not a place to make one's fortune, but can function as a "labor of love."

Only a handful of other sites have adopted the guide model. One is Novalearn's **Writer On Line** (WOL), a Webzine for writers that seeks "Associate Editors" to provide content or recruit contributors. (WOL actually prefers

---

[6] "Answers to Frequently Asked Questions," *The Mining Co.*, online, <www.beaguide .miningco.com/faq.htm>, copyright 1998, accessed 11/21/98.

[7] Mitchell, M. <mamitchell@mindspring.com> "RE: to Moira Allen." 7 April 1998. Personal e-mail.

[8] Curious math: In terms of pay per article, a Suite101 writer is actually paid more for writing less: $15 per month for one monthly feature versus $20 per month for a bimonthly feature ($10 per article) or $25 per month for a weekly feature ($6.25 per article).

its editors to recruit writers rather than to write content themselves.) Editors participate in a profit-sharing plan and may receive a stipend as well. Another site seeking "partners" is **FutureFantastic.net**, which describes itself as "a virtual museum—a museum of the future—filled with artifacts and technologies from humankind's future."[9] FutureFantastic.net also seeks designers and "builders," and divides revenues on a point system based on hits. (At the time of this writing, this particular site had shown no obvious change or development in several months.)

Some Web sites, such as **Inkspot**, follow a more traditional market model for acquiring content: You write an article for the site and are paid a flat fee for its use. Such sites usually request exclusive electronic rights for a specific duration, e.g., one year, after which your material may be removed—or, if it is especially popular, the contract can be renewed.

Distance Education

A final place for writers to turn their talents into cash online is through online classes. Several independent writing sites host or sponsor writing classes and are always on the lookout for experienced writers who can effectively pass their expertise on to others. Though it can be helpful to have some prior teaching experience, this isn't always necessary. What you'll need most are good communication skills and appropriate writing credentials.

Teaching online offers a flexibility you'll never find in a traditional continuing education program. Though some classes include real-time chat sessions, most have no formal schedule. Instructors prepare and deliver lectures, review homework, and discuss questions with students at their own convenience.

Rates for online writing courses depend on the sponsoring site, the reputation of the instructor, and whether the course is part of a degree or accreditation program. Some sites have fixed rates; others allow instructors to set their own fees. **Word Museum**, for example, suggests fees of $40 to $60 per student for a six-week writing course (of which The Word Museum receives 35 percent for providing the host facility).

When you teach an online course, you'll generally be expected to provide the following elements:

- **Course syllabus**. Besides providing the basic title and content of your course (e.g., "Freelancing Basics"), your syllabus should describe what students will learn from the course (e.g., "how to market, outline, query, and develop an article") and what the outcome of the course will be (e.g., "students will complete a marketable feature article by the end of the course"). The syllabus may also list lecture topics, homework assignments, and sources (or URLs) of additional readings.

---

[9] FutureFantastic.net, *www.marketing4technology.com/*

- **Lectures**. Some sites offer a password-restricted Web site where the instructor posts course lectures. In other classes, the instructor e-mails lectures directly to the students, via a central e-mail list. For tips on creating effective lectures, as well as samples of online lectures, see **The World Lecture Hall**.
- **Readings**. The Internet makes reading assignments simple: Just direct students to relevant URLs. You may also want to compile a list of useful URLs that you can recommend to individual students for specific problems, such as grammar sites. Using Web sites for readings also helps avoid the potential copyright problems involved in transmitting "readings" by e-mail.
- **Homework**. Since many writing courses are specifically designed to help students develop or improve their skills, you'll often need to assign (and review) homework assignments. Independent courses usually don't involve grades, but students may expect editorial comments to guide them. Homework assignments may be sent by e-mail or posted on the site's Web page. The assignments themselves are submitted and returned via e-mail.
- **Discussion**. While some courses include real-time chat sessions, most prefer to use e-mail or an online forum for discussion, as this offers more scheduling flexibility. Students post comments and questions to the instructor and to one another online or via e-mail, and the instructor answers on his own schedule. Some courses require students to post or share homework assignments for class critiquing as well.
- **Individual feedback**. In addition to answering discussion questions, you'll also be expected to provide a certain amount of one-on-one guidance to individual students. Students will expect to be able to contact you with questions and will also expect feedback on their homework assignments.

Most of us became writers because of our passion for the written word. Teaching others how to write effectively is a rewarding way to share that passion and to give back some of the lessons and insights we've gathered along the way. It can also bring in a decent paycheck!

To Market, To Market—Today

Markets for writers are in a constant state of change. Editors move, addresses change, publications go out of business—and writers may be none the wiser until their manuscripts come back stamped "undeliverable." Print directories are often months out of date before they even come off the press.

The greatest advantage of conducting market research on the Internet is perhaps its ability to keep writers current with market changes and developments. If your editor leaves your favorite magazine, or a periodical stops accepting e-mail queries, or a book publisher closes its doors to unagented submissions, that information is likely to turn up online within days of the change—which means that you'll be able to find out *before* you waste time and money on an unsuitable submission. You'll also be able to check a publication's guidelines or sample articles when you first conceive of an idea for that publication, rather than having to wait weeks or months for guidelines and a sample copy to show up in your mailbox.

This means, however, that keeping current is more important than ever. Editors will expect their writers to be aware of the latest changes in editorial guidelines, submission policies, or editorial transitions, because those changes *are* posted online for anyone to find. Writers who don't bother to check this information risk appearing unprofessional and out of touch. So even if you still crank out manuscripts on your Underwood portable, be sure to log on before you try to send those same manuscripts to market!

Breaking into Online Journalism:

Some Tips on How to Prepare for a Fast-Changing Field

by J. D. Lasica[10]

A good portion of the e-mail I receive these days is from young people who ask: How do I break into online journalism?

I'm always gladdened by the question, because it suggests that new media have become permanent fixtures in our news and information galaxy. Increasingly, young people see the Internet as a taken-for-granted part of their daily routine—and more relevant to their lives than one-way big media like newspapers and TV.

Net journalism is here to stay. Following are some tips on how to break into the field—and how to last:

- **Bring a passion for Web journalism.** Talent isn't enough. Desire, drive— a willingness to work long hours, often at modest wages, for the sheer love of it—can't be underestimated. The best online journalism sites attract team players with an upbeat attitude and good people skills.
- **Internalize the tenets of journalism.** News judgment is not innate, but is shaped by real-world experience. Work in a newsroom, absorb the daily lessons of interacting with ordinary people, learn the power of words to educate, to uplift—and to cause pain. Learn how to communicate as a writer and reporter.

---

[10] Copyright 1998 by J. D. Lasica. This column first appeared in the November 1997 issue of *The American Journalism Review*. For more information, see *www.well.com/user/jd/*.

- **"Reporting is reporting,"** says Laurie Peterson, former editor-in-chief of Cowles New Media and now supervising producer for iVillage. "Online journalists must have all the skills of those in other media: good interviewing skills, solid research capabilities, tenacity, speed, accuracy, flexibility, a good b.s. detector and crisp and vivid writing."
- **Learn what works on the Web.** Shoveling a forty-five-inch print story onto a Web site and adding links doesn't make it online journalism. How can the story be enhanced through forums, polls, background materials, supporting documents, audio, video, interactive maps and charts, searchable databases, and so on? Develop a sense for how people use the Web for communication, information, and entertainment.
- **"Candidates need to know the difference between an online story and a print story,"** says Robin Palley, an online editor at *Philadelphia Online*. "It's not enough to capture a story in words. You'll need all the skills of a traditional news desk, plus a talent for stepping back and figuring out what other media elements are needed to pull the package together."
- **Show your URLs.** Build your own Web home page. Develop some content and show it to prospective employers. Get an e-mail account. Send your resume by snail mail and e-mail.
- **Get published on the Web.** Write a compelling article and freelance it to a Web publication. Some of them even pay.
- **Learn the tools of the online trade.** Play around with RealAudio, streaming video, QuickTime, Shockwave, Director, along with software applications like Photoshop and Quark XPress. You don't need to learn programming code like Perl or C++ (though it couldn't hurt). Want an inside tip? Bone up on the tools of tomorrow, like Virtual Reality Modeling Language, and apply that 3-D perspective to a real-world news story. That'll blow their socks off.
- **Develop a versatile skill set.** Study HTML and Web design. Learn how to work sound clips. Take a camcorder to a news event and post a twenty-second clip on your site. News media candidates with crossover skills have a decided advantage.
- **Participate in online discussions.** Dive into threads, like Media Rant on HotWired or the Media conference on the WELL. Post messages to Usenet newsgroups, mailing lists, and Web publications' feedback and letter sections.
- **Schmooze.** Network at Internet social gatherings, both online and in person. Develop mentors. Send flattering, but sincere, e-mail to people you admire. Wiggle your way into online newsrooms for an interview, even if there are no openings.
- **Take a chance.** Accept a job that's not your dream job but that can serve as a steppingstone to your ideal. Work as an intern or as a data collector and show initiative by writing stories or reviews.
- **Stay on top of developments.** Read Internet magazines to keep pace

with the fast-changing scene. Subscribe to online mailing lists and free newsletters.

- **Check out job listings online**. CareerPath.com, the Monster Board and America's Job Bank are just a few of dozens of the online resources available to job-seekers.
- **Take the long view**. Start out at a small Webzine, perhaps, and then move on to a better-known outfit like CNet, Wired News, Yahoo! or America Online's Digital Cities. Or start out at a small print publication before moving on to a paper with a new-media department. Remember, CNN Interactive or the nytimes.com aren't going to hire you right out of the chute.

Just a couple of years ago, the road to success in journalism was a predictable, narrow, well-trod path. In today's digital world, the landscape brims with a remarkable variety of career options for would-be journalists.

●

Net Guides: Good for Your Career?

by Marla Hardee Milling[11]

Would you jump at the chance to work as an online contributing editor or net guide? Before you answer, consider that you'll probably be writing for pennies—possibly offset by the potential for good exposure to launch your freelance writing career.

The Mining Co. and **Suite101** are two Web sites that give writers the opportunity to maintain an online presence in a category they feel passionate about. Currently, The Mining Co. has more than six hundred "guides," and Suite101 has more than three hundred contributing editors. The topics run the gamut, from Reptiles to Movie Making to Cigars and Pipes to Baby Boomers.

"At our current growth rate, we should have over five hundred editors before the end of the year," says Suite101 editor-in-chief Jason Pamer. "We're always looking for intelligent experts to join our staff and have no plans to limit our staff to a set number."

"I checked out both companies to write for at one time or another," says Monique Cuvelier. "In short, they left me with a bad taste in my mouth. They don't pay but a pittance. I wonder what kind of service they can really provide with poorly paid writers who seem to be working their tails off supporting them." Writer Dana Nourie had similar feelings, "I considered writing for these companies and decided against it. The low pay was the main reason."

---

[11] Copyright 1998 by Marla Hardee Milling. This article formerly appeared in the October 1998 *The Write Markets Report* (*members.tripod.com/~deepsouth/index-writemkt.html*). For more information, visit Milling's Web site at *www.geocities.com/SoHo/Lofts/3346*.

Suite101 pays $25 a month for weekly articles; $20 a month for biweekly articles; and $15 a month for monthly articles. The Mining Co. pays guides a portion of 30 percent of net ad revenues. The site explains it this way: "If the traffic on a Guide site were 3 percent of the total traffic on The Mining Co. network of sites, the Guide would receive 3 percent of the 30 percent. In addition, 10 percent of The Mining Co.'s net ad revenues are set aside in a bonus pool that is paid out to Guides semi-annually."

Many writers see these sites as a great opportunity to get published on a regular basis. "As a beginning writer that was not published, The Mining Co. has been a wonderful first step for me," says Cynthia Black, the guide for diabetes (*diabetes.miningco.com*). "I think The Mining Co. has great potential and I plan on hanging in there with them.

"I'm really happy with Suite101," says Cleveland freelancer Kelly Ferjutz. "I've been the Classical Music editor (*www.suite101.com/topics/page.cfm/667*) since the end of January. I'll certainly never get rich, but the pay nicely off-sets the cost of the ISP. Best of all is that I get to write about one of my passions—Classical Music."

Jessica Williams says her breastfeeding column at Suite101 (*www.suite101 .com/topics/page.cfm/550*) has led to other sales. "My first sale with *Parenting Magazine* was through a query with attached clips from my column—the only clips I had for breastfeeding at the time. Also, I once called the editor of *Pregnancy Today* to ask if she accepted freelance material. She asked me if I had written for expecting women or new mothers before. I gave her the URL to my Suite101 column. Before I had a chance to send her a query, she e-mailed me. My column landed me a feature article and an assigned baby shower series with her publication."

Former Mining Co. guide June Campbell, who wrote a column on Vancouver, British Columbia, says writers who sign up for these sites must be hobbyists who enjoy doing this work for fun, or for the sake of having it on their resume. "I was consistently told that my site was good and that they were pleased with the quality of my work. After a few months, I received an e-mail saying all local sites that were non-U.S. were being discontinued, as they didn't get enough hits to make it worthwhile. I was offered the opportunity to start all over again in another category. I declined, since I couldn't see any advantage in it for me. I was doing it for whatever money I might make and for the sake of promoting my own talents and my own business. Neither happened."

"While working for The Mining Co. can be a hassle, I believe it's worth the income and the exposure. Mining Co. guides have been written up in trade magazines, in national publications, and even the *New York Times*," says Frances Donovan, the personal insurance guide (*personalinsure.miningco.com/*). "One thing that makes a lot of people nervous is the republication rights. According to my contract, I still own the copyright on all my content, but The Mining Co. holds a perpetual worldwide license on that content in electronic form. In other words, I can't take the stuff I've written for them and put it on another site. Also, a non-compete clause said I wouldn't be able to do similar online content for another publication for six months after quitting The Mining Co. So I could write about gardening for another site, but not insurance."

"The non-compete part of our contract applies *only* to material on the Guide's topic, and *only* on the Internet," says Jacob Levich, Senior Editor at The Mining Co. "Our Guides are free to write books, plays, movie scripts, etc., on the same topic they cover in their Mining Co. sites. They're also free to publish anything they want on the Internet on subjects apart from their Mining Co. interest areas. In addition, they can continue to run their personal Web sites."

If you'd like more information on how to become a Mining Co. guide, go to *beaguide.miningco.com*. For Suite101, go to *www.suite101.com/publish/page.cfm*.

RESOURCES

Print Publications: Lists and Electronic Newsstands

1500+ U.S. Newspapers and Their Links *www.acclaimed.com/helpful/new-add.htm*
Exactly what it says.

AJR NewsLink *ajr.newslink.org/mag.html*
Huge list of links to newspapers around the world, plus a smaller list of popular magazines.

Christian Periodical Publishers *www.colc.com/pubbook/key.htm*
A text list of Christian magazines (no links).

Editor and Publisher Interactive *www.mediainfo.com/ephome/index/unihtm/siteindex.htm*
The site index for *Editor and Publisher* offers links to a variety of magazine and newspaper indexes.

Electronic Newsstand (Enews) *www.enews.com*
Links to thousands of magazines, searchable by title and category.

Media List *www.webcom.com/~leavitt/medialist.html*
Though dated 1995, this is still an excellent list of newspaper sites in the United States (and some international sites), with URLs and e-mail addresses.

NewsDirectory.com *www.newsdirectory.com*
Links to thousands of magazines, searchable by title and category. Also offers links to international media, searchable by title, category, or country.

Newsletter Access Directory *www.newsletteraccess.com/directory.html*
Searchable directory of newsletters (online and off).

Newspapers.com *www.newspapers.com*
Lists and links to U.S. and international newspapers, college newspapers, religious papers, online news services, and more.

Working List of Speculative Fiction Markets *www.bayarea.net/~stef/sf.markets.txt*
Text listing of all major speculative fiction markets (URLs listed but not linked). Probably one of the most comprehensive guides available on the Web.

Guideline Databases

Guide to Online Guidelines *www.snafu.de/~gadfly/*

The Market List *www.marketlist.com*
Covers speculative fiction markets (e.g., science fiction, fantasy, horror).

Markets for Writers: Journals and Magazines Online *www.chebucto.ns.ca/Culture/WFNS/markets.html*
Listing of online markets in a variety of categories.

Writer's Digest *www.writersdigest.com*

Writer's Guidelines *www.writersmarkets.com/index-guidelines.htm*
A listing of paying markets, updated daily, from the publisher of *The Write Markets Report*.

Writer's Guideline Database *mav.net/guidelines/*

The Writer's Place *www.awoc.com/AWOC-Home.cfm*

E-zines and E-mail Newsletters

(For more lists of e-zine directories, see chapter 11.)

John Labovitz's E-Zine List *www.meer.net/~johnl/e-zine-list*
Considered the premiere directory of e-zines and newsletters.

NewJour: New Journals and Newsletters on the Internet *gort.ucsd.edu/newjour/NewJour/*

Newsletters and E-zines *www.copywriter.com/lists/ezines.htm*

Zine & E-Zine Resource Guide *www.zinebook.com/resour1.html*

Writing for Electronic Markets: Information

Contentious *www.contentious.com*
A web-zine for writers, editors, and others who develop content for online media.

Electric Pages: Evolution of Publishing in the Information Age *www.electric-pages.com/artforum/index.htm*
Includes articles and a forum on "writing for interactive media."
Writing for the Web *www.electric-pages.com/articles/wftw1.htm*
Writing for Webzines: Brave New Markets, Same Old Problems *www.nwu.org/aw/97wint/online.htm*

Book Publishers (Lists)

BookWire: Book Publisher Index *www.bookwire.com/index/publishers.html*
In addition to a general listing of book publishers, this site offers both general and genre- or topic-specific listings.
WriteLinks: Commercial Book Publishers *www.writelinks.com/resources/pub/pubsbk.htm*
A comprehensive listing of book publishers in every category, including genre, address, Web site, and e-mail.

International Markets

Canadian Magazine Publisher's Association: Magazine Index *www.cmpa.ca/magindex.html*
Listings of Canadian publications, by title and by subject.
Journalism.Net *www.journalismnet.com/papers.htm*
Lists publications by region.
Magazines in the United Kingdom *www.travelconnections.com/Magazines/Unitedkingdom.htm*
For magazines from other parts of the world, go to *www.travelconnections.com/Magazines/*.
Media and News Resources Around the Globe *www.uct.ac.za/depts/politics/intnew.htm*
Media UK *www.mediauk.com/directory*
Newsdirectory.com: Worldwide Magazines *www.newsdirectory.com/news/magazine/world*

Online Journalism

AJR NewsLink *ajr.newslink.org/news.html*
Journalism Resources *www.moorhead.msus.edu/~gunarat/ijr/journalism.html*
Editor and Publisher Interactive *www.mediainfo.com/emedia/*
Online Journalist *www.online-journalist.com*
Doug Millison's site, which includes a FAQ and an extensive "kiosk" of publications and resources for journalists.
Websites with a Newspaper Connection *MindyMcAdams.com/jaccess*

Web Guides

FutureFantastic.net *www.marketing4technology.com/futurefantastic/*
The Mining Co. *beaguide.miningco.com*
Suite101 *www.suite101.com*

Writing Classes

(For a list of sites that host writing classes, see chapter 7.)

Online Education: Information and Tools

Conferencing Systems *www.hypernews.org/HyperNews/get/www/collab/conferencing.html*
Resources for setting up electronic conferences and meetings.
Diversity University *www.du.org/duSvcs/teachers.htm*
Training for virtual instruction.
Resources for Writing Instructors *www.devry-phx.edu/lrnresrc/dowsc/instres.htm*
Links to a variety of resources on teaching online, including journals on electronic instruction, "computers and composition," and online syllabi.
World Lecture Hall: English, Writing, and Rhetoric *www.utexas.edu/world/lecture/e/*
A listing of online courses (primarily from universities); some post course outlines and lectures. (It takes some hunting.)

4

Electronic
Rights

Ten years ago, it was unusual to see an electronic rights clause in a typical magazine contract. Articles and stories were purchased for print use, and publishers rarely imagined using them in any other medium.

Cyberspace has changed all that. Suddenly, electronic rights have value—though not everyone is certain what that value may be. From a writer's perspective, it seems that many publishers have become desperate to claim those rights, while at the same time denying that such rights have any monetary worth (or that writers ought to be compensated for parting with them).

Electronic Rights and the Tasini Decision

Not surprisingly, the uncertainty surrounding electronic rights has led to a flurry of lawsuits. Perhaps most significant among these was the Tasini case (see the sidebar, "The Tasini Decision"), in which Jonathan Tasini, et al. sued several leading periodical publishers for the "unauthorized" use of electronic rights. The suit was settled against the plaintiffs, but the ultimate outcome might have been the same regardless of the decision: Alarmed by the threat of litigation, many publishers switched immediately to "all rights" contracts, thereby obtaining electronic rights by default. Others now claim that "First North American Serial Rights" (FNASR) "includes" the right to post material on the Internet—despite the fact that the Tasini decision specifically precludes such an interpretation.

One thing is clear: The old language of rights and contracts is no longer adequate to describe electronic transactions. A term such as "First North American Serial Rights," for example, cannot begin to define publication on the Internet, as a Web site is not a "serial," nor can its distribution be confined to the term "North America."

Negotiating a contract today can be a perilous enterprise, as most electronic media are too new to have their own set of standard practices. Writers have a chance to shape those practices, however, by developing and insisting upon terminology that adequately reflects the use of their material and provides appropriate compensation for that use. The first step involves unbundling those rights, so that writers can license some and retain others, rather than losing everything to a catchall electronic rights clause.

Electronic Rights and Your Writing: Some Definitions

Whenever possible, any electronic rights negotiation should include clarifications as to the medium involved, the duration of the use, and the exclusivity of that use:

Medium

"Electronic rights" is currently a catchall term used to define any and all electronic media. In reality, your work might be used in one of several media, including:

- **The Internet.** Many periodicals now offer Web sites that include articles from current or back issues. In most cases, this material is available to consumers at no charge. Consequently, many publishers are unwilling to offer additional compensation for this type of electronic use—and may issue contracts requiring that such rights be transferred along with print rights.

  Other publications exist entirely online, such as e-zines and e-mail newsletters. (With respect to rights, little distinction is made between e-mail newsletters and online publications, especially as most e-mail newsletters also post their content on a Web site.) Online publications also seek electronic rights—though many have no interest in print rights—but the contract terms for those rights can vary widely.

  While many periodicals now demand "Internet" rights, writers should be aware that licensing such rights to one periodical without qualifiers such as "duration" can hinder their ability to sell the same material to another publisher (print or electronic). Many publishers won't accept material that has previously appeared online, even on a personal Web site, or will treat it as a reprint.

- **Databases.** While some periodicals make archived articles available without charge, others compile them into fee-based databases or sell their back-issue material to commercial databases. Such databases often charge hefty fees: a subscription fee, a connection fee while browsing, and a download fee to read or print selected articles.

Despite these fees, however, databases have been reluctant to provide compensation to authors in the way of royalties. The Tasini decision complicated matters by defining certain types of databases as another way of distributing a "collective work" (e.g., a magazine). Controversies have also arisen over commercial databases that have allegedly acquired individual articles from periodicals that did not, in fact, have the right to sell such rights.

- **CD-ROMs.** Several magazines offer collections of back issues on CD-ROM. *Time,* for example, issues annual CD-ROMs in which the articles appear in text format; *National Geographic* has issued a series of CD-ROMs that offer scanned images of every page of every issue. (At the time of this writing, *National Geographic* is also being sued by several photographers who argue that the magazine did not have the right to reproduce their images in this format.) Books and databases are also distributed on CD-ROMs.

  While Web sites and online databases are both accessed via the Internet, a CD-ROM is a tangible publication. It is a physical object, much like a book, magazine, or audio recording, and must be transferred physically from the publisher to the user.

  CD-ROM compilations usually generate direct revenue for a publisher, and a publisher can also track the sales and distribution of a CD-ROM, just like the sale of a book. Consequently, authors argue that material published on a CD-ROM should generate royalties, like material published in a print anthology. Books produced on CD-ROM are usually treated as subsidiary sales, for which the author receives a fifty-fifty revenue split. It has been more difficult to obtain compensation for stories or articles, but at the very least, a writer should look for a flat-fee compensation for such rights.

- **Electronic books online.** Currently, authors who opt to publish their books online can choose from a wide range of agreements, including the option to retain virtually all rights to their work. As electronic books become more accepted, contracts are likely to become more complicated. E-books are often available in many formats, including online files, downloadable files (such as those that can be delivered via FTP or e-mail), disks, CD-ROMs, and most recently, "Rocket Editions" that can be purchased for the RocketBook E-reader. Before signing over "electronic rights" to an e-publisher, be sure you know what formats may be involved—both when you sign and in the future. For more information on e-publishing and electronic rights, see chapter 11.

- **Electronic versions of print books.** Authors who sell their books to commercial print publishers may soon have to address the issue of "electronic books" that are downloaded to a hand reader, such as the **SoftBooks** or **RocketBooks** e-readers. These handheld devices are designed to offer electronic versions of print books. Thus, any book that is issued in print could, conceivably, be issued in an electronic form as well. These and several other e-reader manufacturers have begun negotiations with several major commercial publishers to secure future electronic rights to popular fiction and nonfiction titles.

Don't be surprised, therefore, to see commercial print publishers demanding "all" electronic rights in order to secure this market niche. While some publishers treat electronic editions as a subsidiary right (with a 50/50 split of revenue), others claim that such editions are merely a different form of "distribution" and offer royalties equivalent to print royalties. This, and the issue of print-on-demand books—which could keep your books "in print" indefinitely, regardless of sales—are shaping up as major electronic rights controversies.

Differentiating between different types of electronic media will enable you to license your work to more than one venue, rather than losing all your resale options on a single, nonspecific "electronic rights" clause. For example, you can license a print publisher to post your short story online, license an electronic publisher to include that same story in a fee-based database (such as **Alexandria Digital Literature**), and license yet another to incorporate the story in a "best of" CD-ROM anthology. In addition, specifying which rights are to be licensed will also help you determine whether it is appropriate to seek additional compensation for those rights.

Duration

In print publishing, terms like "first use" were designed to prevent simultaneous publication of the same material in two or more periodicals. A periodical's use expires with the date of issue in which the material appears. This clause has enabled writers to sell material sequentially to several different publishers.

Matters aren't so simple online, however. While publishers still request "first use" (or "first Internet use"), it is no longer clear when that use expires. While your material may appear in a specific issue, it may also end up in an electronic archive of back issues—which, unlike back issues of print publications, remain easily and perpetually available. Consequently, it becomes much harder to ensure that two publishers won't be using the same material at the same time—and publishers who might otherwise purchase material for "second use" may be less inclined to do so when that material is still easily accessible on the Web site of a competitor.

To resolve this issue, the **National Writer's Union** suggests imposing a duration clause on electronic usage: thirty days, sixty days, one year, etc. After the use duration has expired, a publisher should then either renegotiate for an extension, or remove the material from its site. Some publishers have already added a clause that enables an author to request such withdrawal if the author can show that it is necessary for a subsequent sale. Another option is to designate "archival rights" as a separate form of use, again, specifying the duration of those rights or requiring additional compensation if the material is to be archived "indefinitely."

Exclusivity

The issue of simultaneous online publication can be resolved in some cases by adding a nonexclusivity clause (also known as "one-time rights") to your contract. Such a clause makes it possible for more than one publication (electronic or print) to use the same material at the same time.

At present, publishers seem inclined to seek exclusivity in their primary distribution domain. Print publications, for example, may seek exclusive print rights, but nonexclusive electronic rights, while electronic publications seek exclusive electronic rights (usually for a specific duration), but often don't claim any print rights. Other publications accept nonexclusive electronic rights (especially archival rights), enabling the material to appear in more than one location online at the same time. Many publications, however, prefer that material be withdrawn or withheld from other Web sites, including your personal Web site, before and during publication.

Licensing nonexclusive rights can also avoid some of the problems of poorly defined electronic rights. If your contract does not specify whether the material is to be used online or in a CD-ROM, for example, a "nonexclusive" clause will enable you to license your material to more than one medium at a time.

Electronic Rights and Your Web Site

How much of your Web site do you actually own? The answer depends, literally, on what you put into it. A Web site is not a discrete entity, but is often the sum of several components that may each involve separate rights issues.

Design

Web site design can be defined as the layout of the site as expressed through its coding. That design may include the arrangement of elements on each individual page, the navigational pathways within and between pages, the design and structure of the navigational menu, and the arrangement of frames (if any). It also includes such elements as special fonts, logos, background patterns or textures, navigation icons, and graphic elements.

Copyright of a Web site design belongs to the designer. If you designed the site yourself (i.e., wrote the code), you can be fairly confident that you "own" it. This may also be true if you use a software package (such as Adobe Pagemill), but still create your own design rather than using a template provided with the package. If you do use such a template, the design will usually belong to the software company rather than to you, unless it is specified as "copyright-free," in which case it is in the public domain and doesn't belong to either of you. Similarly, you can't claim "ownership" of a site that uses a template provided by a host (such as **SFF Net**). Finally, if you hired a designer, that individual owns the copyright to the design, and you may not be able to modify it without permission.

Besides affecting your right to modify your own Web site, copyright ownership may also affect your ability to transfer your site from one location to another. For example, if your site is hosted by a sponsor such as Suite101 or **The Mining Co.**, you will not be permitted to transfer that site (or its contents) to another location, such as a personal site. You would, instead, be required to build a substantially different site to avoid infringing on the host's copyright. If you hired a Web site designer, that may also limit your ability to move the site, make alterations, or turn the site over to another site manager.

Fortunately, the copyright to a Web site can be transferred just like any other copyright. To do so, you must negotiate a valid, written agreement with your designer, specifying the rights and terms involved. Ideally, you should do this before your site is designed. Later, you may have to pay an additional fee to regain those rights. For more information on design ownership, see attorney Ivan Hoffman's article, "Who Owns the Copyright in Your Web Site?"

Content

If you run a personal Web site, you will generally be the copyright owner of any material you write specifically for that site, such as a column, article, FAQs, etc. Similarly, you own any previously unpublished material, such as a short story or poem, that you choose to post on that site, even if you didn't write it specifically for the site. Be aware, however, that such a posting is generally considered a "first use," which means that you may not be able to sell such material as "new" thereafter.

This rule does not apply, however, if you write material as a Web site guide for a site such as Suite101 or The Mining Co. Though you are the author of that material, the rights belong to the site, much like a work-for-hire agreement. You can't post it elsewhere on the Web or sell it to a print publication. In addition, guide sites also require a "noncompete" or "noncompetition" agreement, which prohibits you from hosting a personal site on the same subject. This agreement may endure even after you've ceased acting as a guide, so check any guide contract carefully.

You may also post previously published material on your site, if you own the necessary rights. You cannot post material to which you have sold all rights, all or exclusive electronic rights (with no reversion or duration limit), or as "work-for-hire." Since most book contracts include an electronic rights clause, you will usually have to obtain permission from your publisher to post a book excerpt.

If you post material written by someone else, it's wise to create a written agreement specifying the rights involved. Even if your agreement is nothing more than an e-mail or letter, it will help prevent misunderstandings.

Be extremely cautious about posting unattributed material on your site, such as the many supposedly "anonymous" stories, jokes, anecdotes, or poems that are circulated on the Internet. Just because no author has been cited doesn't mean the material is in the public domain. Copyright information is often lost when these snippets are forwarded from one person to another.

Graphics

You can claim copyright only to those graphic elements that you have actually created, such as your own photos or drawings. You don't own the copyright to publicity photos taken by a professional photographer or studio (though you may have the license to use such images), and you don't own the copyright to your book's cover image (unless you designed it yourself). Nor do you own any public-domain images that you've downloaded from a Web site or software package. You simply have the license to use them. Since some people assume that any images posted online are copyright-free, it's wise to post a copyright notice on any images that you do own.

Links

While links (URLs) are information and cannot be individually copyrighted, a list of URLs in a "resource directory" can be considered sufficiently "creative" to qualify for copyright protection. This means that you can't simply copy someone else's list of links to your site, or vice versa—but you can use the information on that list as the basis for developing your own resource guide.

Logos

Many sites provide official logos and images for various promotional reasons—e.g., a partnership or associate arrangement, as an award, as a hotlink icon, or as part of a Web ring. If you display a logo belonging to another Web site, be aware that it does not "belong" to you—although you can usually transfer it along with the rest of your site.

Scripts

Many Web sites include CGI or Java scripts that enable a visitor to sign a guestbook, complete a form, search the site, or send a form message. Many such scripts are public domain, but others may be offered by a site's service provider. If you are looking for a script, it's better to find one on a site that provides free CGI scripts than to borrow one from another site. In any event, unless you wrote the script yourself, you don't own that part of your Web site code. If the script was provided by your service provider (e.g., a hit counter), you may have to replace it when you change providers.

Bells and Whistles

Beware of posting music clips, videos, animation, etc., that aren't specifically authorized or listed as public domain. Don't be tempted to download a clip of your favorite Enya CD as a sample of "music I write by" or to provide ambiance. Audio-visual companies tend to be strict about such infringements.

Domain Name

While a domain name can, under certain circumstances, be trademarked, it can't be copyrighted. Thus, while your domain name will be unique on the Internet, there is nothing to prevent someone from using that name in another context (e.g., as a title).

Posting Copyright Notices

To protect the material on your Web site from inadvertent piracy (i.e., from people who simply don't know better), it's wise to post a copyright notice not only on your home page, but on every individual page that you wish to protect. Remember that not all visitors reach your page through the "front door." Search engines and off-site links may lead visitors directly to specific "content" pages on your site, bypassing the home page entirely.

Your copyright should include the title of the site or page being protected, the copyright symbol, the date the material was placed under copyright, your name, and the phrase "All Rights Reserved." If your material was previously published elsewhere, it's a good idea to cite that publication as well.

Copyright Notice

"Great Writing Site" Copyright © 1999 by Ima Good Author[1]
All rights reserved on all material on all pages in this site, plus the copyright on compilations and design, graphics, and logos. For information on reprinting material from this site, please contact *ImaAuthor@myISP.com.*

Electronic Rights and E-mail

Perhaps nowhere else on the Internet are copyrights violated as routinely as through e-mail. You've probably seen numerous postings or "forwardings" of stories, anecdotes, jokes, or poems that may have no accompanying authorship or source information—but that are, in fact, covered by copyright.

It has been argued that passing along such materials doesn't really harm the author and may even be helpful by making an author's works more widely known. This argument is plausible only if the author's name and copyright information are actually included with the work—and still does not alter the fact that the author has not specifically authorized such distribution. It has also been argued that forwarding material by e-mail or posting it to a newsgroup isn't really a copyright infringement, because it doesn't constitute publication, but is only a public display of the material. This argument is also on shaky ground, particularly as many people incorrectly assume that any material posted without attribution is in the public domain.

The same dangers apply to anything you send by e-mail as well. E-mail messages never die. Many become part of permanent archives that may be

---

[1] If you are writing your own HTML, the code for the copyright symbol itself (©) is &#169.

publicly accessible. Even when you send a message to a private individual, you cannot always be certain that it won't be forwarded without your permission. If you send a private e-mail to an individual at a company address, be aware that your message may become part of that company's e-mail archives and will almost certainly be considered "company property." Never assume that your messages will remain private or protected.

The following precautions can help you protect your copyright, and that of others:

- **Don't post anything to a newsgroup or mailing list that you wouldn't want strangers to read.** Once posted, such messages usually become part of an online archive, which may be publicly accessible through such sites as **Liszt** and **DejaNews**. In addition, you never know who will pick up and pass along your message.
- **Don't forward e-mail without the author's permission.** Most newsgroups and mailing lists ask members to refrain from forwarding posts to outsiders.
- **Don't post material from a Web site to an individual or group** (unless the Web site specifically authorizes such use). Instead, pass along the URL.
- **Don't forward e-mail newsletters (or excerpts of newsletters) to individuals or groups unless the newsletter provides written permission.** Instead, provide the URL or subscription information for the newsletter. If a newsletter seems particularly appropriate for a mailing list, ask the editor (and your list moderator) for permission to forward it to the list.
- **Don't post or forward anecdotes, jokes, stories, poems, or similar materials if you're unsure of their source or copyright status.** While many of these materials are publicly available, many others are actually copyrighted, but have been stripped of identifying information. Remember that many less-informed users often assume that such material is public domain if they receive it by e-mail.
- **Be cautious about posting or submitting your own work.** Most critique groups have strict rules about copyright protection and forbid members from passing material along to others. Posting material to a critique group is generally not considered publication—but make sure that the group's archives, if any, are not publicly accessible.
- **If you wish to share your own work with friends or a mailing list, include a copyright notice.**

Finally, if you receive material by e-mail (or find it in a newsletter or other source) that you know came from a copyrighted source, (a) do not pass it along; (b) notify the sender or publisher (e.g., of the newsletter or site on which the material appeared) that the material is copyrighted, and advise the sender of the source; and (c) notify other recipients (e.g., the mailing list to which the material was posted) of the copyright information, and advise members not to pass the material along.

Recent Developments in Electronic Rights

Arguments over rights in cyberspace have wandered into extremes of silliness on both sides—from the assertion that temporarily downloading a copy of a Web page onto your browser constitutes a copyright violation, to the claim that "information wants to be free." The trouble is, silliness can sometimes become legislation.

In the past few years, many bills and proposals have been put forward to regulate—or deregulate—the exchange of information and material on the Internet. A good place to track this legislation, and the ensuing arguments, is the **Association of Research Libraries (ARL)** Web site, which offers links to texts of proposed legislation, summaries, analyses, and formal arguments and testimonies for and against each bill.

Two recent developments of special interest to writers include the Digital Millennium Copyright Act (DMCA) and the ongoing controversy over protection of databases. While the status of any of these issues may have changed significantly from the time of this writing, here is a brief summary of each:

The Digital Millennium Copyright Act

In an effort to address some of the copyright issues raised or affected by today's "digitally networked environment," Congress passed the DMCA on October 12, 1998. Among other things, this Act:

- **Prohibits circumvention of copyright protection systems.** The DMCA prohibits "gaining unauthorized access to a work by circumventing a technological protection put in place by the copyright owner where such protection measure otherwise effectively controls access to a copyrighted work."[2] This means it will be illegal to remove any digitally encoded copyright identification associated with your material, including coding that limits or controls the use or transfer of that material. This provision will take effect in two years, during which time the Librarian of Congress will attempt to determine appropriate exemptions.
- **Prohibits the design, manufacture, and marketing of devices specifically developed to circumvent copyright protection systems.** This prohibition takes place immediately, but contains a number of exceptions and exemptions.
- **Prohibits tampering with "copyright management information,"** which can be loosely defined as any encoded information that identifies the author, source, title, or other copyright information related to a work. It is not clear whether this prohibition applies to "omitting" copy-

---

[2] Band, Jonathan, "The Digital Millennium Copyright Act," online, <www.arl.org/info/frn/copy/band.html>, accessed 10/25/98.

right or source information on material that is transmitted by e-mail or to "innocently" passing along such material that has been stripped of attribution.

- **Protects online service providers (OSPs) from copyright infringement liability** related to material posted or distributed by a client or user. Essentially, this means that OSPs are not liable for copyright-infringing materials posted or transmitted by clients, provided the OSP is not aware of the infringement. This frees the OSP from being responsible for material it "caches" for a user (e.g., by hosting a Web site), and also ensures that OSPs will not have to police Web sites or invade a client's privacy. OSPs are responsible for taking appropriate action, however, if they are informed of a copyright violation. This provision also has a host of conditions, exceptions, and exemptions.

Database Protection

A controversial proposal to provide extra copyright protection for databases—not only for the structure or organization of the database, but for the information contained within it—was removed from the DMCA. This proposal is endorsed by many commercial database proprietors and is hotly contested by universities, libraries, and many other individuals and organizations who are concerned about the proposal's effect on the free flow and exchange of information.

According to the International Council of Scientific Unions (ICSU), the proposal "would protect the contents of databases, i.e., the facts themselves. Thus, all sorts of compilations of data or datasets that have traditionally been in the public domain for lack of sufficient "originality" (to make them copyrightable) will now be protected against unauthorized uses."[3] Most databases do not meet the standards for "creativity in the arrangement of data"[4] in order to be eligible for copyright coverage, and "parts of the information industry believe that a new right is needed to protect their investment in creating databases and to guard against piracy."[5]

Opponents of the proposal argue that protecting information (rather than the expression of information) will have a chilling effect on writers, researchers, scientists, librarians, and anyone else who requires access to data. It is argued that this type of protection would stifle independent research and make it difficult or impossible for researchers to publish, post, or share the results of their work. The proposed legislation makes no allowances for "fair use," and specifically prohibits any use of data that would constitute competition with the marketing interests of the database owner.

Similar legislation has already been enacted in Europe (The European Union

---

[3] ICSU, "Ad-hoc Group on Data and Information," online, <www.nrc.ca/programs/codata/old>, June 22, 1998.
[4] Ibid.
[5] Ibid.

Database Directive, enacted January 1, 1998) and has also been considered and rejected by the World Intellectual Property Organization (WIPO). The DMCA version is only one of several bills proposed in the United States to provide such protections, and it is safe to assume that more such bills will surface in the future. Should such protection come to pass, it could significantly alter the status of information on the Internet and, as well, the free flow of and access to that information that has proven such a benefit to writers.

As these two issues indicate, the status of electronic rights (and rights in general) is highly fluid and in the process of rapid evolution. For writers, the peril lies in the fact that much of the legislation being proposed today is being developed by the groups with the money—publishers, conglomerates, and database companies—who have huge amounts to gain by tweaking the current copyright regulations.

Writers cannot afford to be silent where their rights are concerned. While it may not be practical or advisable to attempt to sue every publisher who offers a work-for-hire contract, it is important to speak out whenever you see your rights threatened. Never assume that your publisher or editor understands copyright law, or that a contract is valid just because it was hammered out by a publisher's legal department. Many publishers have backed down from unreasonable contract demands, and each victory for authors sets the precedent for more. On the other hand, each time writers quietly accept damaging contracts, we lay the foundation for a future in which we may be unable to do anything to secure our rights—or our profits.

●

The Tasini Decision:

How It Affects Your Electronic Rights

by Moira Allen

On August 13, 1997, Judge Sonia Sotomayor issued a ruling in the New York U.S. District Court that would have a profound effect on freelance writers. The case, filed in 1993, was *Tasini v. The New York Times Co.*

Electronic Rights versus Collective Works

Jonathan Tasini, president of the National Writers Union (NWU), and others launched a lawsuit claiming that the New York Times Co. (NYTC) and several other publications violated the plaintiffs' copyright by republishing material on CD-ROM and in the LEXIS/NEXIS database. The plaintiffs argued that they had not granted electronic rights to their material, only first rights.

Sotomayor, however, ruled that no infringement had taken place, because the electronic publications constituted a "revision of a collective work," as defined by Section 201(c) of the U.S. Copyright Act of 1976. Section 201(c) grants "creators of collective works . . . the privilege of reproducing and distributing the contribution as part of that particular collective work, any revision of that collective work, and any later collective work in the same series."

A "collective work" refers to any item that is compiled from a selection of smaller works or data, such as a periodical, a database, an anthology, etc. While the writer may hold the copyright to a contribution within such a work, the creator or publisher of the work itself holds the copyright to the work as a whole and has the right to determine where and how that work is reproduced or distributed. Theoretically, the publisher could issue the same work in a large print edition, a Braille edition, a foreign language edition, etc., without violating the rights of contributors.

Sotomayor ruled that because the CD-ROM in question was not "substantially changed" from the original collective work, it simply represented another form of distribution for that work. As a result, publishers are now authorized to reproduce a collective work in an electronic format—so long as that work is not substantially changed.

Benefits for Writers

While the plaintiffs lost their primary argument, freelancers won several important points:

- The ruling applies only to electronic publications that fall within the definition of a "revision of a collective work." It does not apply to any other form of electronic rights, including publication of material on a periodical's Web site.
- The ruling does not apply to a "new work," such as an anthology or a collection of articles gathered from several different collective works. For example, a CD-ROM that contained "The Best of Magazine X" (i.e., articles selected from several different issues of Magazine X) would not be covered.
- The ruling does not cover the electronic publication of an individual article separated from the "collective work" as a whole.
- First publication rights cannot be taken to mean "first publication in any media." First publication means exactly that; any subsequent use is no longer a first use, even if it's in another medium. Thus, a publisher cannot legally claim that "First North American Serial Rights" for a print publication includes the right to a first use online as well.
- A stamp on the back of a check does not constitute a binding contract. A statement such as, "This check is accepted as full payment . . . and constitutes a transfer of all rights . . ." is not a legal contract and can be deposited with impunity. Sotomayor ruled that to be binding, a contract must be issued prior to the completion of work; a statement issued after the work has been completed and accepted is not valid.

And Now the Bad News . . .

While the ruling itself may seem bad enough, its backlash is proving far more serious. The *New York Times,* for example, now insists on "all rights" contracts. Other periodicals, hoping to avoid similar conflicts, have followed suit.

Consequently, the situation of writers may have gone from "fairly bad" to "much worse." Even if Tasini had won, it is unlikely that revenues from electronic distribution would have compensated for the loss of revenues from subsequent sales of one's material. Now, writers may face the loss of both.

For More Information

- *Tasini, et al. v. The New York Times, et al.; www.igc.apc.org/nwu/tvt/tvthome.htm.* The NWU perspective on the case, including the full text of the complaint.
- *Jonathan Tasini, et al., v. The New York Times Co.; www.ljx.com/topdecision/tasini.htm.* The full text of Judge Sotomayor's ruling.

RESOURCES

Organizations for Writers

American Society of Journalists and Authors (ASJA) *www.asja.org*
National Writers Union *www.nwu.org*

Copyright Information

10 Big Myths About Copyright Explained (by Brad Templeton) *www.templetons.com/brad/copymyths.html*
Berne Convention for the Protection of Literary and Artistic Works *www.law.cornell.edu/treaties/berne/overview.html*
  International copyright laws.
Copyright and Fair Use *fairuse.stanford.edu/*
  Links to articles and other resources on issues of copyright, multimedia rights, and fair use.
Copyright Code *www.law.cornell.edu/uscode/17/*
Copyright for Computer Authors *www.FPLC.edu/tfield/copySof.htm*
Giving Credit and Requesting Permission: Guidelines for Using Material Other Than Your Own
  www.oreilly.com/oreilly/author/permission/
  A book chapter covering issues of copying, quoting, and obtaining permission for use of other authors' materials.
Internet Law Simplified (by Ivan Hoffman) *www.online-magazine.com/copyright.htm*
Publishing Law and Other Articles of Interest *publaw.com/articles.html*
  Articles on a wide range of copyright, trademark, and rights issues.
U.S. Copyright Office *lcweb.loc.gov/copyright*

Electronic Rights

ASJA Contract Watch *www.asja.org/cwpage.htm*
  "A free [biweekly] electronic newsletter about the latest terms and negotiations in the world of periodicals, print and electronic."
Association of Research Libraries *www.arl.org*
  The ARL is involved in, and keeps track of, a variety of electronic and copyright issues relevant to writers; this site is a good place to look for the latest legal developments.
Authors in the New Information Age: A Working Paper on Electronic Publishing Issues *www.nwu.org/docs/aniabeg.htm#173*
Contract Tips for Freelancers *www.asja.org/asjatips.htm*
Copyright Protection in the New World of Electronic Publishing *www.press.umich.edu/jep/works/strong.copyright.html*
Electronic Publishing: Protecting Your Rights (by Moira Allen) *www.inkspot.com/feature/epublish.html*
  Article based on a 1997 survey of print and electronic magazines' approach to contracts and electronic rights.
Journal of Electronic Publishing *www.press.umich.edu:80/jep/*
Journalist Electronic Rights Negotiation Strategies *www.nwu.org/journ/jstrat.htm*
SFWA Statement on Electronic Rights *www.sfwa.org/contracts/ELEC.htm*
  The Science Fiction Writers of America position on electronic rights, including an open letter from a lawyer on rights issues involved in handheld "e-readers."

Web Sites and Electronic Rights

"C" Rights in "E" Mail *www.ivanhoffman.com/derivative.html*
Clearing Rights for Multimedia Works *www.ut.system.edu/ogc/intellectualproperty/multimed.htm*
Copyright Protection: Understanding Your Options *www.seyboldreport.com/Specials/Copyright.htm*
  Includes information on "digital watermarking," a method of protecting image copyrights.
Derivative Rights and Websites (by Ivan Hoffman) *www.ivanhoffmann.com/website.html*
Electronic Publishing and the Potential Loss of First Serial Rights (by Ivan Hoffman) *www.ivanhoffmann.com/website.html*

Proper Use of a Domain Name for Trademark Protection *www.arvic.com/library/domanuse.asp*
Who Owns the Copyright in Your Web Site? (by Ivan Hoffman) *www.ivanhoffmann.com/website.html*

Digital Millennium Copyright Act

Copyright and Intellectual Property *www.arl.org/info/frn/copy/copytoc.html*
Sponsored by the Association of Research Libraries, this site offers an extensive set of links to current legislation on copyright and related issues, including the DMCA, proposed database legislation, protection for ISPs, and more. Also provides links to official arguments and testimonies for and against proposed legislation.
The Digital Millennium Copyright Act (summary) *www.arl.org/info/frn/copy/band.html*

Database Protection Issues

Myths and Facts about S2291 *www.arl.org/info/frn/copy/myth.html*
Information about proposed database protection legislation.
Primer on the Proposed WIPO Treaty on Database Extraction Rights *www.essential.org/cpt/ip/cpt-dbcom.html*
Though the WIPO treaty was rejected in 1996, this article contains a good overview of the general issues involved in database protection proposals.

COMMUNICATING

ONLINE

5

Netiquette: E-mail Queries, Submissions, and Interviews

Of all the advantages of being connected to the Internet, e-mail is perhaps the greatest. It offers the most significant savings to writers in terms of time and money, enabling a writer to contact an editor anywhere in the world, submit a proposal, and deliver a manuscript—all without licking a stamp. It also enables writers to conduct interviews at the convenience of both parties and conduct surveys that would otherwise involve hundreds of dollars in mailing costs.

Advantages of E-mail

While e-mail won't replace every form of correspondence, it offers the following advantages, not only to writers, but to editors and publishers as well:

- **It saves postage.** When you send a query or manuscript by e-mail, or a request for information or a response to such a request, you're saving at least one stamp and usually two. On manuscripts, you may save several dollars.
- **It saves paper.** E-mail may not be the ultimate act of recycling, but it certainly helps! Each time you submit a manuscript by e-mail, you've saved the paper needed to print the piece and the envelope required to mail it. You also save paper at the other end by enabling an editor to reply to your e-mail rather than having to compose and mail a formal response.
- **It saves time.** E-mail transmissions usually arrive instantly. That means you can send a query or an article to an editor anywhere in the world

without wondering whether it will arrive or when. This makes manuscript tracking easier, as you no longer have to factor delivery time into your estimate of response time. It also means that you can add precious days to your deadline, because you can transmit material literally on the day it is due.

- **It encourages an immediate response.** The ability to simply type a line or two and hit the "reply" button encourages many editors to reply to e-mail queries more quickly than to traditional mail. E-mail eliminates the need to draft a formal response, type a letter, find a reply form, locate your SASE, or type an envelope. Consequently, you may receive a reply to an e-mail query within days, or even hours, rather than having to wait weeks or months. E-mail also provides a good way to follow up on a query or submission.
- **It provides a convenient means of exchanging information.** Do you have a question for your editor? Does your editor have a question for you? With e-mail, you can exchange information without having to play telephone tag, send a fax, or compose a letter. Information exchanges are usually informal. The question and the answer may be little more than a line or two apiece.
- **It streamlines negotiations.** E-mail makes it possible to conduct an entire contract negotiation in days rather than weeks. The original contract can be transmitted by e-mail, whereupon both parties can "snip" clauses that require further discussion or change and send their comments back and forth until a final agreement is reached. Once the contract has been finalized, a paper copy should be drafted and faxed or "snail-mailed"—e-mail as yet offers no commonly accepted way to transmit a legally binding signature.
- **It enables editors to download documents.** With e-mail, you don't have to worry about translating your documents into a program your editor's computer can read. (This is especially good news for Mac users in a PC world!) No more sending disks back and forth; e-mailed material can be copied directly into your editor's word processing or formatting program.
- **It opens doors to international markets.** No one likes dealing with International Reply Coupons (IRCs). Writers have to visit the post office to buy them; editors have to go to the post office to redeem them. Consequently, international publications are often more than happy to bypass this hassle and do business electronically. Many U.S. publications will accept e-mail submissions from non-U.S. authors, even if they don't accept them from domestic writers.

In addition to its general advantages, e-mail offers special benefits to writers in four key areas: queries, submissions, interviews, and surveys.

E-mail Queries

Amazingly, some books and articles still warn writers not to submit queries by e-mail. While it is true that many publications don't accept material via e-mail, hundreds of others do. To find out just how many, I surveyed 720 consumer magazines that listed e-mail addresses in the *1999 Writer's Market*. Of the 360 publications that responded, 318 (88 percent) were willing to accept e-mail queries, while 313 (87 percent) accepted assigned manuscripts by e-mail.[1] Interestingly, many that wouldn't accept e-mail queries were often willing to accept assigned manuscripts, and vice versa. The moral: If you don't know whether or not a publication accepts electronic queries, ask. Send a brief, polite e-mail inquiring whether an e-query will be acceptable. If you don't receive a response, assume the answer is "no."

Besides saving paper and postage, e-mail queries save time. You don't have to wonder when, or whether, your query was received; you know that it reached the editor's "desk" within seconds of leaving your own. If it did not, you should receive a "bounce back" notification of undeliverable mail within a few minutes.

In addition, many editors tend to answer e-mail queries more quickly than traditional queries. It only takes an instant to type a response to an e-mail—whether a rejection, an acceptance, or a request for more information. Editors that you work with regularly are likely to respond even more quickly, and you don't have to wait for them to dig your envelope out of a pile of snail mail.

E-query Format

Just because an editor can respond quickly and informally to an e-query, however, doesn't mean that the query itself should be hasty *or* informal. When you're approaching an editor for the first time, the only real difference between an e-query and a traditional query is the mode of transmission. The content should be composed as carefully as that of any paper query.

An electronic query letter involves three basic sections: the header, the body, and your signature.

The Header

The header of your e-query includes such information as the editor's e-mail address, your return address, the date sent, and the subject of the e-mail. Some of these fields are automatic; others must be filled in. As the header contains the first information an editor will see, it's important that every

---

[1] In all, approximately 840 consumer listings in the *1999 Writer's Market* included an e-mail address. Of these, approximately 120 addresses were invalid or no longer active, bringing the total of delivered surveys to 720. It's also quite possible that the remaining 360 editors who *didn't* respond absolutely loathe e-mail communications of all kinds!

aspect of this section (including the automatic fields) reflect your professionalism. Pay special attention to the following fields:

- **To:** Besides inserting the e-mail address of the editor, you can personalize this field by adding the editor's name and title. Type the name and title first, without commas (use colons or dashes for punctuation or this information will be treated as part of the address), followed by the e-mail address in angle brackets:

  To: John Smith - Editor - GREAT MAGAZINE <jsmith@greatmag.com>

- **From:** If you use an e-mail alias, it will appear in this field, so be sure your alias is appropriate for a query letter. Calling yourself "Studmuffin" or "Firesinger Dragonheart" is fine among friends, but will not endear you to an editor! (Some programs allow multiple aliases or "personalities" for different types of correspondence.) Also, if your alias is uninformative (e.g., MQW@isp.com), consider entering your full name in parentheses following the e-mail address. Or, enter your real name in the "real name" option within your e-mail settings.

  From: MQW@isp.com (Mary Q. Writer)

- **Subject:** Make sure the editor knows this is a query and what it is about:

  Subject: QUERY: Feline Heart Disease

- **CC:** Send yourself a copy of the query, both as a record for your files and to retransmit if the first transmission doesn't succeed. (To save time and typos, make yourself a mailing "nickname" such as "Me," or set your e-mail program to automatically save a copy of all outgoing mail.)
- **Attachments:** Under no circumstances should attachments be sent without permission. Never attach electronic "clips" or any other information to an unsolicited query letter.

The Body

The body of your query begins with the salutation and should proceed like any traditional query. In fact, you may find it easier to maintain the right mindset by composing your query on your usual word processing program and then pasting it into the body of your e-mail.

The primary difference between an e-mail query and a paper query is format. Be sure to observe the following guidelines:

- Don't use special formatting commands, such as boldface, italics, or underlining. Instead of underlining titles, use all caps or quotes, or indicate formatting with asterisks (for *boldface*) or underscores (for _underlining_ or _italics_).
- Turn off "smart quotes" (also known as "curly quotes"), and avoid the

use of characters or symbols that require a combination of keys. (See the sidebar, "Ten Tips on Effective E-mail.")

- Double-space between paragraphs. Bulleted paragraphs are also acceptable.
- Don't use emoticons, smileys, or abbreviations (e.g., "BTW" [by the way] or "IMHO" [in my humble opinion]).
- Limit your query to a single printed page, if possible.
- Let the editor know whether clips are available (but don't attach them). An editor who wants to see samples of your work will request them by snail mail. Or, you can post representative clips on a Web site and provide the URL in your query (see chapter 8 for more information).

The Signature

If you use a signature block, make sure it is appropriate for this type of correspondence. Don't include a block that lists the names of your nine cats, your favorite *Star Wars* quote, or your "Firesinger Dragonheart" alias. The basic rule is easy: If you wouldn't use your e-mail signature to sign a traditional query, don't use it on an e-mail query either!

Sign your query with your full name. You may also wish to include your snail mail address, a telephone number, and a fax number. If you'd like the editor to visit your Web site, include the site's title and URL.

Once you've built a good working relationship with an editor, your e-queries will undoubtedly become less formal. As a rule, editors appreciate brevity from writers they already know and who have already established their credentials and abilities. Until then, keep your e-queries professional, and they'll impress editors as thoroughly as anything on paper.

E-mail Submissions

If there is a single rule about e-mail submissions, it is this: Never send an unsolicited manuscript by e-mail! No editor wants twenty unsolicited pages in her inbox—or worse, an attachment that takes five minutes to download.

Many editors welcome assigned manuscripts by e-mail, however, and often prefer them to hard copies or disks. An e-mail submission allows an editor to download a manuscript file directly, without having to worry about compatible word processing programs or platforms. Such submissions also enable writers to turn in manuscripts at literally the last minute. However, it should be noted that, when sending a manuscript as an attached file, compatible word processing might be necessary.

When e-mailing a manuscript, always include all sections of the manuscript (including sidebars and any other information) in a single document. Place a brief cover memo at the beginning of the document to provide any necessary information to the editor, including the word count of the submission.

With the exception of longer manuscripts (e.g., full-length books), you can transmit the manuscript within the text of the e-mail itself, even if you are also sending it as an attachment. This ensures that the material will arrive in a readable form. Attachments are notoriously unreliable; some programs can read them and others can't. Never send a manuscript attachment until you've checked with the editor and confirmed that it will be readable. Most MS Word documents, for example, can be read by any recent MS Word application, whether produced on the Mac or the PC. Or, you can convert documents to "text only," which is readable by any word processor but holds no formatting or special characters.

Make sure that your manuscript does not include any special formatting, that you've turned off smart quotes, and that you haven't used any special characters or symbols. Provide a subject line that describes the manuscript (e.g., its title), and mail a copy back to yourself so that you have a record of the transmission and a copy to retransmit if necessary.

E-mail Interviews

E-mail can be an effective and convenient way to conduct an interview and is often appreciated by busy experts who don't have time for a face-to-face or telephone interview. It enables you to compose questions carefully rather than "on the fly" and gives your interviewee time to respond carefully as well. E-mail also offers a good way to follow up on a traditional interview, when seeking clarification or additional information.

E-mail interviews are especially useful when the interviewee's information will constitute a very small part of your article or, alternatively, when the article will be based almost verbatim on the interviewee's words, as in a "Q and A" interview or similar piece. They may also be appropriate when:

- The interviewee specifies a preference for being interviewed in this fashion.
- The interviewee is too busy for a traditional interview.
- Conflicting schedules and/or time zones make telephone interviewing difficult.
- You know exactly what questions you want to ask. (This often requires some background knowledge of the subject.)
- The subject is relatively impersonal. (An e-mail interview wouldn't be appropriate for discussing a tragic or deeply personal issue.)
- The interview can be conducted with a limited number of questions.

E-mail interviews are less effective when you're trying to develop a profile or catch a personal glimpse of the interviewee—a profile that would include not only the individual's words but also your observations of the person's appearance, actions, skills, emotions, tone of voice, etc. They are less effective if you don't know enough about a subject to develop useful questions, or when you're more likely to get information from the natural flow of questions and answers than from a predefined script. In an e-mail interview, you can't change direction if a more promising tangent emerges from the conversation; you can't nudge the interviewee back on track if the conversation strays or ask follow-up questions if your first questions don't elicit enough information; and you can't ask for immediate explanations or clarification.

The following strategies can help you develop and refine an e-mail interview:

- Determine your goals before writing your questions. Decide exactly what you need to know, then develop questions that will best elicit that information.
- Ask open-ended questions rather than questions that can be answered "yes" or "no." For example, instead of asking, "Do you enjoy writing children's books?" ask, "What do you enjoy most about writing children's books?" or "What are some of the things you enjoy about writing children's books?"
- If necessary, explain why you are asking a particular question, so the interviewee has a better idea of the response you're looking for.
- Let the interviewee know what audience or market you're writing for, so she will know how detailed or technical the information should be.
- Keep your questions as clear, uncomplicated, and short as possible.
- Keep your list of questions as short as possible. Ten is good; twenty is likely to tax an interviewee's patience.
- List your questions numerically, and leave space between each question for the interviewee to insert the answer.
- Include a final "open" question (e.g., "Is there anything else you'd like to say on this subject that hasn't been covered above?") that will enable the interviewee to add information or ideas that weren't covered by your script.
- Let the interviewee know how soon you need the answers. If you need to follow up on a late interview, be polite. Remember that the interviewee is doing you a favor and is under no obligation to comply with your request or meet your deadline.

E-mail interviews don't work for everyone or in every circumstance. They may not be appropriate, for example, if your interviewee is uncomfortable with written questions (they may look too much like a test) or doesn't enjoy expressing ideas in writing. Under the right conditions, however, e-mail can add an extra level of convenience to an interview—and give you a written record of the conversation.

E-mail Surveys

Another way to gather information via e-mail is to conduct a survey. Once again, the Internet offers an unparalleled opportunity: You can send a list of questions to hundreds of potential respondents at no cost.

At the same time, caution is in order. Some respondents may regard a survey as a form of spam. Your e-mail should state the nature and purpose of the survey as quickly, succinctly, and courteously as possible. Assure respondents of privacy, and guarantee that you won't cite anyone by name or organization without permission. If you're soliciting comments as well as statistics, ask respondents to indicate whether or not they may be quoted and how they should be cited.

Like interview questions, survey questions should be short, clear, well organized, and limited in number. Unlike interview questions, however, survey questions should encourage "yes/no" or multiple-choice options. Respondents are also more likely to answer a short questionnaire than a long one.

An easy format is to follow each question with the answer options (e.g., "Yes" or "No") on a separate line or lines. Place a set of parentheses in front of each option, with space for a response:

> 1. Do you accept e-mail queries?
> ( ) Yes
> ( ) No
> 2. How do you prefer to receive manuscripts?
> ( ) Hard copy (printed)
> ( ) On diskette
> ( ) By e-mail, in the body of the e-mail message
> ( ) As an e-mail attachment

This enables the respondent to simply insert an "x" in the appropriate space and mail the form back as a reply. If you are offering a multiple-choice question that could have more than one answer, indicate whether you want the respondent to "check only one" or "check all that apply."

To ensure your respondents' privacy, place all your survey addresses in the "BCC" (blind copy) field of your header. Leave the "TO" field blank, or enter a generic title in that field (such as "editor" or "director"). That title will then show up as the "addressee" on each survey form, but addressees won't be able to see the addresses of your other respondents. (You'll receive a notice that this "blank" e-mail was undeliverable, but the blind copies will go through.) If you have a large number of addressees, send the survey in several batches rather than all at once.

When you mail your survey, several may bounce back immediately as undeliverable. Keep track of these bounces so that you know exactly how many surveys went out. This will enable you to calculate the correct percentage of responses. For example, if you send out one hundred surveys, get ten back as undeliverable, and receive fifty responses, you have a 55 percent response rate.

The bulk of your responses will typically arrive in a flood within the first two or three days of your mailing. After that, the flow will taper to a trickle. At some point, you'll have to decide when it's time to cut off the survey and tally the results, even if you're still getting an occasional response. It's also helpful to set up a separate mailbox to store your responses until you're ready to tally them.

Once you've completed the survey, make a list of the respondents and send them a thank-you note for participating. If respondents are interested in the results of your survey, let them know when and where the article will appear.

Perhaps more than any other electronic invention, e-mail has changed the way writers and editors do business. Like any technology, however, e-mail can easily be abused. Its simplicity often fosters an inappropriate attitude of informality, an inattention to detail. Traditional mail contains a number of steps (composing, typing, proofreading, mailing) that act as safety buffers, offering the opportunity for second thoughts about tone or content. E-mail, with its "type and send" capability, removes those buffers, making it easier to send an ill-considered or poorly edited message.

Because e-mail costs virtually nothing, it can also be overused. Editors have no more wish to be bombarded with e-mail messages than with phone calls. Authors, experts, and others who post an e-mail address on a Web site still value their privacy and are under no obligation to reply to every message they receive. And absolutely no one appreciates unsolicited writing samples— especially when sent as attachments!

Simple courtesy and professionalism, however, can eliminate most of the negatives from e-mail communication and will go far toward keeping those lines of communication open between writers and editors. For both, the negatives are generally far outweighed by the positives!

●

Ten Tips for Successful E-mail

Whether you're e-mailing a query, a manuscript, a set of research questions, or an informal letter, be sure to observe the following Netiquette rules. Breaking these rules can result in unreadable correspondence and irritated editors.

1. **Compose your message with care.** E-mail lives forever—you never know where your message may turn up. Read twice before hitting the "send" button!
2. **Proofread and spellcheck.** Some newer e-mail programs have spell-checkers, but many don't. Visually proofread any message you send.
3. **Remove or convert all quotes, symbols, and special characters.** The most common problem in e-mail is the use of "curly" (or "smart") quotes and apostrophes. A "curly quote" is any quote or apostrophe that automatically curves to the left or right, depending upon where it is placed. In most e-mail programs, these are translated into bizarre symbols (or commas) that make text very difficult to read. If possible, avoid them

altogether by turning them off in your word processing program (look under Format Preferences, Tools, AutoCorrect, or AutoFormat menus for details[2]). Another problem character is the em dash (—), formed by a combination of a control key and a hyphen on PC or shift, option, and hyphen on Mac). Simply use two hyphens (--) to indicate a dash. Never try to insert special characters, such as copyright (©) or trademark (®) symbols. Otherwise, your text may come across looking like this:

☐YouΣre crazy!☐he shoutedβand slammed the door. ∉ I wonder why heΣs so mad,α she mused.

4. **Remove all special formatting from your text.** If you've composed your material on a word-processing program, be sure to remove all formatting commands such as italics, boldface, and underlining. Otherwise, the commands that turn formatting on and off are likely to be translated into strange symbols at the receiving end. The easiest way to do this is to save your file as "text only" and then paste the text version into your e-mail. To indicate italics or underlining, use an _underscore_ character on each side of the word or phrase; use *asterisks* to indicate boldface. (It's also perfectly acceptable, in e-mail, to place a book or publication title in "quotes" or ALL CAPS.)

5. **Indicate paragraphs with an indent or a blank line.** If your material consists of short paragraphs, set them off with tabs or indents. If it consists of very long paragraphs, however, separate them with blank lines. Also, make sure that your e-mail program is not set to compress messages by removing those lines, or your recipients will receive a huge, undivided block of text.

6. **Turn off any special e-mail formatting functions.** For example, turn off any option that converts your e-mail into HTML-formatted text. For most recipients, this simply results in a double message, one in text and one with HTML coding. This doubles the length of the transmission and is particularly annoying on longer messages, such as manuscript submissions. Also, make sure that your e-mail doesn't automatically compress files by removing blank lines. In some cases, this will cause your paragraphing to be lost.

7. **Set your line length, if any, to "wrap" or to no more than sixty-five characters.** Longer lines tend to wrap incorrectly at the receiving end and will be hard to read.

8. **Don't type in ALL CAPS. This is considered shouting.** Use caps sparingly for emphasis or to indicate a title (which can also be set in quotes). Use asterisks and underscore characters to indicate *boldface* and _italics/underlining_.

---

[2] In Microsoft Word, for example, look under Tools » AutoCorrect » AutoFormat as You Type, and uncheck the box under **Replace as you type:** "straight quotes" with "smart quotes".

9. **Keep your messages as short as possible.** When replying to a message, include only those portions of the original message that you are actually responding to, and "snip" the remainder. Similarly, remove older messages from an exchange that is being sent back and forth or forwarded to others.

10. **Never send attachments without permission.** Many recipients may not be able to open an attachment, and lengthy attachments can take considerable time to download (which only exasperates the recipient). If you are submitting a manuscript for critique or to an editor, include it within the body of your e-mail, even if you have permission to send an attachment as well. This ensures that a readable copy will be received. Make sure that your e-mail program does not automatically send messages as both text and attachment, and turn off any options that send a "vcard" attachment with every e-mail.

●

E-mail Glossary

by Mary Houten-Kemp[3]

Autoresponders (Mailbots): Automated programs that are established to return a prewritten message upon receipt of e-mail. Program will grab the return address from the "header" of the message. Typically, these programs will send out the canned message within seconds of receipt.

Aliasing (Redirecting): Using a fictitious address with which to send and receive e-mail. Typically done to avoid having people write to long "real" e-mail addresses or if underlying e-mail address is subject to change. Provides a permanent address.

Bounced Message: A returned, undeliverable e-mail message.

E-mail Acronyms: When sending off a quick message, these acronyms can help. Don't overuse.

2L8	too late
AAMOF	as a matter of fact
AFAIK	as far as I know
B4N	bye for now
BTW	by the way
CMIIW	correct me if I'm wrong
CUL	see you later
FWIW	for what it's worth
IAC	in any case
IKWUM	I know what you mean

---

[3] Copyright 1997, 1998 by Mary Houten-Kemp. All Rights Reserved. From "Everything E-mail," *www.everythingemail.com/*.

IMHO	in my humble opinion
IOW	in other words
KWIM	know what I mean
LOL	laughing out loud
NBIF	no basis in fact
OTOH	on the other hand
ROTFL	rolling on the floor laughing
ROTFLMAO	rolling on the floor laughing my a** off
RTFM	read the f...... manual
SIG	special interest group
TIA	thanks in advance
TNX	thanks
TTFN	ta ta for now

Emoticons: Also referred to as smileys, these symbols help convey the tone or emotion of an online message. Examples:

:-)	happy
:)	smile
:-(	sad
;-)	wink
:-o	shocked, surprised
:->	devilish
:/	hmmm . . .
$-)	just won the lottery

Encoding: A method of sending binary (nontext files) with e-mail messages. Common encoding options include: Mime, BinHex, UUencode, etc. Sender and receiver must both use the same method.

Flame: An angry or rude e-mail message, often posted as a public response on a discussion group. If you become the target of a flame, avoid responding or you might incite a flame war.

Header: The first part of a received e-mail message, which contains information about the routing of the message while traversing the Internet. Much of this may not be displayed if the e-mail software program keeps it hidden (usually an option).

IMAP: Internet Message Access Protocol. A method to access and manipulate e-mail that is stored remotely on another computer. Messages do not get transferred to the user's computer, making it easier to manage e-mail when accessing from multiple computers.

Lurk: To observe an online discussion without participating. Good idea when first joining a Mailing List.

Mail Bomb: Hundreds or thousands of e-mail messages sent to the same address, sometimes to the central posting address of a discussion group causing an avalanche effect that can bring down a server with the heavy load it causes.

Mailer Daemon: A Unix program used in the management of e-mail messages. Not generally encountered by a user unless the user gets a bounced message.

Mailing List: A collection of e-mail addresses of people who have asked to receive regular mail discussions on a particular topic, and for which they can sometimes submit messages for disbursement to the entire group.

Mailing List Manager: An automated program to handle the administrative functions of adding/removing subscribers, disseminating the message postings, sending topic related and help files, etc., for the entire Mailing List. Example MLMs include Majordomo, Listserv, ListProc, Mailbase, etc.

Moderator: Someone who controls the postings of messages in a Mailing List to ensure conformity with the topic and list policies.

Netiquette: Network Etiquette. Acceptable practices of using various Internet resources. Example: DON'T USE ALL CAPS. IT APPEARS AS IF THE WRITER IS SHOUTING.

POP/POP3: Post Office Protocol. A mail protocol used to service intermittent dial-up connections to the Internet. Mail is held until the user accesses the account, at which time the mail is transferred to the user's computer.

Postmaster: The person to contact at a particular server/site to get help, or information about that server/site. Also the person to contact to register a complaint about a user's behavior.

Signature Line: A set of four to eight lines of text placed at the end of a mail message to provide the reader with the author's contact information, favorite quote, special of the month, autoresponder/Web site address, etc. The signature line is composed and placed into the e-mail software's signature file for automatic appending.

SMTP: Simple Mail Transfer Protocol. The most common protocol used for transferring e-mail across the Internet.

Spam: To send unsolicited commercial e-mail, usually in large amounts and indiscriminately, to discussion groups or subscriber bases.

Thread: A written conversation on a particular topic in a larger group discussion.

●

RESOURCES

Tips on Using E-mail

The Basics of Internet E-mail *www.wwwscribe.com/ebasics.htm*

E-mail Attachments—Your Questions Answered *everythingemail.net/attach_help.html*

E-mail File Attachments *telacommunications.com/nutshell/email.htm*

   In a nutshell, why e-mail attachments often fail to work. (Yes, it's "tela.")

Everything E-mail *everythingemail.net/index.html*

   A site addressing a host of e-mail-related topics, including software, Netiquette, handling mailing lists and discussions, news, and more.

6

Joining the Online Community: Discussion Lists and Newsgroups

The Internet has been described as an "electronic community." That community includes a number of "writing neighborhoods," in the form of e-mail discussion groups, newsgroups, forums, and chat rooms. These are places where writers meet to discuss topics of mutual interest, share information, and provide mutual support.

Discussion groups are excellent sources of information, not only on writing but on a host of other topics. They also provide valuable opportunities for networking. Many top-name authors and editors participate in newsgroups and lists dedicated to their particular area of writing.

Nor are these opportunities limited to writing discussion groups. Among the thousands of special-interest discussion groups online, you're bound to find one that covers your favorite topic (and the topic you're most likely to write about), whether that topic is Arthurian lore or auto mechanics.

Like any community, online discussion groups have certain rules and social customs. Some of these are spelled out in the "welcome" message you'll receive when you join, while others remain unspoken until broken. To get the most from a group, you need to know how such groups work, what to expect from them, and what they will expect from you.

Advantages of Online "Talk"

As a writer, you can benefit from a discussion group (writing-related or otherwise) in a variety of ways. Before you get involved, it's wise to have an idea of the benefits you're looking for, so that you can evaluate a group in terms of your specific needs and interests.

The benefits of discussion groups include information, networking, writing advice, marketing tips, diversity, and encouragement.

Information

Both writing and special-interest groups are excellent sources of research and background information. You never know what sort of experience group members have. Consequently, a simple question like, "Does anyone know . . . ?" can bring unexpectedly rich results.

A writing e-mail list to which I subscribe, for example, recently covered such topics as wound management (with information contributed by a former U.S. Navy field corpsman) and what really happens to the human body in the vacuum of space (with information contributed by a vacuum physicist). When list members don't have first-hand information on a topic, they can often provide useful references and URLs or refer you to a list that would be more helpful.

While writing groups excel in the breadth of information available, special-interest groups are the place to look for depth on a specific topic. A cat-lovers' discussion group, for example, is the place to turn for information on a particular feline malady—whether you're looking for technical information or anecdotal experiences of cat owners who have coped with the disease. For an idea of the range of topics available, check the directory page of **ListServe.com**.

Networking

One of the benefits of joining a discussion group is getting to know people in your field and letting them get to know you. While some writing groups are primarily for amateurs, others are frequented by well-known authors and editors and expect a correspondingly high degree of professionalism from all participants. While a discussion group is not the place to solicit a critique from a top-name author or to pitch a story to an editor, it is a place to be "seen." If you've posted useful, worthwhile, professional comments or critiques, chances are that an editor will remember your name when your submission arrives by normal channels. (A word of caution: If you post under an e-mail pseudonym, such as "Cloudwalker Dragonstorm," be sure to include your real name somewhere on your messages if you're hoping for name recognition later!)

Discussion groups are also an excellent place to search for professionals, experts, and other potential interview contacts and sources of information. One way to find contacts is to post a general query, such as, "Is there anyone I can talk to about . . . ?" If you're seeking anecdotes on a topic, consider asking members to share their experiences on the subject—if it's appropriate to the group. If it's not, ask members to contact you personally. If you've already discovered a group member who seems appropriate for an interview, contact that person privately with your request. Most group members are eager to share information on their area of interest or expertise.

Writing Advice

One advantage of a writing group is the opportunity to get advice on style, technique, plot, character development, and a host of other writing skills from experienced writers and editors. Some groups focus entirely on discussions of technique, including such issues as how to develop a novel synopsis or an agent query. While some groups welcome amateur queries, others don't. It's a good idea to "lurk" (listen in) for awhile to determine what sort of subjects are considered appropriate.

Marketing Tips

Some writing groups are good sources of marketing information, including announcements of new markets, market changes, contests, markets to avoid, and more. A word of warning, however: Groups can also be hotbeds of rumor, so be sure to check any suspicious-sounding information (or information that begins, "Did you hear about . . . ?").

Diversity

Online discussion groups boast a membership roster that can never be equaled by a local group. Here, you'll talk with writers from around the world, with a range of interests, viewpoints, and experience that is truly global. You may find yourself discussing character viewpoints with a writer from Singapore, or examining issues of social violence with a writer from Sweden. Such diversity can only help expand your own view of the world, and consequently, your ability to write about that world effectively.

Encouragement

Some writing groups go beyond "neighborhood" to become the equivalent of "extended family." In such groups, you'll find people who genuinely understand what it means to be a writer: how it feels to be rejected, to be accepted, to be afraid to send your work to market, to experience writer's block, or to work for months on a story that just won't come together. You'll find support for your efforts, applause for your successes, sympathy for your failures, and perhaps a well-needed boot to the rear if you're having trouble putting your work in the mailbox. You may even find yourself building some genuine friendships.

The Downside of Discussion

All discussion groups have their disadvantages as well as their benefits. The most common problems with discussion groups include off-topic chatter, "fluff," mailbox clutter, and flames.

Off-Topic Chatter

Often, a group (or members of a group) may become involved in a discussion that bears no relationship to the stated topic. One writing list, for example, became involved in a lengthy discussion of cockroaches (and they weren't talking about Kafka). Members of another list were reprimanded for ongoing discussions of *Titanic*. Often, a polite request to take an off-topic discussion off-list will suffice. If it doesn't, an appeal to the group moderator (if there is one) may be necessary.

Some lists also consider posts of humor, jokes, inspirational stories, or similar items to be off-topic. Some prohibit such postings entirely; others permit them if enough members express an interest. Whenever such items are posted, however, attention should be paid to issues of copyright. If at all possible, attribute such items to their original source.

Fluff

What I call "fluff" is the tendency to clutter a discussion group with relatively meaningless personal posts: thanks, congratulations, personal wishes, "got your message" messages, and so forth. Most groups encourage their members to send congratulatory and similar personal messages privately, but this advice is rarely heeded. Fluff is the downside of camaraderie, and often leads to:

Mailbox Clutter

This problem affects e-mail discussion lists, on which you receive every message posted to the group as a whole. It is not always pleasant to find that you have one hundred waiting messages—half of which are off-topic or personal fluff. One way to alleviate mailbox clutter is to request the "digest" option, which compiles each day's message traffic into a single (often very long) e-mail. While receiving your messages in digest form has the advantage of reducing your message traffic, it also has a downside: You cannot simply delete unwanted messages, but must scan the entire digest to find the topics that interest you. You also cannot use the automatic "reply" function to respond to messages within a digest, as you can to individually posted messages.

Flamers and Flame Wars

The most significant problem on any type of discussion list is the proliferation of antagonistic, hostile, or offensive messages, called "flamers." Flamers often attack not only the opinions being expressed by an individual, but the individual as well. "Flame wars" arise when the attacked person (or others) respond to the original flame. Flamers and flame wars create a hostile environment and reduce the opportunity for serious discussion. Some groups act quickly to extinguish such wars, but others allow them to rage unchecked.

One question you may wish to ask before joining a discussion group is whether it is moderated or unmoderated. A moderated group has a human host who either monitors message traffic (and screens out inappropriate messages) or who can be contacted by group members if a problem arises. When problems do arise, a moderator can take action against the offender(s), either by issuing a warning or by removing the offender from the group. Unmoderated lists have no such "higher power" to deal with problems such as flamers or off-topic chatter. Members of such groups must fend for themselves, working out their own problems—or not, as the case may be.

Four Types of Talk

Discussion groups come in four basic formats: e-mail discussion lists, newsgroups, forums, and chat. Each involves a slightly different technology and slightly different ground rules.

E-mail Discussion Lists

E-mail groups are simplicity itself: Members post messages to a central e-mail address, and those messages are then forwarded to everyone on the list. You can opt to receive your messages individually or in a digest format (a single daily message that incorporates that day's mail traffic).

Since anyone with the right software can host an e-mail group, thousands of private lists have sprung up on every imaginable topic. Some have hundreds of members; others have fewer than ten.

All you need to participate in such a list is an e-mail handler. Most groups offer a Web site that provides membership details and subscription instructions. To subscribe, you'll need to send the appropriate command to the group's administrative e-mail address (which is not the same as its posting address). Once your request has been received, you'll receive a "welcome" e-mail that describes the purpose of the list, its rules and guidelines, and the types of commands that can be used with the list. Keep a copy of this message; it will also tell you how to unsubscribe if you want to leave the list.

Newsgroups

Newsgroups function as electronic bulletin boards and are hosted on Usenet, a "world-wide distributed discussion system"[1] that is transported through (but is not actually a part of) the Internet. You'll need a newsreader to access newsgroups. Most browsers, however, are equipped with this software.

Newsgroups are forums for either discussions or announcements (e.g., items for sale). While most are open to the public, some are moderated, which means that messages are screened before being posted. Messages to moderated newsgroups must often be sent to an e-mail address for screening rather than posted directly on Usenet.

You can also visit and post to newsgroups through the Internet via such sites as **DejaNews** and **Reference.com**. These and similar sites enable you to

---

[1] Mark Moraes, "What is Usenet?" *News.announce.newusers official archive*, <http://www.netannounce.org/news.announce.newusers>, January 16, 1998.

read or post messages, search for specific groups, or search for specific topics of discussion.

Newsgroups are divided into eight subject categories (see the sidebar, "Newsgroup Subject Headings"). Writing groups are usually found in the "Rec" category. Support groups often meet under the "Alt" heading, making this a good place to search for personal experiences and anecdotes.

Newsgroups are posted chronologically (from newest to oldest) and hierarchically by "thread" (subject heading). Responses to a particular thread are grouped beneath the originating message, as shown below:

- Newest Thread
- Previous Thread
  - Response #1 to "Previous Thread"
    * Comment on "Response #1 . . ."
  - Response #2 to "Previous Thread"
- Earlier Thread
  - Response #1 to "Earlier Thread"
  - Etc. . . .

There are two ways to conduct research via newsgroups. The first is to use a resource such as DejaNews to search for a particular topic. The results will often include the e-mail address of the person posting, which will give you the opportunity to follow up for more information. The second is to post your question on a relevant newsgroup, then check back in a day or so to read the responses. You don't have to subscribe or unsubscribe, and you won't be bombarded with unwanted messages; you can read only the posts that interest you.

Forums

Forums are organized much like newsgroups, but are hosted on specific Web sites rather than on the Usenet. Many writing sites contain discussion forums. Some sites offer unrestricted read-only access to their forums, but require that you register and choose a user name to post messages. Others require registration before you can read messages.

Forums are simply Web pages. Consequently, if a forum contains a large number of messages, downloading time can be extremely slow. Forums are often used as an alternative to real-time chat (in fact, some sites mislabel their forums as chat rooms). Since forums are often associated with "fan" sites (e.g., *Star Trek, X-Files*), they are a good place to conduct research on trendy topics.

Chat

Live, real-time discussion on the Internet is called "chat." Chat can take many forms, depending upon the host's software and your own. If you are a member of an online service such as AOL or Prodigy, for example, it's easy to simply visit a chat room "writing workshop." If you are operating independently, you'll often need additional software, such as Telnet or IRC, to participate in a chat. Another alternative is the ICQ ("I Seek You") software or AOL Instant Messenger. These programs allow you to "talk" online with anyone else with the same software who is online at the same time.

Many writing sites host chat functions or chat rooms that are open at specific hours. Online classes often have a chat component, enabling the instructor and students to "meet" at a specific time. While chat has its limitations as a research tool (though it can be used to conduct interviews), it can be a good way to network with writers, editors, and perhaps your readers as well.

Twenty Tips on Effective Discussion

While every discussion group has its own guidelines, the following strategies will help you make the most of a group and its resources:

1. **Lurk for a period of time before becoming an active participant.** This will give you a chance to determine the tone, style, and content of the group.
2. **Read everything.** That is, read any FAQs, instructions, and other information provided by the list or newsgroup before participating (or asking questions). This will prevent you from annoying the group by posting a question like "how do I unsubscribe?" or "how do I receive messages in digest format?" Some FAQs also include "content" information that a member is expected to be familiar with. For example, a newsgroup on science fiction might include a definition of science fiction in its FAQ and would expect a new member to have read this definition rather than posting a question such as, "Say, what is science fiction anyway?"
3. **Make an introduction.** When you decide to participate, introduce yourself with a brief description of your background, as it relates to the group.
4. **Compose your messages with care.** Remember that newsgroups and e-mail lists are forever. Messages posted to newsgroups can be publicly accessed in perpetuity, while e-mail lists generally keep archives. Think before you hit that "send" button. It's easy to send off a hasty reply without thinking about how others may interpret your message.
5. **Check your sending address!** More than one list member has been embarrassed to discover that a message that was meant to be private was accidentally sent to the entire group.
6. **Be courteous!** And do so at all times, even when others are not courteous to you.
7. **Use text-only in e-mail messages.** Turn off any special formatting programs, including programs that convert e-mail into HTML format. Otherwise, such messages come across in HTML code (or not at all).
8. **Avoid special characters.** Don't use characters that require a keyboard

combination, such as an em dash (use a double hyphen instead) and smart quotes. These rarely translate properly and usually come across as distracting symbols.

9. **Don't type messages in ALL CAPS.** This is considered shouting. Use asterisks and underscore characters to indicate *boldface* and _italics or underlining_.

10. **Use emoticons.** Indicate your tone or emotion, especially if your wording might be misinterpreted otherwise :) . But use them sparingly! (See the "E-mail Glossary," chapter 5, for a list of common emoticons.)

11. **Limit line length to sixty-five to seventy characters.** Otherwise, your text may be wrapped incorrectly by the receiver's program.

12. **Try to keep messages short.** Not everyone has inexpensive or free e-mail, especially recipients in other countries.

13. **Cut and Snip.** When replying to a message, include only those passages of the original message that you are actually responding to and "snip" the rest. (You can use the word "snip" to indicate that sections have been cut.) A common complaint on e-mail lists is the continual and unnecessary reforwarding of lengthy messages.

14. **Never send attachments to an e-mail list.** This irritates (a) those who must pay for bandwidth, (b) those who can't open your message with their software, and (c) just about everyone else on the list.

15. **Use concise, interesting, accurate subject headings.** If you change a topic, change the subject heading.

16. **Don't post or e-mail copies of Web pages.** Instead, cite the complete URL (including the http:// prefix). Some e-mail programs enable a user to click directly to the Web page link from the e-mail message.

17. **Don't advertise.** If you have a Web site or product that you believe would be of interest to the group, include a discreet signature block at the end of your message that lists the URL or product name (e.g., book title). Posting advertisements to a group is considered spamming.

18. **Be sure to sign your e-mails, or use a signature block.** That way, if your original e-mail attribution is lost through replies or forwarding, people will still know who wrote the original message. When you use an alias, many groups appreciate the use of a signature with your real name.

19. **Get permission before forwarding group messages.** Do not forward messages from one group to another without the original author's permission, and do not post personal messages from outside the group.

20. **Provide sources.** When posting material such as jokes, anecdotes, humor, etc., to a group or mailing list, provide an attribution or source whenever possible. Many groups are extremely sensitive about issues of copyright violation.

Finally, be sure to follow the "Ten Tips for Successful E-mail" listed in chapter 5!

Writing, by its nature, is often an activity conducted best in seclusion, but that same seclusion can take its toll upon the writer. While discussion groups are not a substitute for participation in the real world, they can alleviate a writer's sense of isolation. It can be comforting to know that others who share your feelings, anxieties, and passions are just a mouse-click away.

Of course, even this benefit has its downside. When other writers are just a mouse-click away, it can be terribly tempting to spend your day reading and responding to posts and e-mails (all in the name of research!) instead of actually writing. And that is perhaps the biggest danger of all!

Newsgroup Subject Headings

Newsgroups are divided into the following categories:
- **Comp**—topics relating to computers, computer news, products, etc.
- **News**—topics relating to the Internet news network
- **Rec**—topics relating to hobbies, recreation, sports, the arts (most writing groups will be found under this heading)
- **Sci**—topics relating to any area of science, including medicine, astronomy, natural sciences, physical sciences, etc.
- **Soc**—social and sociological topics, including current and international social issues, cultural issues, world cultures, etc.
- **Talk**—groups focusing on debate
- **Misc**—topics that aren't easily classified under any other category
- **Alt**—Groups that have chosen to bypass the classification system listed above. While the "Alt" category includes a large number of controversial topics, it also includes many hard-to-classify groups such as support groups, pet-related groups, etc.
- **ucb**—newsgroups distributed through U.C. Berkeley
- **clari**—newsgroups distributed through ClariNet, a fee-based service that distributes newsfeeds

RESOURCES

Searchable List Databases

The following sites enable you to search for a particular type of list or, in some cases, to search all discussion groups for messages on a specific topic. Results vary, so try several sites and be creative in your use of search terms.

CataList, the Official Catalog of LISTSERV Lists *www.lsoft.com/lists/listref.html*

This list produced the best results for discussion groups on the subject of "writer" or "writing."

DejaNews *www.dejanews.com*

Search for newsgroups or specific subject content.

E-mail Discussion Groups/Lists and Resources *www.webcom.com/impulse/list.html*

Everything E-mail: Mailing List Discussion Groups/Newsletters *everythingemail.net/discussion.html*

Useful articles, charts, and lists of commands to help you get the most from newsgroups and discussion lists.

ListServe.com: Publicly Accessible Mailing Lists *www.neosoft.com/internet/paml/bysubj.html*

Check the topic directory for an idea of the types of lists available online.

Liszt, the Mailing List Directory *www.liszt.com*

Navigating the Net: E-mail Discussion Lists *www.delphi.com/navnet/faq/listsub.html*

Offers a useful FAQ on discussion lists at *www.delphi.com/navnet/faq/mlistsq.html*.

Reference.COM Usenet and Mailing List Archive *www.reference.com*

Articles on how to use lists and forums. Offers searchable database of Internet discussion lists, for content or list type.

Tile.Net *tile.net/listserv/*

A reference guide to all standard Usenet Newsgroups on the Internet. Every newsgroup has its own page on Tile.Net, offering statistics, FAQs, and links to newsgroup Web sites.

Vivian's "List of Lists" *www.catalog.com/vivian/interest-group-search.html*

A directory of e-mail discussion lists and newsgroups.

Writers' Groups *www.writers.com/groups.htm*

A selection of writing groups and classes. Includes a helpful participation FAQ.

Chat Software and Resources

AOL Instant Messenger *www.aol.com/aim/promo/73010/aim_download.html*

Free downloadable program that enables you to "talk" with others online.

ICQ *www.icq.com*

Another free "talk" program.

Softseek.com *softseek.com/Internet/Chatting_and_IRC/*

Links to several downloadable chat and online communication programs.

Writing Chats[2]

America Online *www.aol.com*

Chats are held in several areas, including "Writers Club Romance Group" (Keyword: WCRG), "Fictional Realm" (Keyword: Books), "Book Central" (Keyword: BC), "Other Side of Creativity" (Keyword: OSC), and "Amazing Instant Novelist" (Keyword: Novel).

Byron's Romance Port *www.geocities.com/Athens/8774*

Chats for writers include "Bookaholics," "Kensington Interactive," and "NovelTalk."

Compuserve *www.compuserve.com*

"Litforum" offers several areas and chat groups for writers.

Delphi *www.delphi.com*

Look for writer chats (in both Java and HTML) in the "Creative Arts" area, which includes the Painted Rock Writer's Colony.

---

[2] Much of this information is drawn from Lori Soard's article, "Writing to Talk About," in the December 26, 1998 issue of *Inscriptions*.

From the Heart Online *www.delphi.com/FTH*

    Romance Writers of America holds a weekly public chat on Thursdays at 9:00 P.M. EST. It also hosts a number of workshops open only to members.

The Mining Co. *www.miningco.com*

    Visit the "Art/Entertainment Area" for a list of guides that host chats and forums. Java required.

Romance Central *www.romance-central.com*

The Romance Club *www.theromanceclub.com*

    A "writers' chat" hosted every Thursday from 9:00–11:00 P.M. EST.

TalkCity *www.talkcity.com*

    Offers chat on a variety of subjects, including author interviews.

Word Museum *www.wordmuseum.com*

    Word Museum's Friday chats (10:00 P.M. EST) frequently feature guest authors, agents, and editors. Transcripts from such sessions are often available.

Writer'sClub *www.writersclub.com*

    Features daily writing chats and a wide range of scheduled special interest and author chats.

Your Weekly Kiss *www.mindspring.com/~driordan/kiss*

    Romance chat.

Online Learning: Two Ways to Improve Your Writing Skills

If you'd like to become a better writer or learn skills in a new area of writing, such as a different genre or field, the Internet is a good place to look for help. No longer does one need the resources of a big city to attract quality instructors or lecturers. You can find experts throughout the world teaching in a host of online classrooms. You can also learn on your own schedule—no more drives to late-night classes in rotten weather!

Two skill-building methods that writers find particularly useful are critique groups and online classes. Both are excellent ways to become a part of the online writing community.

Online Critique Groups

Online critique groups or workshops work via e-mail and give writers the chance to submit their work for review while reviewing the work of others. As with discussion groups, members must subscribe to a list in order to participate and post submissions and critiques to the central list address. However, critique groups are not places for discussion; off-topic chatter is strongly discouraged, and some groups don't even permit members to enter into a discussion of a critique. If you want to discuss a critique or submission with another member, you will often be asked to do so off-list.

Dozens of critique groups are now available online. To find the group that is right for you, you'll need to make three important decisions:

- **Subject or genre.** Some critique groups are open to any submissions, including fiction and nonfiction, short stories, and ongoing novels. Most, however, are more specialized, open only to materials within a specific genre or field. Fiction groups are far more common than nonfiction groups. In some cases, a single sponsor will host critique groups in a variety of genres. If the group has a Web site, you will be able to check the guidelines for participation. Otherwise, you may have to e-mail the sponsor for information.

- **Experience requirements.** Some groups accept members of any level of experience; others require members to be of a comparable level of expertise. The latter will ask for a writing sample and an outline of your writing history before accepting you as a member. Each has its advantages and disadvantages. In a group where members share similar levels of expertise, your work will be critiqued by someone at your own level of writing ability—which can be an advantage if you are an experienced writer looking for feedback from peers, but a disadvantage if you are a new writer looking for feedback from more experienced pros. In a mixed group, however, you may receive feedback not only from seasoned writers, but also from writers with absolutely no experience or understanding of your type of work (though even "newbies" can offer insights that might be overlooked by more seasoned writers). Both types of groups generally give you an opportunity to mentor and to be mentored.
- **Participation requirements.** Most critique groups have participation requirements, some more intense than others. Members may be expected to critique (or "crit") a certain number of submissions per week or month. You will usually be expected to critique a certain number of submissions before you can post your own work to the group, and you may also be expected to maintain a certain "crit-to-sub" ratio (e.g., three crits for every submission). Some groups are very strict about these requirements and may suspend you from active membership, or eventually drop you from the list entirely, if you don't meet your quota. If you join such a group and go out of town or, for any other reason, are unable to critique for a time, it's wise to inform the list moderator so that you won't be automatically placed on an inactive list for nonparticipation.

Advantages of Online Critiquing

Like real-world writing groups, online critique groups are not created equal. Some are considered highly effective; others aren't as well reviewed. The effectiveness of a group can also be a matter of personal taste. Online groups offer certain advantages over real-world groups—as well as some unique disadvantages that arise from the electronic environment.

- **It's free.** Perhaps the greatest advantage of this type of feedback is that you don't have to pay for it. It's far cheaper than hiring a tutor, a book doctor, or a personal editor to review your work. Nor do you have to pay dues, which some real-world groups require to pay for room rental, refreshments, etc. or worry about who's bringing the coffee and donuts. Nor do you have to make copies of your manuscript to hand out.

- **It's convenient.** Online groups fit easily into one's writing schedule. You don't have to drive anywhere or wonder how to grab a hasty dinner before meeting with your group. You can participate at any time, reading submissions on your own schedule and in the comfort of your own home.

- **It offers a broad membership base**. Members of your online group aren't drawn from your local community. Instead, they may literally come from around the world. This brings an amazing diversity of backgrounds, cultures, educational levels, and interests to the group—which in turn leads to an amazing diversity of perspectives and viewpoints. It can also provide a much broader range of factual feedback—don't be surprised if your big fight scene is critiqued by a reader with actual weapons training or medical expertise.

- **It offers rapid feedback**. In a real-world group, you hand out your material at one meeting and wait until the next for feedback. If your material is part of an ongoing project, or if you have a deadline, this can be frustrating—you may not receive feedback for an entire month. Online, however, you may see responses to your submissions within hours, and if you're on an active list, you'll never have to wait longer than a day. This enables you to incorporate feedback into your ongoing writing schedule.

- **It offers individual attention**. Most real-world critique groups attempt to give a few minutes of time to everyone at each meeting. The larger the group, therefore, the less actual feedback you're likely to receive. In an online group, however, each submission is handled individually, so the critiquer can spend as much time as necessary to give adequate feedback.

- **It offers multiple points of view**. Some real-world groups tend to move toward a consensus. Some members may not speak up if their opinions differ significantly from the rest of the group. In an online group, members may not see the critiques of other members, or may choose to ignore them, and so are less likely to be influenced by the opinions of the rest of the group. In addition, no single voice will be drowned out by disagreement or silenced by lack of time.

- **It allows multiple submissions**. Some groups allow you to submit new material as often as once a week (or as often as you meet the crit-to-sub ratio). This enables you to get feedback on more of your work, more quickly than you could ever obtain from a real-time group.

- **It's anonymous.** If you're shy about sharing your work, the facelessness of an online group may make you feel more at ease. You don't have to sit squirming in your chair as critiquers tear your prose to shreds. In many cases, no one else will even see the feedback you receive, and no one will ever see your blushes. You can also be sure that critiquers are responding solely to your work, and not to you as a person.

Disadvantages of Online Critiquing

- **Amateur feedback.** While some groups accept only experienced writers, others are open to all. That means you may receive feedback from someone who knows little or nothing about the actual craft of writing or who may be unfamiliar with the type of material or genre you're submitting. You may receive feedback from someone who lacks your vocabulary, and therefore who considers the material "too hard to understand," or who inaccurately attempts to correct your grammar. You may receive feedback from someone with no knowledge of the markets you're writing for, and who therefore cannot give you any useful feedback on whether your material is suitable for those markets. Finally, you may receive feedback that says little more than "Gee, I really liked this piece."

- **Amateur submissions.** Any open group will have its share of amateur, unskilled writers whose material is riddled with grammatical errors, misspellings, and structural and conceptual flaws. You may find it difficult to critique such material in a constructive fashion. The best approach is usually to find something that works at least moderately well ("good story idea" or "interesting characters") and work from there.

- **Anonymity.** While the facelessness of an online group can be comforting to a shy author, it can create as many problems as it solves. It may, for example, bolster the courage of the "hypercritter" who confuses critiquing with shredding—and whose feedback ranges from a sarcastically dismissive paragraph to a line-by-line vivisection of your work. It may also encourage the "hypersensitive submitter"—the author who can't accept any negative feedback without lashing out in anger or whining of ill-treatment. Personality conflicts are bound to arise in any critique group, and while real-world groups have an incentive to resolve those conflicts, that incentive is sometimes lacking in the electronic environment. Consequently, some groups fail to deal appropriately with flamers, complainers, members who flood the list with inappropriate submissions, or other problems. Conversely, other groups take a very strong stance against problematic members and will either reprimand or, if necessary, remove a member who refuses to play by the rules.

- **Submission overload.** Some groups impose a queue system that limits the number of submissions to the list; others allow unlimited posts. While you may feel tempted, or even obligated, to reply to every submission, doing so can often cut significantly into your own writing time. As you become more familiar with the group, you may find it easier to determine which submissions you will review and which you would prefer to pass. Whatever the reasons for your choices, decide what your limits should be and stick to them.

- **Fear of theft.** Note that the disadvantage listed here is "fear" rather than "theft." Many writers are concerned about posting their material online for fear that it will be copied or stolen. Part of this fear arises from loudly voiced concerns about piracy online and the growing impression that anything posted is likely to be stolen.

Thus far, this has not proven a peril for online groups. Most groups have firm guidelines on issues of plagiarism, copying, or distributing materials in any form without permission (i.e., it would be against the rules to print out a story to pass to a friend). Perhaps more importantly, participants in such groups tend to be serious, if sometimes inexperienced writers who are more interested in receiving feedback on their own work than in trying to pick up a story from someone else.

The very fact that your work is posted electronically can actually mitigate against the risk of theft. When you post a story to a critique group, it is viewed by a large number of people, all of whom could later verify your authorship if a question of theft or copying actually arose. Many groups also archive messages, which provides a permanent record not only of your authorship, but of the date of your submission. Thus, any issue of theft could quickly and easily be resolved in your favor by a variety of mechanisms. In addition, ISPs now have a tremendous responsibility to deal quickly with cases of copyright infringement and will remove material from their server at the first indication of possible infringement, even before a case of infringement is actually proven. In short, your risk of having material stolen in an online group is no greater than of having it stolen in a real-world writers' group—and in some cases, possibly less.

Five Tips on Submitting

One way to endear yourself to fellow members of your group, and to improve your chances of positive feedback, is to observe the following submission guidelines:

1. **Always submit your best work.** Polish your material as carefully as if you were submitting it for publication. Never submit something you would consider a rough draft (i.e., a story that still has holes to be filled or problems to be resolved). It's perfectly acceptable to ask, "Does this work?" but not, "What do you think my character should do here?" Also, be sure that your work meets the content guidelines of the group. If your group specifies "romance only," for example, don't submit a horror story or a sample of your science fiction novel.

2. **Always spellcheck and proofread.** Many of the errors I've seen on submissions could have been caught by a basic spellchecking pass, let alone an actual proofreading. Failing to spellcheck sends a message of laziness—it implies that you aren't bothering to do your best for the group. Remember, as well, that spellchecking won't catch grammatical and punctuation errors, so give your material a thorough proofreading as well. If you don't and post material that contains numerous spelling or

grammatical errors, you risk alienating your critiquers, who will either take you to task for every single error or advise you (sometimes harshly) to review the basics before submitting more work.

3. **Observe the group's length restrictions.** Some groups specify a maximum number of words per submission. If your submission is longer, ask the moderator for permission before submitting. It's usually wise to divide longer submissions into two parts. Otherwise, recipients' e-mail programs may split your text anyway, which can create awkward breaks. By dividing a longer message yourself, you'll make your work more readable. Be sure to specify how many parts are being sent, and in what order—e.g., "Part 1 of 2, Part 2 of 2."

4. **Don't submit revised work to the group without permission.** Most groups prefer not to see the same material twice, especially if you've only made minor grammatical revisions. In addition, when you submit a revised piece, your critiquers will quickly see whose advice you've accepted and whose you've ignored—so why stir up that particular pot? It's usually best, if you would like a specific reviewer to take another look at your work, to contact that reviewer directly and ask if he would look at the revised piece off-list.

5. **Always thank your critiquer(s).** Even if you don't agree with a critique, thank everyone who took the time to review your work. (On some lists, this is handled off-list.) If a critique seemed rude, hostile, or unduly negative, don't bother to respond angrily to the critiquer. Instead, discuss the problem with the list moderator; you may not be the only one experiencing a problem. Many lists will reprimand or remove a member who submits inappropriate critiques.

In addition to these guidelines, be sure to follow the "Ten Tips for Successful E-mail" listed in chapter 5.

Ten Tips on Critiquing

While every group has its own guidelines for critiquing (which can either be found on the group's Web site or will be e-mailed to you as part of your "welcome" message when you join), all share certain basic expectations. The first rule, of course, is to behave courteously and professionally at all times and under all circumstances. Beyond that, a good critiquer should:

1. **Be specific.** Critiques should say more than "I liked it" or "I didn't like it." Members want to know why you liked a piece and, more specifically, what sections you liked and what sections you didn't. Let the author know what works and what doesn't. On the positive side, are the characters believable? If so, can you list specific details or incidents that make a character believable? On the negative side, does the author skimp on description? Can you point to a paragraph where added detail would

have helped the reader "see" the scene or setting? Point out sections that seem unclear or confusing, that contradict one another, or that are rough or hard to read. Many critiquers use the "reply" function to go through a submission paragraph by paragraph, noting parts that work and parts that seem awkward.

2. **Be constructive.** It's often easier to point out the flaws in a piece than its positive qualities. Even if a piece is badly written, it's important to find some element to praise. Try focusing on areas that could use more development, and describe those areas in a positive tone: "I really liked the character of Zelda and would have liked to see more of her in the story. Perhaps you could give her a few more scenes or some additional dialogue." Or, "You have a talent for imagery, and your piece is loaded with vivid descriptions. A few times, however, I found that the descriptions got in the way of the story, as in the paragraph where . . ."

3. **Suggest "fixes" when appropriate.** If you have factual information that could help an author correct a scene, by all means provide it—most authors will thank you for it. If you can suggest a way to make a passage run more smoothly, perhaps by varying sentence structure or changing punctuation, don't hesitate to do so. If a scene could benefit from more (or less) description, provide suggestions on what to cut or what to add. Often, an author may recognize that a scene has problems, but may have run out of ideas on how to make changes. Your suggestion may be just what the author needs to look at the scene from a new direction or perspective. Just remember that the author is under no obligation to actually use your suggestions!

4. **Be sensitive.** Even experienced authors can have thin skins, and beginning authors can have extremely fragile egos. When dealing with a new author, remember that while this person may be writing truly appalling material now, she may well improve with practice. A badly timed shot, however, can often discourage a budding author from seeking feedback in the future. Try to take into account an author's level of experience when critiquing. Encourage an amateur author's strengths, and choose no more than one or two problem areas to focus on—e.g., point-of-view errors or faulty dialogue tags.

5. **Be unbiased.** Members of your group may write about ideas, subjects, themes, or viewpoints that you disagree with—perhaps passionately. The purpose of a critique, however, is not to argue the merit of an idea, but to assess how well that idea is presented. If you find that you truly can't deal objectively with certain themes (and this can happen—passion is an important quality in a writer), simply avoid critiquing those materials.

6. **Focus on presentation, not plot.** You may not like a particular type of story, plotline, or theme; however, it's never appropriate to respond with a negative critique based purely on personal taste ("I thought this was a

boring story, like all *Star Trek* stories."). Instead, focus on specifics: Does the story start in the right place? Is the conflict effective? Are the characters well developed? Is the dialogue believable? Is the resolution appropriate? Address the manner in which the story is written, rather than the story itself.

7. **Avoid nitpicking on grammar.** Some groups welcome grammatical corrections, especially if you can explain the rule behind the correction. Others don't. It's a good idea to lurk for awhile and see how others handle this issue before plunging in with the electronic equivalent of the red pen. When you do comment on grammar, don't undertake to proofread an entire submission. Instead, focus on areas of consistent error—for example, a writer who consistently confuses "its" and "it's," or who misuses dialogue tags ("I wonder what that means." He said.), or something similar. Point out consistent spelling errors, but don't quibble over mistakes that might well have been typos (though if you see a lot of those, you could politely recommend that the writer spellcheck material before submitting).

8. **"Snip" whenever possible.** To save downloading time, don't simply hit "reply" and send the entire submission back to the submitter. Instead, "snip" (delete) those paragraphs that you aren't specifically responding to, retaining only those that you are commenting on.

9. **Resist reviewing other critiques before submitting your own.** Reviewing what other people have said about a piece can sometimes influence your own thinking—you may not approach the piece with a fresh outlook. It may also cause you to omit certain comments because they have already been made by others—but it can be precisely this sort of repetition that convinces an author that a problem actually exists.

10. **Respect the author's confidentiality.** Besides the obvious rule of no plagiarism, most groups also have rules against sharing submissions with anyone outside the group. If an author shares personal information with you, perhaps to clarify events in a story, be sure you don't pass that information along to the group (e.g., by inadvertently mentioning it in your critique). Respect the author's privacy at all times.

Many groups also have unspoken guidelines—a set of mutual understandings that evolve as the group learns to work together. It's always a good idea to lurk for awhile when joining any group, without actively participating, so that you can get a feel for the types of submissions and critiques that are considered appropriate—and for the group dynamics. You'll soon learn whether submissions are amateur or professional, whether critiques are detailed or cursory, and whether inappropriate behavior (such as flaming) is ignored, tolerated, encouraged, or politely quelled.

It's also important to remember that no matter how experienced your critiquers may be, or how urgently they advise you to make changes, you are the final judge of your own work. You are not required to agree with anyone else's opinion or follow anyone else's suggestions. A good critique group can offer you valuable tips on improving your writing, but it is up to you to determine how (or whether) to apply those tips.

Online Education

A more intensive approach to improving your writing skills is to take a class online. On the Internet, you can find courses to help you build skills in your current field or to teach you how to write in a totally new field or genre.

Online classes (also referred to as distance education) offer a number of benefits to the busy writer, including the following:

- You don't have to live near a major city or university to have access to high-quality courses and reputable instructors
- You don't have to drive to a campus at night, park somewhere in the dark, walk through the rain, and sit in a too-small desk in an odd-smelling classroom[1] for two or three hours, wishing you'd had the sense to pack a dinner like the one your neighbor is enjoying
- You don't have to fit an evening or weekend course into your already busy schedule
- You don't have to choose between family and school on evenings and weekends
- You can conduct every portion of the class at your own convenience
- You receive one-on-one feedback from the instructor
- You don't have to feel shy about asking a question in front of the rest of the class—it's just you and the prof

Of course, there are disadvantages as well. Besides the fact that courses may vary widely in quality, there is no class participation. You can't sit with a group, interact with other writers, make friends, and hear the questions and discussions raised by other class members (which may cover issues you wouldn't have thought of). Some people find it easier to learn in a group environment and may find that convenience doesn't compensate for the loss of human dynamics.

Writing courses are available from a number of sources, including major universities, private companies, and writing sites. Costs vary on an equally wide scale. While a class at the **Word Museum** might cost $40 to $60, a course from UCLA might cost as much as $550. With such a range of prices, it's important to know what to look for while shopping for a class and what to expect when you find one.

---

[1] This is not an exaggeration. Once I was asked to teach a writing class in a chemistry lab. After one evening of perching on stools by lab tables amid some extremely odd and potent odors, the class and instructor rebelled en masse and demanded better quarters.

How Online Classes (Generally) Work

As little as two years before this book was written, online courses were highly experimental. Colleges and instructors were still struggling to develop a template that would work for both instructor and student—and ensure that the student received an appropriate level of instruction.

That template has now evolved into a fairly standard structure for online instruction. Most online courses include the following elements:

- **Lectures**. Instead of speaking in front of a crowded room, online instructors "lecture" via a Web site or e-mail. In other words, the lecture is basically a reading assignment. Lectures vary in length; some online samples are no more than a few paragraphs, whereas others are considerably more substantial.
- **Readings**. An instructor may post materials on a Web site for students to read or, more typically, direct students to specific URLs for reading materials. (Using URLs also helps instructors avoid copyright issues.)
- **Discussion**. Some courses attempt to bring the entire class together in a chat room for real-time discussions. Most, however, recognize that much of the benefit of an online course is the freedom from any preset schedule, so "discussion" is conducted via e-mail or a Web site forum (which works much like a private newsgroup). Students and instructors "talk" back and forth, asking questions and making comments, but not in real-time.
- **Homework**. A good writing course should ask you to write. One of the advantages of learning online is the ease and speed with which you can submit your homework to the instructor and have it evaluated and returned. Some instructors post homework assignments on the course Web site, others deliver them by e-mail. Some courses also ask students to post or share their homework assignments for class critiquing.
- **Individual feedback**. Your instructor will generally provide detailed comments on your homework assignments and will also be available to answer your questions by e-mail (personally rather than through the group forum or list). If you raise a question that would benefit the rest of the class, the instructor may ask your permission to share the question and answer in the public discussion.

Questions to Ask When Choosing a Class

- **Does the topic match my needs?** If you're looking for a course on screenwriting, for example, don't just jump at the first screenwriting course you see. Review the course description and the syllabus for the course (which will usually be posted online). Remember that you're not limited by geography to the courses offered by your local college; you can pick and choose, finding the one that is right for you.
- **How advanced is the course?** Make sure the course matches your level

of expertise. Is it described as beginning, intermediate, or advanced—and what do those terms actually mean? Are there prerequisites for the course, such as previous courses or a demonstrated level of writing ability? Is the course part of a series?

- **Who is the instructor?** Have you ever heard of this person? What credentials are listed? How much experience has this instructor had in the actual subject area of the class? For example, if the instructor is offering a class on "Writing for Magazines," how many articles has he sold? An instructor who has sold two hundred articles can probably share more market tips than one who has sold two, or even twenty.
- **Who is the sponsoring organization?** In some cases, this may be of little importance. Many writing sites now offer hosting services for instructors, which enable any qualified writer to offer a class by using the site's resources. Still, it won't hurt to ask around in newsgroups or mailing lists to find out whether anyone has had an especially positive (or negative) experience with any particular organization.
- **What are the requirements of the class?** How long (and comprehensive) are the lectures? How much reading material will you be expected to review? Will you be expected to write? Since online education greatly facilitates personal feedback, it seems almost pointless to take a writing course that doesn't provide writing assignments. Again, review the syllabus carefully—and find out if you can review sample lectures or assignments from previous classes.
- **Does the class offer credit toward a degree program?** Many colleges offer online courses as part of the requirements for an MFA (Master of Fine Arts). These courses are usually more expensive than ordinary writing classes (which are often the online equivalent of a continuing education course), but may offer more instruction and add specific education credentials to your resume.
- **Can I get my money back?** Find out whether the sponsoring organization has a drop option that enables you to reclaim your tuition (or a prorated portion of your tuition) if you find that the course is not what you expected or that you can't participate for some reason.

Two Other Sources of Help

For the self-motivated, the Internet offers two additional skill-building resources: Online Writing Labs (OWLs) and sources of grammatical help.

OWLs are sponsored by a number of universities—usually through the English or Communications department—and offer a range of instructional tools. Some post dozens of handouts on grammar, effective writing, and related topics. Others offer exercises and quizzes to help you build your writing skills. Still others offer actual online writing help, though most limit that assistance to students of the sponsoring institution. With dozens of OWLs to choose from, the best approach is to surf through the different options and find the facility that offers the tips or instruction you need.

Grammar sites come in all shapes and sizes. Some are sponsored by universities, while others are hosted by writers or private organizations. No matter what your particular grammatical bugaboo may be, you can find the rules to set you straight. Some of the grammatical offerings on the Web include:

- **"Answer people."** Sites hosted by authors and experts who will answer your questions or discuss grammar issues with you directly
- **Basic guides.** Articles and guidelines on grammar, punctuation, usage, and writing style
- **Interactive guides.** Online minicourses, exercises, and quizzes that walk you through specific grammatical issues
- **Hotlines.** Yes, places where you can actually call to ask a question about grammar
- **Newsgroups.** Grammar newsgroups that discuss issues of spelling, usage, and similar topics
- **Stylebooks.** Tips on writing effectively, appropriate word choice, and modern word choice (e.g, **The Gender-Neutral Pronoun FAQ**)
- **Reference tools.** Dictionaries, thesauri, and, yes, *The Elements of Style* (1918 edition), all online

One of the fears writers and readers have shared about the growing popularity of the Internet is that it would spell the end of good writing. With hyperlinks, multimedia, and whiz-bang effects designed to delight the attention-span–challenged, who would care about good writing? Would it be relegated to the attics of eccentric fussbudgets who still cared whether people knew the difference between "its" and "it's"? Would the Internet encourage and contribute to the demise of good (i.e., grammatically correct) writing?

The reality should quickly dispel that fear. Badly written Web sites may abound, but good ones draw a steady crowd. Writers have more opportunities than ever to check their work and get vital feedback. Far from encouraging literary sloth and error, the Internet offers an explosion of writing sources, courses, and resources—and leaves virtually no excuse for bad writing!

RESOURCES

Critique Groups

Critters Workshop *brain-of-pooh.tech-soft.com/users/critters/*
This highly recommended workshop focuses primarily on speculative fiction, though it offers other workshops as well. The site offers sample critiques, tips on critiquing and participating in a group, and market information, including the "Black Hole" page that lists response times for speculative fiction markets. Considered a "high-intensity" group with high workload demands.

Del Rey Online Writing Workshop *www.randomhouse.com/delrey/workshop/howitworks.html*
A workshop for speculative fiction writers, sponsored by Del Rey Books.

IRC Undernet Writer's Page *www.getset.com/writers*
This site offers several critique lists, a "live" critique group, chat, and a newsletter. To subscribe to any of the lists below, send a message to the address listed with the word "subscribe" in the subject line.

- Romance writers: *RomanceCrit-request@niestu.com*
- Freelance writers: *FreelanceCrit-request@niestu.com*
- Religious writers: *InspirationCrit-request@niestu.com*
- Mystery writers: *MysteryCrit-request@niestu.com*
- Mainstream Fiction: *FictionCrit-request@niestu.com*
- Short Stories: *ShortsCrit-request@niestu.com*
- Science Fiction, Fantasy, and Horror: *SpecFicCrit-request@niestu.com*

SFNovelist Workshop *www.crayne.com/victory/sfnovel.html*
A critique group for writers of "hard science fiction" novels.

Writeria: Online Workshops *wkgroup.com/zeugma/writeria/workshops.html*
A list of free and fee-based critique workshops.

Writers' Groups Online *www.writerswrite.com/groups.htm*
A list of critique, support, and chat groups for writers.

Writer's Internet Exchange (WRITE) *www.writelinks.com/write/index.html*
A discussion list and critique group "for professionals only." A writing sample is required. Click "The Friendly Pencil" for information on coaching services for less experienced writers.

Writer's List *web.mit.edu/afs/mbarker/www/faqs/writers.html*
A writing sample is required to establish skill level. For submission guidelines, go to *web.mit.edu.afs/ mbarker.www/faqs/subfaq.html*; for critique guidelines, go to *web.mit.edu.afs/mbarker.www/faqs/ critfaq.html*.

Tips on Effective Critiquing

Hardcore Critique Advice *www.crayne.com/victory/download/casiltip.txt*
An excellent, detailed article by Amy Sterling Casil on how to write an effective critique.

How to Critique Fiction *www.crayne.com/victory/howcrit.html*
Most critique groups recommend this article by Victory Crayne as *the* reference to review before undertaking a critique, as well as to help you interpret critiques of your own work. The rest of the site also has a number of useful critique and writing resources.

Writing Courses

Freelance Success Institute *www.freelancesuccess.com*

Gotham Writers' Workshop *www.write.org/frame_main.html*
This is an excellent place to acquaint yourself with how online classes work. It offers a "sample" class on its Web site that enables one to explore a syllabus, posted lectures, student forums, homework assignments, etc.

NovelAdvice *www.noveladvice.com/craft/index.html*

UCLA *www.onlinelearning.net/w99*

Word Museum *www.wordmuseum.com*

Writeria: Online Workshops *wkgroup.com/zeugma/writeria/workshops.html*

Writers Club University *www.writersclub.com/wcu/catalog.cfm*
Writers on the Net *www.writers.com/classes.htm*
> This group also offers tutoring and editing for a fee; go to *www.writers.com/classes.htm/tutors.htm.*
Writer's Village University *4-writers.com*
Writers Write University *www.writerswrite.com*

OWLs and Instructional Materials

The Arrow *www.wport.com/~cawilcox/mainpath/page1.htm*
> Helpful tools for writing papers and essays, including advice on the outlining and development process.

National Writing Centers Association *departments.colgate.edu/diw/NWCAOWLs.html*
> A comprehensive directory of OWLs, handouts (by category), and online tutoring services. (For handouts and tutoring, click the "Resources for Writers" link.)

The UVic Writer's Guide *webserver.maclab.comp.uvic.ca/writersguide/Pages/MasterToc.html*
> Designed primarily to assist in writing essays and papers, this site contains many useful tips on style, presentation, organization, and similar topics, as well as various reference tools.

Writing Labs and Writing Centers on the Web *owl.english.purdue.edu/owls/writing-labs.html*
> A directory of nearly fifty online writing labs.

Grammar Sources

The Arrow *www.wport.com/~cawilcox/mainpath/page1.htm*
> Focusing primarily on student papers and essays, this site provides tools that can help with outlining and topic/content development.

Bartlett's Quotations *www.columbia.edu/acis/bartleby/bartlett/*
Common Errors in English *www.wsu.edu:8080/~brians/errors/spellcheck.html*
> A list of commonly confused/misspelled words, usage errors, and "other strange and amusing word confusions."

Elements of Style *www.columbia.edu/acis/bartleby/strunk/*
Garbl's Writing Resources On Line *pw1.netcom.com/~garbl1/writing.html*
> An extensive list of grammar resources, including basic and interactive guides, advice columns, texts, quizzes, and more.

The Gender-Neutral Pronoun FAQ *www.lumina.net/gnp/*
> A general and specific discussion of gender-neutral pronouns.

Grammar and Style Notes *andromeda.rutgers.edu/~jlynch/writing*
> An English professor's "miscellany of grammatical rules and explanations, comments on style, and suggestions on usage."

Grammar Hotline Directory *www.tc.cc.va.us/writcent/gh/hotlinol.htm*
> A searchable list of grammar hotlines that can be contacted by phone or e-mail for answers to "short questions about writing."

Grammar Lady, The *www.grammarlady.com*
> An online columnist who answers grammar questions, hosts a grammar hotline, and sponsors a forum on grammatical issues and questions.

Guide to Grammar and Writing/Ask Grammar *webster.commnet.edu/HP/pages/darling/original.htm*
> Another huge grammar site, including lists of basic grammar tips, interactive quizzes, a hotline, quotes, links, and a log of grammar FAQs.

Interactive Grammar Quizzes *webster.commnet.edu/HP/pages/darling/grammar/quiz_list.html-ssi*
> More than one hundred (fun) grammar quizzes. (Most require Java.)

The King's English *www.columbia.edu/acis/bartleby/fowler/*
The Linguistic Fun Page *www.ojohaven.com/fun/*
> Links to amusing and helpful references on grammatical use and misuse, such as misquoted quotes, funny translation errors, "The Book of Clichés," and more "linguistic humor."

One-Look Dictionaries *www.onelook.com*
> One of the most comprehensive dictionary sites, with links to more than three hundred dictionaries in a range of fields, including literary, technical, scientific, linguistic, business, and more.

On Line English Grammar *www.edunet.com/english/grammar/index.cfm*
Tips, exercises, a "grammar clinic," and practice pages.
Research-It! *www.iTools.com/research-it/research-it.html*
A collection of look-up tools, including dictionaries, thesauri, language translators, biographical information, quotation directories, and more.
WWWebster Dictionary *www.m-w.com/info/info.htm*
Look up words or phrases, or search the thesaurus, vocabulary builder, or other tools on the Merriam-Webster site.

8

Do You Need a Web Site?

Do you want to impress editors? Do you want to attract more readers and sell more books? Do you want readers and editors to know that you are an expert in your field? If you answered "yes" to any of these questions, you've answered the title question as well: Yes, you need a Web site.

For the first time in history, writers have access to something they've craved since the first cuneiform was chiseled: worldwide publicity at almost no cost. The Internet offers writers an opportunity to promote their books, become more accessible to their readership, establish their expertise, and enhance their professional standing with editors (and other writers)—all for the cost of your ISP connection and a little time spent learning HTML.

Before you rush out to post a home page, however, stop and take a deep breath. The Internet is flooded with sloppy, unimpressive, cutesy, and trivial "writer" home pages. As a professional, you want something that says more than, "Hi, my name is Bob, click here to read my stories, click here to see a picture of my dog!" Before you launch, you need to make some important decisions about your site.

Five Great Reasons for a Web Site

A professional Web site requires a professional purpose: It should, in some way, advance your career (or your dreams). Your first step, therefore, is to determine what writing goal is most important to you at this time. Is it to sell more articles to magazines? To sell more copies of your nonfiction book? To attract more readers to your novels? To interact with your readership? To educate and inform your readers? To become more involved in the writing community?

Keep in mind as well that visitors aren't impressed by sites that are little more than electronic ads for your books. Purpose must be supported by content, just as content must be guided by purpose. Choose both with care, and you'll be able to give readers a reason to stop by, to stay and browse, to come back—and to tell their friends.

Following are five of the more common purposes for writers' Web sites and the types of content that can help support those purposes:

Reason #1: To Post Clips

One of the downsides of electronic queries is the impossibility of attaching clips. The easiest solution is to post a selection of appropriate articles on a Web site and provide the URL in your e-query. A clip site should include:

- **An introductory home page** that indicates the type of articles that will be found on the site. It's a good idea, if possible, to organize a clip site around a particular theme (e.g., science fiction), rather than "shotgunning" your site with copies of clips on a host of unrelated topics. Another option is to cluster clips around two or three separate categories (e.g., pets, travel, writing). Your home page should also list your name and provide an overview of your credentials.

- **Selected clips of your best work.** Before posting clips of previously published work, be sure you own the necessary rights. If you've sold all rights, produced the material as work-for-hire, or do not own electronic rights, you won't have the right to put the material on your personal Web site. Nor should you simply scan clips and post them as image files, for two reasons: First, image files are cumbersome to download, and second, a magazine clipping may contain copyrighted elements that don't belong to you (such as artwork, advertising, etc.). If you prefer to scan your clips before posting them, translate them into text files first.

- **Copyright information on every page.** Since the point of clips is to let editors know where and when you were published, be sure to include complete copyright information with each article. In your copyright notice, list the title of the material, the copyright date, your name, the name of the publication in which it appeared, and the date of publication. (This information will also be useful to anyone using your material for research.) Your copyright notice might look something like this:

"Ten Ways to Get the Most from the Internet"
© 1997 by Ima Good Author.[1]
Originally published in **Write Write Write**, October 1997
All rights reserved. For reprint information, contact
IGAuthor@myisp.com.

---

[1] The HTML code for the copyright symbol (©) is © simply type this into your text and the symbol will appear when viewed online.

Reason #2: To Establish Your Expertise and/or Educate Readers

Some writers focus upon a particular area of interest, expertise, or passion. Others pursue writing as a secondary interest, in support of or in the context of a special interest, hobby, career, area of study, or similar area of expertise. In such situations, your goal may not be to convince editors that you are a brilliant writer, but that you are an expert on a particular subject. Similarly, you may be as interested in promoting a general understanding of your field as you are in promoting your own writings in that field. In this case, an expert Web site may work better for you than a purely writing-focused site and would be likely to include the following elements:

- **A home page that describes the subject area itself.** Title this page in such a way that anyone interested in your topic or area of expertise is likely to find it. Choose keywords that would be chosen by a searcher, and put those words at the top of your page, so that they will be properly indexed by search engines. Make sure your home page clearly describes the subject area of the site, the types of materials that will be found there, and how to access those materials.
- **An array of information resources.** The best way to establish your expertise is to provide expert information. This could include articles that you've published on your topic, a set of FAQs developed specifically for the site (e.g., "Ten Ways To . . ." or "Questions People Ask About . . ."), or full-length articles written for the site. You might also consider posting a regular column, such as a news column that keeps visitors up to date on developments in your field or a Q and A column in which you answer questions posed by visitors to your site. Archive back issues of your column elsewhere on your site. Whatever materials you choose, your goal is to ensure that anyone who comes to your site with a question is going to leave with a worthwhile answer.
- **A selection of top-quality links.** To position yourself as a vital resource site in your field, you'll need to surf the Web for the best links to other sites in that same field. This accomplishes two purposes: It adds to the value of your site and encourages other sites in the field to link back to you (thereby increasing your traffic). Remember that your visitors rely on you to screen sites—don't add any link that you haven't personally checked.
- **A bookstore.** If your goal is to establish expertise, consider offering a bookstore of titles related to your subject or field. While such a bookstore may compete with your own title, it will also give readers the added benefit of your expert recommendations—and show editors that you have done your homework and are familiar with the top titles in your field. If you set up an "associates" program with an online bookstore, this portion of your site can also earn money—see chapter 10 for more details.
- **Your credentials.** Keep your bio short, sweet, and professional. Focus on anything that supports your standing as an expert: education, cre-

dentials, job history, personal experience, and so on. Let visitors (and editors) know that they can trust you as a source.

Reason #3: To Promote Your Novel(s)

Novelists are finding the Web an excellent place to highlight past, current, and forthcoming novels of all types and genres. A novelist's Web site will often contain many of the following elements:

- **An introductory home page** that clearly lists your name (e.g., "Welcome to the Joan Q. Novelist Web Site"). Keep in mind that most fans will search for your work by author name, not by title, so your name should be prominently listed toward the top of your home page. Otherwise, it may not be indexed properly by search engines (see chapter 9 for more details). This page may also include your table of contents (TOC), perhaps a list of your novels (with click-throughs to pages with more information), and perhaps some images of your covers. It should also include your copyright statement (see "Five Things Every Web Site Needs," below).
- **An author bio.** Fans will want to know more about you, so satisfy their curiosity with a brief, professional biographical sketch (and a photo, if you wish). This is a good place to discuss how you began writing, why you write the types of books you do, your expertise relating to those books, your future writing plans—and, of course, how many cats you have.
- **A bibliography.** Many authors provide a list of all their writings, including short stories, awards, and any other credits.
- **Descriptions of your books.** This is your chance to give readers a better summary (and teaser) than they will find on the backs of your books. Try to include images of your book covers as well. If you can't obtain image files from your publisher, you can scan in your covers yourself, or take them to a commercial printer for scanning. If you are providing lengthy descriptions of more than one novel, consider using a separate page for each, with a second-level TOC listing all the titles you've included.
- **Excerpts.** Selections from current or forthcoming novels are often a major attraction on novelists' sites—and an excellent sales tool as well. Such excerpts give readers something free to take away, but also leave them hungry for more. Choose an excerpt that a reader can understand without having read the rest of the book—but ends with a cliff-hanger that will make the reader *want* to read the rest of the book. (You'll probably need your publisher's permission to post such an excerpt.)
- **Background information.** Is your novel set in a particular historical period, locale, or cultural milieu that readers might want to learn more about? Your Web site is an excellent place to answer questions, post background history or details, explain unfamiliar terms and concepts, and provide links to other sources of information on the Web.

- **Writing tips.** Many of your fans undoubtedly dream of writing the types of books you write. Give them a hand by offering some advice on writing in your field or genre. Such a section will also improve your chances of receiving links from other writers and organizations in your field, because other writers and organizations will regard it as a useful site for writers as well as readers.
- **A news page.** Let readers know when your latest book is coming out, what awards you've won, when you'll be appearing on television or radio talk shows, when and where you're giving talks or book signings, and anything else of a newsworthy nature. Some authors also provide links to fan sites, book reviews, and online interviews.
- **Links.** No site is complete without a few links. Choose those that relate to the general purpose and content of your site—other sources of background information or other sites for writers in your genre. You might also seek reciprocal links with other authors in your field.
- **Other works.** Some authors use their Web sites to archive previously published stories. This works well if the stories are relevant to the novel you're trying to promote. Be careful, however, about posting material that is likely to shatter the image your fans have of you as an author; this could have a negative effect on the works you're currently trying to promote.
- **Ordering information.** Make sure that visitors can find out where and how to get your books. One easy way to prompt sales is to link your book title(s) to an online bookstore, such as Amazon.com (see chapter 10 for more details).

Reason #4: To Promote Your Nonfiction Book(s)

The key difference between a fiction and a nonfiction author site is that while fiction readers tend to be author-focused, nonfiction readers tend to be subject-focused. A Web site designed to promote a nonfiction book, therefore, should usually focus on the subject of the book, and include:

- **An introductory home page** that will attract visitors searching for information on your subject area. Your name may be less important than keywords that describe the subject. To be indexed properly in search engines, those subject keywords should be close to the top of the page.
- **Information of value to readers.** Perhaps the best way to promote a nonfiction book is to offer useful *free* information. Turn your site into a resource on the topic of your book. Offer FAQs, articles, and other forms of information that will help the reader immediately. Avoid, at all costs, the appearance that the information is just a plug for your book or that you're manufacturing some sort of hype or crisis that your book will solve. Make sure that visitors can benefit from your site itself, whether they buy the book or not; this will also encourage referrals.
- **Links.** One way to make your site a genuine resource is to include a list of links to other sites covering similar topics. This will help convince

visitors that you are genuinely interested in sharing information, rather than simply trying to peddle a product.

- **Your credentials.** Before accepting your advice or information, readers will want to know why they should trust you. Readers won't want personal details here, but information about your education, experience, background, and anything else that will demonstrate your qualifications.
- **A summary of your book.** On a nonfiction site, it helps to keep book promos low-key. Offer a summary of the book, along with a cover image, on a separate page that also includes ordering information (such as a link to an online bookstore).

Reason #5: To Educate and Inform Writers

Initially, one of the most common features of any author site was a selection of writing tips. Now, sites for writers have proliferated beyond count (the resource appendix at the end of this book just scratches the surface). There's still room on the Web, however, for high-quality writing advice.

The best approach to a writing tips site today is to move beyond general "how to write" (or "how to format your manuscript") topics and focus on your area of specialty. What can you offer writers that isn't easily found elsewhere? Focus your site on writing for a specific genre, category, or field.

For example, if you're a mystery writer, share tips on how to become a mystery writer—or how to become a better mystery writer. Be creative: Don't just talk about writing techniques, but tell your readers where to find helpful research information, such as sites that cover forensics or police procedures. Offer links to publishers of mystery books or short fiction. Seek reciprocal links with other mystery sites. Offer a "contest" page that lists writing contests for amateur mystery authors. Offer links to mystery e-zines. Offer a bookstore of how-to books for mystery writers.

A writing site will need much the same type of content as an expert site, including:

- **An informative home page** that describes the types of writing tips that will be offered. If your name is well known in the field, make sure it is prominently displayed on the page. If readers are more likely to locate your page through an information search than an author search, however, move your name and biographical information to a lower position on the page and keep the topical information toward the top.
- **An array of top-quality information.** Again, consider posting previously published articles, FAQs, a column, and anything else that will help writers (and would-be writers) improve their skill. An important consideration to keep in mind is the quality of your own writing: Be sure that your information not only discusses good writing, but models it as well! Nothing will detract from a writing page as quickly as flawed grammar, spelling and punctuation errors, or errors in content.
- **Links.** If you're offering a general writing site, you can go crazy with links. If you're specializing in some field, however, limit your links to

the area that your site addresses. For the mystery writing example, one might include links to mystery writers' organizations, sites of other mystery writers, sites that address the how-tos of mystery writing, and sites that provide useful research or reference information for mystery writers. A good selection of links helps establish you as a resource site and will encourage related sites (such as other mystery authors and organizations) to link back to you.

- **A bookstore.** Rare is the writing site that doesn't offer a selection of the best writing books on the topic. If you've published (and are promoting) your own writing book, consider listing it both on your bookstore page and also on a separate page of its own, where you can offer an expanded summary and a cover image.
- **Writing samples.** If you're a novelist, you may wish to incorporate a "tips for writers" section into a site designed primarily to promote your novels. If you write short fiction, consider posting samples of some of your previously published works. These can serve several purposes: to attract readers, to serve as clips for future editors, and to stand as examples of the techniques you discuss in your "tips" section. Again, be sure that you own the relevant rights to the material you post.
- **Your credentials.** If you're a fiction writer, describe your writing background and feel free to add some personal information. Consider including a bibliography page of published works, along with cover images of your books. If you're discussing nonfiction writing, keep your bio professional, listing credentials and credits but leaving out such personal details as how you started writing. (However, it's perfectly OK to mention that you have a spouse and twenty cats!)

Needless to say, these aren't the only reasons writers launch Web sites— and in many cases, these reasons may overlap. You're certainly free to mix and match the items listed above, as well as to add items of your own. Be cautious, however, about attempting to develop a Web site that serves too many purposes at once (e.g., to promote your novel, showcase nonfiction clips, help writers, and establish your expertise in a completely unrelated area). Many writers have several separate career tracks. If you're one of them, consider creating a separate, stand-alone Web site (with its own home page) that supports each of your career goals.

Five Things Every Writer's Web Site Needs

No matter what the purpose of your site, certain elements are essential, including:

A useful table of contents.

Whether you think of it as a table of contents, a menu, or a site index, your site needs one (or several). A typical approach is to offer a general, first-level

TOC on your home page that provides an overview of the contents—e.g., Articles, Bibliography, Resources, etc. A second-level TOC can then be developed for each section—for example, under "Articles," you should list all the articles posted on your site. However, beware of building in too many layers of menus (e.g., Articles » Articles for Writers » Fiction Articles » Short Fiction » Finally, The Actual Article List). Remember that each layer of menus adds an extra barrier between your visitors and your content—and another opportunity for that visitor to grow impatient and move on to a more accessible site.

In addition to your main TOC, be sure to include a version of the top-level TOC on each page of your site. This enables visitors to navigate within your site without having to return to the home page.

Annotated links.

Every site needs links—and one of the best ways to please visitors is to annotate those links with a brief description. Let visitors know, in a line or two, what to expect when they visit the recommended site. In addition, it's a good idea to include not only the title of the site, but the actual URL. Then, if visitors print off your material to read later, the links will still be useful. (I learned this the hard way when I distributed copies of my own articles at a conference—and realized that a list of underlined sites with no URLs wasn't terribly helpful!)

Check your links regularly to make sure they are still active. If you're daunted by the thought of doing this manually, don't despair: There's an easier way. Simply submit your URL to a diagnostic site such as **Site Inspector**, and you'll receive a list of inactive or inaccurate links within minutes. If you have more than twenty-five links on your site, you'll need to repeat the process until all the links have been checked.

A copyright notice.

Actually, you may need not just one, but several copyright notices on your site. The first should be a blanket copyright notice that covers your entire site. This should be posted prominently on your home page and might read something like this:

Keep in mind, however, that many visitors may arrive at your site indirectly, either through a link or a search engine that takes them to one of the subordinate pages on your site rather than the home page. If you post articles, columns, or clips on your site, therefore, you may also wish to include a separate copyright notice with each article. (See "Reason #1," above, for an example of a single-page copyright notice.)

A hit counter.

The best way to find out whether your site is serving its purpose is to track the number of visitors it receives. To do this, you'll need a counter not only on your home page, but on each separate "content" page. This will enable you to determine which aspects of your site are attracting attention and which are being ignored. For example, if your home page registers two hundred visitors in a single month and your article on "The Importance of Flossing" registers only two, you know that only 1 percent of your visitors are interested in this article—a good clue that you might want to swap it for something more enticing.

Your hit counter should provide some indication of the longevity of your site. For example, you might want to incorporate it into a phrase such as, "You are visitor number (XXXXX) since January 1, 1999." This is also a good place to include a "last updated" date, to let visitors know how fresh your material is. On the other hand, if you don't update your pages, leave this information off, or visitors will get the impression that your material might be old news, no matter how timeless it is.

Contact information.

Unless you prefer to toil in seclusion, include an e-mail address so that your visitors (and fans) can contact you. On your bookstore or links pages, you may want to invite visitors to suggest additional references or links. (It's wise to have a policy about the types of links you will accept—for example, no commercial links—so that you can explain, if necessary, why you are choosing not to add a particular link.) Another way to solicit feedback from your visitors is to incorporate a guestbook into your site.

Three Things Your Web Site Can Do Without . . .

In developing a Web site, as in writing itself, it's as important to know what to leave out as what to leave in. Certain elements can significantly detract from the professionalism of your site, including:

Unpublished writings.

Many would-be writers view the Internet as the ideal place to self-publish material that they have been unable to market. Unfortunately, the only result has been to convince savvy surfers that self-published stories, poems, or novels on a Web site are an indication, not of professionalism, but of desperation. Even if your unpublished materials are of the highest quality, posting them online is likely to tarnish your professional image. (Note that this does not apply to materials written specifically for the site itself.)

Another issue to consider when posting unpublished materials is the question of rights. Increasingly, publishers are regarding material posted on a Web site as previously published—which means that once you post something online, you may no longer be able to sell first rights to that material (if you can sell it at all). The best rule when it comes to rights, therefore, is to sell the piece first and post it later.

Too much personal information.

If your goal in developing a Web site is to advance your writing career, be sure to keep it as professional as possible—which means making sure that it won't be confused with a holiday newsletter to friends and family. This is not the place for news about your grandchildren or photos of the family pets. That doesn't mean that you can't develop a personal site, but you'd be wise to keep it separate from your writing site. At most, add a discreet link that points readers to "Joan Q. Novelist's personal home page."

Links to everything.

Resist the temptation of offering links to every site on the Web that interests you, no matter what its subject. No matter whether you are a veteran rock-climber, an armchair archaeologist, or a connoisseur of filksinging groups, leave those personal-interest links off your professional page, unless they somehow relate to its focus.

And Finally, the Greatest Danger of All . . .

The greatest danger of a writer's Web site is not what you put on or leave off. It is the speed with which such a site can consume your writing time.

The temptation to tinker with a Web site is hard to resist. There's always the urge to redesign your pages, add new elements, rewrite your menus, add better graphics, or simply to surf for new links or new ways to promote your site. Moreover, it's easy to justify such tinkering as "working to promote my novel" or "gathering important information."

Before you quite know what has happened, however, you'll have spent the entire day tinkering—without adding a single word to that article or story you're trying to complete by deadline. (Trust me. I know.) Designing and maintaining a site can be an excellent way to promote your writing and advance your career, but it should not be allowed to *replace* writing. High-tech procrastination is still procrastination. If necessary, ration yourself to only so many hours of site development per week or month. Otherwise, you may end up with the perfect writer's Web site—and nothing for it to promote!

Sixty Ticks for a Good Website

by Richard Waller[2]

Impression on first entry
- ☐ The URL/domain name is appropriate and meaningful
- ☐ The surfer sees something meaningful within 8 seconds
- ☐ The site name and product/purpose come up instantly
- ☐ The first page is less than 20K, and images are kept small
- ☐ Text is visible while graphics are loaded (WIDTH=, HEIGHT=)
- ☐ Graphics are named (using ALT=) with full text content

The Home Page is exciting, interesting, attention-grabbing
- ☐ There is useful information on the home page
- ☐ The home page looks good, and has a clean, uncluttered look
- ☐ The important information is on the first display seen

The Home Page contains the key facts
- ☐ Name of organization (preferably in H1 heading)
- ☐ Shows business, products, where based
- ☐ Shows the sort of information available in the site
- ☐ Shows how to contact the company [or individual]
- ☐ A mail to: reply form
- ☐ What to do about faults, comments, suggestions
- ☐ TITLE is meaningful
- ☐ META statements are accurate
- ☐ Site description mirrors the TITLE and META description

Links are clear and meaningful
- ☐ It is clear which are internal and which are external links
- ☐ Not more than seven options on any menu
- ☐ Image-links are appropriate
- ☐ Image-links are supported by text-links and ALT tags
- ☐ External links are shown with the full URL

The whole site has a structure
- ☐ It is clear what the structure of the site is
- ☐ Useful content is not more than three clicks from the home page
- ☐ There is a List of Contents or a Site Map with links to every page
- ☐ Each Web page has links back to the Contents or Site Map
- ☐ There are appropriate links to other useful pages

All the pages obey the same rules
- ☐ Each Web page has a proper title
- ☐ The title shows why users should look at this page
- ☐ Titles are consistent with the words used in links to this page

---

☐ META statements are provided where appropriate
☐ Text is shown in centered tables (say 500 pixels wide)

Long Web pages have their own structure

☐ Long Web pages are used when it is useful to print as a whole
☐ Avoid long centered tables; use several short ones
☐ Users are warned if access time is likely to be long
☐ Each displayed part of the Web page has a heading or color
☐ There is a list of contents for the page
☐ At useful intervals there is an escape link back to the contents

All Web pages have a reference

☐ Author and name of organization on each page
☐ Accreditation or acknowledgement of the source of data is shown
☐ Web page URL is shown for reference if page is printed
☐ Date created or last updated on each Web page
☐ Pages that may be printed have company and/or contact information

Useful external links are provided

☐ Links are provided to relevant sources of information
☐ Links to associated organizations are provided
☐ Information readily available elsewhere is not repeated
☐ There is a description of who each link is to, and why

The Web site achieves its purpose

☐ It is clear what the purpose of this Web site is
☐ The apparent purpose has been achieved
☐ There are appropriate images and color
☐ It has a professional, planned, workmanlike, friendly image
☐ There is appropriate scope for user interaction, Java, JavaScript
☐ The reply forms are easy to use and relevant to the need
☐ There is some humor or light relief
☐ I am tempted to return in the future

The whole Web site has been tested on several browsers

☐ Netscape
☐ Internet Explorer
☐ At least one portable or heritage browser

Score: 40–50 is excellent. 20–40 is only average. Less than 20, and you have a problem.

●

RESOURCES

Articles on Web Site Development

Be Succinct! (Writing for the Web) *www.useit.com/alertbox/9703b.html*

Building a Writer's Website *www.sff.net/people/victoriastrauss/*
Ideas and design tips from fantasy author Victoria Strauss.

Concise, Scannable, and Objective: How to Write for the Web *www.useit.com/papers/webwriting/writing.html*
The results of a study by John Morkes and Jakob Nielsen on how users "read" online, with tips on writing for an online audience.

How Users Read the Web *www.useit.com/alertbox/9710a.html*
Tips on making your page more "reader-friendly."

Jakob Nielsen's Alertbox *www.useit.com/alertbox/*
A column on Web site design, content, development, navigability, and related issues.

Resources for New Web Authors *darkwing.uoregon.edu/~lincicum/resource.html*
Links to Web publishing guides, FAQs, HTML tutorials, style guides, publicity, and more.

Usable Web: Guide to Web Usability Resources *usableweb.com/index.html*
"A collection of 422 links and accompanying information about human factors, user interface issues, and usable design specific to the World Wide Web."

Web Authoring Resources *www.wwwscribe.com/resource.htm*
Links to domain registration agencies, HTML tools, and many other useful Web site development tools.

Writing for the Web: A New Resource for Writers *www.wwwscribe.com/webwrite.htm*
Overview of Web authoring techniques and tools, plus a list of software.

(For HTML and Web site development resources, see chapter 9.)

9

Your Web Site II:
Construction and Promotion

While content is all-important in attracting visitors to your Web site, design can make the difference between keeping those visitors and driving them away. A poorly designed site, with pages that are difficult to download or navigate or that offer no clues as to their content, is likely to be dismissed as not worth the effort.

Building a Web site doesn't have to be intimidating or expensive. While some writers hire designers to develop and maintain their sites, the truth is that if you can handle basic word processing tasks (let alone desktop publishing), you can easily construct a Web site. The key word is "construct." The issue is not so much how your Web site looks, but how easily the user can access the information you consider important.

I'll share a little secret with you: The only people who are really, truly impressed by glitzy site designs are other designers. The rest of us may think a Java-based fire-breathing dragon is cute, but it's not what we came for. And for some of your visitors, too much design can actually get in the way.

Think of assembling your Web site as similar to assembling a book. No matter what your content may be, certain elements need to go in certain places. You'll need a table of contents that will enable a reader to quickly locate your material. You'll need chapters, or a similar division of content. You might also want an index, a copyright notice, an author bio. You may wish to include illustrations, but those should be chosen to enhance your content and not simply to dress up the page. Finally, your site must be accessible. If the Internet is analogous to a vast electronic library, you want its patrons to be able to locate your book on its shelves.

Making Your Site "Search-Engine Friendly"

Search engines are to the Internet what card files are (or once were) to libraries. If those search engines can't find you, many potential visitors won't be able to find you either.

The problem is, no two search engines work exactly the same way. A good overview of how different engines retrieve, index, and rank sites can be found at **Search Engine Watch** ("How Search Engines Work"). It's also important to know how they *don't* work: Certain design elements can actually prevent you from receiving a high ranking or from being indexed at all. The following tips will help you ensure that your site can be located, retrieved, and indexed effectively:

Don't hide your menu in an image map.

Many search engines can't read image maps, and therefore can't index keywords from your menu. Thus, if your home page consists of nothing but an image map, it might not be indexed at all—and if it is, it may not be associated with relevant keywords.

Image maps also prevent many engines from "crawling" from your home page to your secondary pages. Most engines use your links to explore the rest of your site—but if those links are hidden in an image map, those secondary pages may not be retrieved or indexed. Since those pages often contain important content that may boost your site's ranking in a listing of search results, it's vital to make them accessible to search engines.

If you want to use an image map, be sure you also provide a text menu on the same page. This will not only ensure that search engines can index and explore your site, but will also help visitors whose browsers don't handle graphic files well—or who simply prefer not to download large graphic files just to determine what's on your site.

Think twice about frames.

Frames can also create problems for search engines. Like image maps, they may hinder an engine's ability to link to your secondary pages from within a framed menu. In fact, many search engines don't "see" frames at all. A frame is composed of several separate files, including a master file that tells browsers how to assemble those files into the frame displayed on the screen. A search engine may locate only that master instruction file—which often doesn't have the information that needs to be indexed. And since the instruction file doesn't include your internal links, the search engine won't be able to explore the rest of your pages.

One way to bypass this problem is to incorporate indexing information under a "noframes" tag on the master page. More information on this option, along within links to frames resources and tutorials, can be found on the Search Engine Watch site ("Search Engines and Frames").

Use META tags.

Some articles claim that you should always use META tags; others claim that they don't help. The truth is that some search engines use these tags and others don't. Since you won't be penalized for incorporating META tags, this simply offers you another chance to improve your index ranking.

A META tag is a line of HTML code placed within the <HEAD> section of your document. Two META tags are used in indexing: the "description" tag and the "keywords" tag.

The "descriptions" tag consists of up to 250 characters that describe your site. For those engines that use tags, this is the description that will appear in your listing. Make sure your description is tailored toward the audience you are trying to attract. Determine how your site can benefit that audience, and list those benefits or resources in the tag.

The "keywords" tag lists the keywords under which your site should be indexed. For example, if you write romance novels, you might include such keywords as "romance," "romance writing," "romance fiction," and perhaps your name and the title of your novel(s). Spend some time brainstorming all the possible keywords someone might use to locate a page about you and your writing, and include those in the tag.

Here's an example of the placement of META tags:

```
<HEAD>
<TITLE>Tips for Writers</TITLE>
<META name="description" content="Articles on writing skills, finding a
publisher, copyright issues, and electronic rights; resources for fantasy/SF
authors; contests; critique groups; research and writing links.">
<META name="keywords" content="writing, writers, writing tips,
freelancing, freelance writing, publishing, fantasy, science fiction, writing
contests, writing resources">
</HEAD>
```

Never use META tags to "spam" a search engine. "Spamming" means repeating the same keyword dozens of times, in hopes of obtaining a higher ranking. Most search engines are programmed not only to ignore spam, but to reject pages that include it. Other spam techniques include placing keywords in a "comment" tag that is read by search engines, but not by browsers, or in "hidden" text (text that is the same color as the background and can't be seen by the viewer). Again, these tricks may result in the rejection of your page.

Choose an effective title.

Actually, each of your pages will need two titles: the hidden title that serves as the official label for your Web site (but isn't viewed onscreen) and the title you choose for the page itself. These titles don't have to be identical.

Your hidden title is included within the <HEAD> section of your document. This is the title that will be listed in a search engine, at the top of a user's browser window, and in a user's navigation menus and bookmark files. If you don't choose a title, search engines and browsers will use the first readable characters of your page, which may not be descriptive or informative.

If you want to include the same master title on each page of your site, use subtitles to distinguish one page from another. This will help users locate and return to specific pages while navigating your site. For example, you might title your home page:

<TITLE>ANNIE AUTHOR'S BOOK PAGE</TITLE>

but label your bookstore page:

<TITLE>ANNIE AUTHOR'S BOOK PAGE: Books for writers</TITLE>

In addition to your hidden title, you'll also want to give appropriate titles to your pages themselves, just as you'd title an article or story. Since these titles are also likely to show up in your search engine listing (because they're near the top of your page), think carefully about the impression they'll make. A title like "Links for Romance Writers," for example, is more likely to attract serious writers (and romance readers) than "My Favorite Links to Really Cool Stuff."

Place descriptive content toward the top of your page.

Search engines that don't use META tags will index the first 100 to 250 characters of your text as your site description. It's important, therefore, to make sure the first readable text on your page is also descriptive of its content. That text should be something other than image tags, menu items, or similarly noninformative material.

The easiest option is to simply provide a brief description of the page's content as a sort of abstract beneath the title. You could even repeat your META description tag, since it won't be visible to browsers. If your first item is a menu, make sure its contents are descriptive: "Articles on Writing" instead of simply "Articles," and "[My Book Title] Excerpt" instead of simply "Book Excerpt."

Keep in mind as well that many search engines (like **WebCrawler**) index every single word on your page, up to 1MB of text. Such engines often determine keywords not by META tags, but by the number of times a word appears on a page. To improve your chances of being included under the right keywords, therefore, make sure your entry page uses those keywords frequently (and appropriately!). Move content that doesn't relate to your central topic to another section of your site.

If you're determined to have a graphics-only entry page, place descriptive information in a comment tag or hidden text, so that it can be indexed by a search engine without appearing on the user's screen. Or, consider submitting a different page for indexing purposes that is more reflective of your content.

Test your site.

After you've done everything possible to ensure that your site is indexed properly, test it. Several sites on the Web will examine your site, free of charge, and report on its effectiveness in several areas (such as search-engine readiness, accessibility, design, HTML accuracy, and link problems). One is **Meta Medic**, which analyzes the suitability of your META tags and provides a simulated example of how your site will be listed in a typical search engine index. Another is **Site Inspector**, which provides detailed reports on HTML problems, identifies inaccurate links, and rates your site on design and searchability. These reports will give you additional hints on how to improve and upgrade your site.

Making Your Page "User-Friendly"

Some of the same issues that affect a search engine's ability to index your site may also affect a visitor's ability to navigate it. While today's array of multimedia bells and whistles can be tempting, it's vital to remember that not everyone has the fastest modem, the most sophisticated processor, the latest browser. If your site takes so long to download that a visitor could brew a pot of coffee while waiting, or if your rotating globe or fire-breathing dragon causes the user's browser to crash (taking the system with it), visitors will move on. More importantly, they won't recommend your site to others or link to your page.

Whether your goal is self-promotion or a desire to educate and inform others, it simply doesn't make sense to erect technological barriers between your material and your audience. The following elements all have the potential to create such barriers and should be considered carefully:

Image maps

Besides creating problems for search engines, image map menus can also hinder users. Often these maps involve sizable graphic files that take time to download, which means that the slower the user's modem or processor, the longer it will take to determine what your site is about. Some browsers, such as Lynx, don't support images at all, which means your menu may be completely inaccessible. Other visitors prefer to surf with images off to save download time and don't appreciate being faced with an entry page that is nothing more than an unidentified icon (or flock of icons) that offers no navigation clues.

If you want to use a graphic-based menu, offer the user a text alternative somewhere on the page, or offer a text-only version of your site. This will ensure that anyone can access your site, regardless of their level of technology (or tolerance for image files).

Frames

Some browsers (such as Mosaic) can't "read" frames, and others don't handle them well. Since frames often make it impossible to use a browser's navigation buttons (such as "forward" and "back"), they can be frustrating to users, who must constantly return to the main menu rather than choosing their own path through a site. Frames also bypass the "history" and "bookmark" functions of many browsers, so users can't relocate pages they've visited or bookmark other sites accessed through your frame.

Another problem with frames is the question of what is being framed. While you may ensure that your own Web pages fit within the frame, other pages that are displayed as the result of links from your site may not work as well. A page that contains "hard" formatting elements (such as fixed line lengths, tables, or large images) won't adapt to a frame window, so the user may have to scroll both horizontally and vertically to view a single paragraph or image.

This has raised a new concern about frames: the legal implications of importing someone else's page into your own frame format. Such a display, some have argued, violates copyright by removing a page from its original context and placing it within the context of the framer's site, or even making it appear that the imported information "belongs" to the framing site. Several court cases have already arisen over this issue.

The bottom line is that some users love frames and others hate them. An easy solution, therefore, is to offer both a frames and a no-frames option, making your site equally accessible to all.

Graphics

Used effectively, graphics enhance a site's content; used ineffectively, they can detract from a site's usefulness and appeal.

The primary problem is the size of many graphic files. Image files often require large amounts of memory, and consequently require lengthy download times. For this reason, many users surf with images off, choosing to download graphics only after determining whether the site's content is of interest.

Even smaller graphics, such as lines and bullets, can slow loading time, especially if a page includes a number of graphic elements. Image-heavy pages affect a user's ability to move easily between different sections of your site, especially if the user must repeatedly return to a graphic-laden (and slow-loading) menu or list of links to select new options.

Some browsers don't allow users to turn images off, which creates additional downloading problems. Some, for example, load images automatically during the print function, which creates delays and may hinder a user's ability to navigate while that function is in operation. Users who must pay for connect time (a common problem outside the United States) won't welcome such delays.

While it would be absurd to suggest that one avoid images entirely, one can take steps to make graphics easier for all users:

- Use only those images that contribute to a site's content. Avoid graphics that are little more than bells and whistles that add no functionality to a site.
- Keep graphic files as small as possible. Use a "GIF wizard" program to streamline larger files, such as images that you have scanned (see Resources).
- Include an "Alt" ("alternate text") tag with every image icon so that users can determine the content or purpose of a graphic before downloading it. This tag is especially important for visitors who can't download images or who surf with image loading turned off (often because of slower modems or connections). The "Alt" tag enables you to give your image a title or caption that will be displayed when the image itself has not been loaded. It is particularly useful if you incorporate navigation functions into images—for example, your "contact me" image button could have an "alt" tag of "contact." The HTML for an "Alt" tag is included in the image tag. For example, a line of HTML such as <IMG SRC="Contact.gif" ALT="Contact"> will ensure that the word "contact" will be associated with the image icon when the image itself is not displayed.
- Keep graphics to a minimum on pages that a user is likely to have to reload frequently, such as a menu or list of links.
- Specify height and width sizes for images. This enables text to download first.
- When embedding menu or navigation instructions in graphics, provide an alternate, text-only set of instructions.
- Consider offering a text-only version of your site for users whose browsers (or patience) don't handle graphics well—especially if you use lots of images or if you're using frames.

Java

At one point, Java was heralded as the future of the Internet. Soon, it was thought, every site would have applets and interactive scripts.

That future has not materialized. While Java has its uses, it can also create problems for browsers that aren't Java-enabled. Embedding Java applets within a page will automatically produce error messages on such browsers and, at times, will cause a crash. Java-based menus may not be accessible to older browsers, which means that those users won't be able to navigate your site. Animation applets that require continual refreshing or downloading can interfere with a browser's operation (or a slower processor) and cause a crash.

Before adding Java to your site, ask whether it is really necessary. Will the application add genuine value to your site by enabling users to accomplish a task more easily or to interact with your site more effectively? If not, either omit the application or make sure users can bypass it.

Audio and Video

Recently, I visited a site that greeted me with the warning that I needed a Real Audio plug-in to fully appreciate its content. A second warning told me that I should also download a MIDI program. A third warning then popped onto my screen—but before I could read it, my browser crashed. Needless to say, I haven't gone back.

There's nothing wrong with adding audio or video elements to your site—but make sure that they don't interfere with a browser's operability. Even newer browsers may not have all the plug-ins needed to handle such functions. Audio and video extras should be just that: optional extras that users can choose to explore or ignore.

After constructing your site, it's a good idea to test it—not only with your own browser, but with others, including older programs. If you don't have access to other browsers, use a program like Site Inspector to determine your site's accessibility from different platforms and programs.

More Construction Tips

While there is no single right way to construct a Web site, certain considerations are likely to win the hearts of your visitors and encourage them to recommend your page to others:

Make your site easy to view.

Ideally, a page should fit within the width of a typical computer screen or browser. (Keep in mind that some users may access your site through a laptop with a small screen.) If a page is too wide for the screen, users must scroll horizontally as well as vertically to view your material.

An easy guideline is to think of your page as just that: a page of paper. If your material won't fit within the width of a normal sheet of paper, it won't fit certain browser windows either. While many elements of your site may be flexible and adapt to different window widths, make sure "fixed" items (such as tables and large images) can be contained within that page size.

Keep in mind that if you use frames, this will further limit the amount of space available for viewing your page. An oversized left-hand menu frame can cause your viewing frame to shrink dramatically. Some pages that look fine on a full screen don't work nearly so well when shrunk to a three-inch window.

Make your site easy to print.

The same guidelines apply to printing: If your material won't fit on a sheet of paper, it will have to be reduced or printed horizontally. Reductions may make parts of your page hard to read, and horizontal printing is just plain annoying.

Always test your site's printability. Check your images: Do they print properly or create black boxes on the page? Tables with a colored background may also print as black boxes with some browsers, which means the user won't be able to read the content. Light fonts on light backgrounds may print as "shadow fonts" that are hard to read. Background images and "wallpaper" may also interfere with the text overlay, and while white text on a black background usually prints properly over a background color, it may not print correctly over an image.

Use colors and fonts wisely.

Though it may seem boring, dark type on a pale background still creates the most readable page. Be cautious about mixing colored fonts and backgrounds. What looks good on one browser may not work well on another, and what appeals to one user may seem absolutely ghastly to another.

Pale fonts on pale backgrounds are notoriously hard to read. Patterned backgrounds can also interfere with readability. The smaller the font, the more difficult it will be to read—and italics reduce legibility even further.

Some people find white (or light) fonts on black extremely hard on the eyes, while red or glaring yellow text on black can be positively painful. Colors that possess a comparable "grayscale" (i.e., they would appear as the same shade of gray on a black-and-white monitor or printer) cause a "jitter" effect as the eyes struggle to distinguish between them.

Be conservative with font sizes as well. While a huge headline may be appropriate for the top of a page, it will be distracting anywhere else. Italics can be difficult to read; consider using boldface or caps for titles or emphasis. Tiny font sizes should be avoided—remember that they will become even smaller if the page must be reduced for printing.

Promoting Your Site

Once you build it, will they come? Constructing an accessible, navigable, attractive site is only half the battle; the other half is promotion. Fortunately, there are several steps you can take to promote your site that cost nothing more than time:

- **Register your site with all major search engines,** including Lycos, Infoseek, AltaVista, HotBot, and Excite. Don't rely on a program that promises to submit your site to all the major engines. Instead, visit each site yourself and follow the instructions under the "add URL" option.
- **Use free site registration programs to submit your URL to additional search engines and directories.** While most registration sites want you to purchase a registration package, many (such as **Register-It!** and **Auto Submit**) still offer a limited range of free submission services. While it's not clear how effective these registration services are, they can't hurt.
- **Register your site with major directories.** While Yahoo! is the best-known directory on the Web, you can find many others through sites like **Internet Sleuth**, which lists more than three thousand directories

and databases. Directories like the **Librarians' Index to the Internet** and the **Argus Clearinghouse** offer hundreds of categories to choose from. You can also submit your URL to various categories within smaller directories, such as **Handilinks** or **My Virtual Encyclopedia.**

- **If your site includes writing tips, invite the major writing resource sites (such as Inkspot or Zuzu's Petals) to add your URL.** If appropriate, offer a reciprocal link in your own resource section. But don't stop at the majors. Actively solicit links from any writing site you come across, including those hosted by individual writers like yourself.
- **Submit your site information for inclusion in author lists,** such as the miscellaneous author list maintained by **SFF Net**.
- **If your site includes nonfiction topics, search for sites that cover similar topics.** Ask for reciprocal links whenever appropriate, but don't hesitate to suggest a link to your site even when you can't offer one in return. For example, many pet owners offer links to my pet loss site because of their interest in the topic, even though I don't offer links to personal pages in return.
- **Watch for potential link sites whenever you surf the Internet.** When you add a site to your page, contact the site host and inform them of the link, and invite them to link to you in return.
- **Look for newsletters or e-zines that cover topics relevant to your site, and submit your URL for review.**
- **Join newsgroups and discussion lists relevant to your site.** Don't advertise your site on such lists; however, if someone raises a question that your site answers, it's usually acceptable to provide the URL. If not, send the URL information by private e-mail.
- **Exchange links with authors of books similar to your own,** either of the same genre or on related topics.
- **Ask your publisher to post a link to your Web site.**
- **List your site name (or book title) and URL in your e-mail signature block.** This is considered a discreet, acceptable way to advertise your site to newsgroups and discussion lists—as well as to anyone else with whom you correspond.
- **Include your URL and e-mail address on your business card and letterhead.**

Finally, be sure to check your promotional efforts regularly. To find out whether your site is indexed in the major search engines, for example, run a periodic keyword check to determine whether (and where) your listing appears. If it doesn't appear, resubmit it. If it doesn't appear within the top one hundred listings (or even the top ten), use a program such as Site Inspector to help you determine whether you can improve its ranking. Also, visit the sites that *do* receive high rankings and see if you can determine ways to improve your own site's rating. Download the source code for high-rated sites, for example, to determine what META tags they use.

You can find out how many people have added links to your site by conducting a URL search. On Infoseek or AltaVista, for example, all you have to do is enter *"link://www."* as the search parameter. You can enter a specific page's URL (*link://www.domain.com/mydirectory/mypage.html*) to find the results for that page, or enter your directory information (*link://www.domain.com/mydirectory/*) to retrieve results for your entire site.

Keep in mind that search engines can't keep up with changes to your Web site. When you remove a page, it may remain in a search engine's index for months—but potential visitors won't be able to find it, or you. You can solve that problem by replacing any page you delete with a "redirect" message (using the same URL) that offers a link back to your main menu:

> Hello! You have reached a page that has been moved or deleted from this site. Click here to return to <u>Annie Author's Tips for Romance Writers</u>; click here to reach the <u>main menu</u>.

Web sites don't become popular overnight. Most become popular through word of mouth—but it's your job to get that word started. Be patient, be diligent, create the best site you can—and one morning you'll check your hit counter and be astonished by the results.

●

RESOURCES

HTML and Web Site Design

The Bare Bones Guide to HTML *werbach.com/barebones*
   A listing of every known HTML tag, plus tutorials and links to other Web design resources.

A Beginner's Guide to HTML *www.ncsa.uiuc.edu/General/Internet/WWW/HTMLPrimerPt1.html*
   An excellent primer on HTML, with easy instructions and examples of how formatting will appear on the page. Includes instructions on tables and graphics, plus links to other resources.

Color Specifier *www.users.interport.net/~giant/COLOR/1ColorSpecifier.html*
   An easy-to-use chart of colors for use in backgrounds or fonts, showing the color, the name of the color, and the HTML code.

GIF Wizard *uswest.gifwizard.com*
   This software program streamlines and reduces the file size of your graphics, which can save file space and download time. You can test the software on your graphics for free, but will be charged a fee if you actually use the "reduced" images on your site.

HTML Goodies *www.htmlgoodies.com*
   Tutorials, primers, images, software, and a host of other resources on HTML, Java, and Web site development.

Matt's Script Archive *worldwidemart.com/scripts*
   Free CGI scripts that can be used to create forms, feedback messages, forums, visitor counters, site search tools, and more. Also offers links to other free script and shareware pages.

Miscellaneous Web Tools *www.lib.msu.edu/harris23/general/webtools.htm*
   HTML and Web design tools and resources.

Robin's Nest: Web Site Development *www2.netdoor.com/~smlady/Websitedevelop.html*
   Links to advanced Web site development tools, including clip art archives, HTML guides, scripts, and programs for such tasks as checking links. The main site also includes writing links.

TableMaker *www.bagism.com/tablemaker/*
   Just type in your design requirements, and this site will automatically generate the HTML code for your tables—free! The site also includes links to a number of other useful tools.

Top Ten Mistakes in Web Design *www.useit.com/alertbox/9605.html*

Web Authoring Resources *www.wwwscribe.com/resource.htm*
   Links to various tools and software, including domain registration tips, HTML guides, etc.

Web Style Guide *info.med.yale.edu/caim/manual/contents.html*
   A useful tutorial on designing Web sites, with illustrated examples.

Web Wonk: Tips for Writers and Designers *www.dsiegel.com/tips/index.html*
   A variety of tips and resources to improve one's Web site.

Willcam's Comprehensive HTML Cross Reference *www.willcam.com/cmat/html/*
   A helpful listing of HTML tags and what they do.

META Tags and Search Engines

META Tags *northernwebs.com/set/*
   Tips on adding META tags to your site, including how to target your audience and achieve higher rankings in search engines.

Search Engine Watch *searchenginewatch.internet.com/webmasters/*
   This site offers a host of resources and information on search engines, including "How Search Engines Work" (an overview of how search engines retrieve, index, and rank sites); "How to Use META Tags" (tips on developing effective tags, plus links to tag tutorials); "Search Engines and Frames" (how to solve interaction problems between search engines and frames); and a "Search Engines Features Chart" (comparing features and performance of major search engines).

Site Analyzers

Bobby *www.cast.org/bobby/*
A free service that analyzes your Web page and provides an analysis of its accessibility and compatibility with various browsers.

did-it detective *www.did-it.com*
Check search engines to determine whether your site is indexed and how it is ranked.

Free HTML Validator *www.iaehv.nl/users/fpieters/validate.html*
Links to sites that validate HTML coding, links, spelling, and other aspects of your Web site.

Meta Medic *www.northernwebs.com/set/setsimjr.html*
Check your META tags for validity, length, and repetition. The program generates a simulated "search engine listing" to demonstrate how your site is likely to appear in a search.

Site Inspector *siteinspector.linkexchange.com*
An excellent, free service that analyzes and rates your site's META tags, HTML, spelling, links, and browser accessibility. This is a quick and easy way to verify whether your links are accurate. The program provides a detailed report on each area.

Registering Your Site

Automated registration programs register your site with various search engines. You can also visit search engines directly and list your site in various topical directories (see chapter 2).

1 2 3 Add-It! *www.123add-it.com*

Auto Submit *www.autosubmit.com/promote.html*

Cozy Cabin *www.cozycabin.com/add.html*

did-it.com *www.did-it.com*

Register-It! *www.liquidimaging.com/submit/*

Web Site Promotion

Go Net-Wide *www.gonetwide.com/gopublic.html*
An extensive list of URL submission sites and other promotional links (some free, some fee-based).

Internet Promotions MEGALIST *www.2020tech.com/submit.html*
Lists registration/submission sites, directories, search engines, and other promotional tools and resources.

Virtual Promote *www.virtualpromote.com/*
This site offers a number of promotion techniques and tools, including a free newsletter (the *VirtualPROMOTE Gazette*). Though aimed at commercial sites, many tips also apply to writing sites, especially if you're promoting a book or product.

10

Promoting Your Book Online

If you're the author of a book, the Internet provides a marketplace that you can't afford to ignore. Dozens of promotional opportunities are available online—and unlike old-fashioned marketing methods that involve printing hundreds of flyers and paying for hundreds of stamps, many of these opportunities are absolutely free. At most, they are available for the cost of a connection and Web site space.

Ten Ways to Promote Your Book on the Web

The first step in book promotion is often to develop an effective "author site." Chapter 8 discusses a variety of ways in which you can use such a site to promote your book(s). Once you've built that site, however, don't stop. You can use it as the focal point for a variety of promotional efforts, including the following:

Write articles for other sites.

An excellent way to attract readers and build name recognition is to offer content to other sites. Whether you write fiction or nonfiction, you can develop informational articles that will be valuable to visitors and act as a lure to bring those visitors back to your own page. Consider the following possibilities:

- **Offer nonfiction articles or FAQs on the topic of your nonfiction book.** Look for both specific and general sites. For example, if you've written a book on breast cancer, look not only for sites that address that specific issue, but sites on health in general, women's health, nutrition, stress, and other topics that could relate to your own. Offer an article or FAQ that focuses on the interests of visitors to that specific site.

- **Offer nonfiction features on topics relating to the background of your novel or other fiction**. For example, if you've written an Arthurian novel, look for sites that cover history, folklore, British travel, and related topics. If you've written a Victorian romance, consider covering various aspects of the period for sites likely to be visited by enthusiasts of Victoriana. For example, you might include sites covering costuming, collectibles, and other topics not clearly related to reading or writing.
- **Offer tips for writers that relate to your writing expertise or genre**. Consider offering a brief article or FAQ to one or more of the many writing sites online. You could discuss writing techniques that relate specifically to your work (e.g., "How to Research Victorian Customs") or general writing issues ("How to Find a Publisher").
- **Use your imagination**. What other topics could you address that might interest potential readers of your book? As you surf the Web, keep your eyes open for sites that such readers are likely to visit, and ask yourself what you could provide for that site that would then attract a reader to click the link to your own page. One way to find potential sites is to do a search for sites that already include a link to your page. On Infoseek or AltaVista, for example, just enter "*link://your address*" as the search parameter. To locate pages that link to any portion of your site, rather than a certain page or to your home page, leave off the specific "*page.html*" at the end of your address.[1] Another way to find sites that might appreciate your input is to search on your own name.
- **Provide your URL!** Many sites can't pay for content, but they will provide a direct link back to your page. Consider including your e-mail address for questions and feedback as well.

Write for newsletters.

No matter what subject you write about, there's likely to be a newsletter (or e-zine) that covers it, or at least something closely related. Search for newsletters and e-zines in one of the many directories online (see chapter 11 for a list of such directories). Most are free, so you can read a sample copy to determine the focus of the publication at no cost. Many newsletters post the most recent issue and/or archives of back issues on a Web site; others ask you to subscribe to receive the most recent issue. Once you've familiarized yourself with the style and content of the publication, contact the editor with an

---

[1] For example, if I wanted to locate all sites that link to a specific Inkspot column I've written, I would enter "*link://www.inkspot.com/moira/myarticle.html*". If I wanted to locate sites that link to any of my Inkspot columns, however, I would simply enter "*link://www.inkspot.com/moira/*". If I wanted to locate sites that link to Inkspot, but not necessarily to me, I would enter "*link:// www.inkspot.com*".

article idea. While many newsletters can't pay for material, they will list your URL, and some will provide a free classified ad for your book in exchange for your article.

Submit your book for review.

Many sites and newsletters review books. Look for book review opportunities in newsletters, e-zines, and sites that cover topics related to your book. Look also for book review sites that cover specific genres. Some of these are related to genre organizations; others are independent. Search for sites that focus entirely on book (or media) reviews. Look into The Mining Co. and Suite101; these sites offer pages specifically dedicated to literature, books, authors, and genres, as well as subject-specific pages that might also be willing to review your book. Develop a list of potential online reviewers and ask your publisher to include them when sending out review copies (most publishers are less likely to do this research on their own).

Add your URL to "author" lists and links.

A number of sites list links to author pages on the Web, including pages hosted by authors and pages about authors. Look for author lists on genre-specific sites, general writing sites, and sites devoted to reading or literature. Join author Webrings, both general and specific. If you write nonfiction, look for Webrings that focus on the topic of your book. (Most author lists focus on fiction.) Visit **Yahoo!** and look under the "genre" directories for author listings; then submit your own URL for inclusion.

Join discussion groups.

Use newsgroup "search" pages (such as **CataList** or **Liszt**) to find newsgroups and e-mail discussion lists that relate to your writing. Be creative. Don't stop at lists that focus on writing or literature. Look for lists that discuss subjects you've addressed in your writing, whether fiction or nonfiction. For example, if you've written a novel about an abusive relationship, consider looking for lists that discuss abuse issues, psychology, or related topics. Don't "advertise" your book to the list, but instead, become a participant and offer helpful advice in response to questions. Include your book title and URL in a discreet signature block to let participants know who you are and where to look for more information.

Provide information about your book to online bookstores.

Amazon.com provides a number of opportunities for authors to promote and even "hand-sell" their books (see below). Other online bookstores also offer promotional opportunities. Some feature author interviews, and most provide a "review" section where you can include information about your book. Check a book-search site such as **BookFinder.com** to find out what online bookstores carry your book. Then visit each of those stores to find out what you can do to promote your title. Ask friends and customers to provide reviews. If you choose to place your own book description in a "review" section, be sure to note that you are the author; don't try to fool readers into thinking that you're a "happy customer." Keep your description short and free of hype. You can also use a book-search site to make sure that your title is listed correctly. One bookstore inaccurately listed one of my books at twice the actual price! Since such sites also provide lists of those bookstores that *didn't* list your title, you can use this list to encourage your publisher to promote your book to those stores.

Participate in organizations related to your writing.

Search for sites that relate either to the type of writing you do (e.g., a genre organization) or to the subject of your writing. Find out how you can become active in the organization.

Look for opportunities to "chat" with readers.

Dozens (if not hundreds) of "author chat" opportunities exist online. The challenge is to find them and to get yourself onto the program. Some "hosts" seek only big-name authors or authors of the latest bestsellers, but others are interested in authors of all types. Look for author chats in the following areas:

- **Online bookstores. BarnesandNoble.com** and **Borders.com**, among other online bookstores, offer chats with authors. You can also read transcripts of previous chats to get an idea of how they work and what types of questions are asked.
- **Publishers.** Find out if your publisher hosts author chats online or would be interested in doing so. Many major publishers now have a regular chat feature on their Web sites.
- **Writing sites.** Many writing sites offer chat rooms where writers can gather to discuss specific or general topics. Some already host author chats whereas others might welcome the opportunity to do so if you offer to volunteer your time.
- **Book and literature sites.** Many book-related sites have chat rooms where readers gather to talk about their favorite books or types of literature. Again, if such a site doesn't already offer author chats, offer your services and see what happens.
- **Major book review sites.** Sites such as **CNN** and **MSN** (Microsoft Network) offer author interviews and chats.
- **Genre organizations.** Check with sites and organizations related to your genre for chat possibilities.
- **Topical sites.** Many sites that have nothing to do with writing or books still offer chats. Approach these sites not so much as an author but as an "expert" willing to discuss a topic of importance to visitors.
- **"Chat" sites.** Some sites, such as **TalkCity**, are dedicated to chat and other forms of discussion. Most such sites will have an "Arts and Literature" section. Send an e-mail to the Web master or host of that section to indicate your availability.

- **Guide sites.** Both The Mining Co. and Suite101 have chat rooms where fans of a particular page can meet for discussion. Look for pages that relate to your genre or topic, and contact the page "guide" about the possibility of participating in a chat.
- **Internet services.** AOL, Compuserve, and Prodigy all have "areas" for authors and author chats. You don't have to be a member of the service to gain a "guest spot" in a chat room or forum.

Make yourself available for interviews.

Many sites are willing to interview authors. Look for interview opportunities with online bookstores, genre organizations, writing or topical newsletters and e-zines, and "guide" sites such as The Mining Co. and Suite101.

Promote your book through individual "bookstore" pages.

Search for personal and professional sites that offer a "bookstore" page (usually in conjunction with an associates or referral program sponsored by an online bookstore). Contact the host of the site to suggest that your book be added to the page. One way to find sites that might host your book is to search on a related or competing, title.

Whatever method of promotion you use, be sure to include your URL. Keep track of sites that list your URL, so that if it ever changes, you can contact them to update it. If possible, provide a link from your own site to the site that is promoting you. Link to articles you've written, interviews that you've given, and transcripts of author chats. If you're going to give a chat, announce it on your own site in advance.

Be sure to promote your online efforts offline as well. Add your URL and e-mail address to your business card and professional stationery. Make sure that it is included on any promotional materials for your book, such as postcards of your book's cover, handouts, flyers, and so on.

Promoting Your Book on Amazon.com

Online bookstores are one of the greatest boons to authors and small publishers. By linking your title directly from your Web site to its electronic bookstore page, you greatly increase the chance of catching those impulse buyers who want your book *now*. If you're distributing your own books, selling them through an online bookstore bypasses the problem of accepting credit cards on your Web site.

The trouble with online bookstores, however, is that buyers cannot browse before they buy. They can't hold your book in their hands, examine the cover and "blurbs" (including reviews), and flip through its contents. To buy a book online, one must take the risk of buying sight unseen.

Recognizing this problem, Amazon.com is taking steps to help authors and publishers (including small presses) promote their books more effectively. The site that calls itself "the world's largest online bookstore" has launched programs that enable self-publishers, small presses, and authors who distribute their own books to compete on virtually equal terms with the major presses—"leveling the playing field," as merchandising manager Dan Camacho puts it.

To get a sense of the possibilities, it's a good idea to read both the Author and the Publisher guides from Amazon.com, no matter which category you fall into. As an author, you can contribute significantly to the way your title is displayed—and you can encourage your publisher to take additional steps to enhance sales

Here are some of the options recommended by Amazon.com:

Make sure your title is actually listed in the Amazon.com catalog.

Most books that have an ISBN and are available from a North American publisher, wholesaler, or distributor are added to the Amazon.com database automatically. However, if you're a self-publisher, or if a small press without major distribution outlets published your book, you may need to add the information yourself. See, "Listing your titles in our catalog" for full information on how to submit titles.

Encourage "impulse purchases" of your book by linking your title directly from your Web site to its "detail page" on Amazon.com.

This page lists basic information about your book, including the title, author, publisher, price, discount (if any), and how long it takes to ship. To find your "detail page," search for your title or ISBN.

Add material directly to your detail page.

Amazon.com offers two ways to add information to your book's page: You can use the interactive commands you'll find on the page itself (which lead to forms that you can complete online), or you can submit directly to Amazon.com. The interactive commands allow you to add the following information:

- **Author comments.** At the bottom of your detail page, you'll see a link that says, "I am the Author and I want to comment on my book." Use this link to provide a basic description of your book: an overview, a narrative summary, a brief table of contents. Think of yourself as a reviewer—what can you say about your title that would encourage a browser to pick up the book? If you have more information on your Web site, include the URL (and your e-mail if you wish).
- **Publisher comments.** Does your publisher have something worthwhile to say about your book? At the very least, the publisher could include your book's catalog information, so suggest that your publisher complete this form.
- **Reader reviews.** Few things are as gratifying as revisiting your page and discovering that someone has written a rave review of your book. But

why wait? Contact readers you know and ask them to write an honest review for you.

- **Author self-interview.** An online interview form will walk you through several questions about your books, your motivation, your writing life, and your plans for the future. You will have the opportunity to provide both a hotlink to your Web site and an e-mail link. Your author interview will be linked to every book under your name—but you must be sure that you list your name *exactly* as it appears on your titles. Even omitting a middle initial can prevent the interview from being linked correctly.

Send additional material for your detail page to Amazon.com.

Besides the information listed above, you can send additional items directly to Amazon.com to be added to your page. These items include:

- Your cover. You'll need to provide an appropriate image file of your cover, such as a TIFF or JPEG file. If your cover was created electronically, your publisher should have an image file. If not, you can get your cover scanned at a print shop for a small fee, or you can pay Amazon.com to scan it for you.
- A description of your book, up to 1,000 words
- An excerpt of your book, up to 1,000 words
- A table of contents (omitting page numbers, formatting, etc.)
- Reviews of your book or, more accurately, quotes of published reviews of up to 150 words each, including the name and date of the publication in which the review appeared
- Back cover copy, up to 1,000 words
- Inside cover flap copy, up to 1,000 words
- Your author bio, up to 1,000 words
- Author comments, up to 1,000 words (if you haven't already completed this information online)

This material must be sent to Amazon.com on disk (Mac or PC) or uploaded via FTP. Read the information in The Catalog Guide carefully for the precise format in which to submit your information.

Send your book to a "subject librarian" for more publicity.

Amazon.com has twenty-three "Browse Subjects" categories, which function like mini-bookstores within the main site. Each of these categories is divided into various topic areas, where the visitor can browse through best-selling titles, top recommendations, author lists, and more.

Getting your book into one of these categories will help improve its visibility. To submit your title for review, mail it, along with any supporting materials, such as published reviews, to:

[Subject] Editor
Amazon.com
1516 Second Avenue
Seattle, WA 98101

Join the Amazon.com Associates program.

When you do, you'll be given a code to add to your book link that enables you to receive a commission (up to 15 percent) on every copy of your book (or any book) sold via your Web site.

Amazon.com can now track all purchases that originate from your Web site, rather than only those titles that you have linked to the store directly. Thus, if a visitor connects to Amazon.com through one of your hotlinks and then travels around the store, every book purchased by that visitor will earn you a commission, whether it's one of your hotlinked recommendations or not. Another new feature is a search program that you can add to your Web site, which enables visitors to search the Amazon.com bookstore directly from your site and, again, earns you a commission on all sales originating from that site.

If you are a self-publisher or distribute your own titles, join Amazon.com's Advantage program.

When you become a member of this program, Amazon.com will stock a small quantity of your titles, so that books can be shipped from their warehouse immediately. The Advantage program includes the following services:

- Inclusion in the appropriate "Browse Subjects" category
- Cover scanning
- Immediate shipping
- Online order tracking
- Monthly payments
- Marketing assistance

As of the time of this writing, no other online bookstore has offered authors the same opportunities for self-promotion as Amazon.com. This may change in the future, as other bookstores recognize the role authors can play in promoting (and increasing the sales of) their books. In the meantime, it's still a good idea to get your book listed by as many online bookstores as possible, simply to make it available to as wide an audience as possible.

On the Internet, as anywhere else, the key to a successful promotion is persistence. Think of the Web not as a giant shopping mall, but as the world's biggest library. Your contribution to the flow of information will be the best possible advertisement for your writing—and with luck, you should see the difference on the bottom line of your next royalty statement.

RESOURCES

Author and Writer Chat Sources

Barnes & Noble: Authors Online *www.barnesandnoble.com/community/community.asp*
 Look for a calendar of author chats, plus a list of more than seven hundred transcripts of previous chats.
The Chat Hole *www.geocities.com/SouthBeach/Breakers/5257/Chathole.htm*
 A site listing links to a wide range of chat topics, along with useful articles on how to participate in a chat.
CNN Interactive Interviews *www.cnn.com/chat/*
 "Multimedia interviews with your favorite authors."
MSN (Microsoft) Web Communities *communities.msn.com/reading/chat.asp*
 "A chat for every genre, every day."
Reader's Choice Book Chat *www.thegrid.net/dakaiser/books/chat.htm*
 "An online community created by book lovers for book lovers."
TalkCity *www.talkcity.com/communities/art_books.htmpl*
 A site dedicated to talk and discussion, including author chats and general reading chats (e.g., "SF&Lit Chat, a discussion of the best and brightest in SF&F literature"). Transcripts of previous chats also available.
The Literary Times *www.tlt.com/news/itiner.htm*
 Provides a place for romance authors to post events, such as chats and book signings.
WordsWorth *www.wordsworth.com/www/present/interviews/*
 A bookstore that hosts author interviews and author promotional pages.
The Writer's BBS *www.writers-bbs.com/chat.html*
 Offers chat rooms, discussion forums, and an e-zine entitled, "Fish Eggs for the Soul."
Writer'sClub.com Chat Schedule *chat.writersclub.com*
Writers Write Chat *www.writerswrite.com*
 (See chapter 6 for a list of chats related to writing.)

Genre Organizations That Host Web Sites

Horror Writers Association *www.horror.org*
Mystery Writers of America *www.bookwire.com/mwa/*
Romance Writers of America *www.rwanational.com*
Science Fiction Writers of America *www.sfwa.org/site_index.htp*
SFF Net *www.sff.net*
 Hosts author pages in a variety of genres, plus links to other author pages.

Pages Listing Author Sites

Author Web Sites *www.geocities.com/~bookbug/home.html*
 A list of primarily romance author sites.
Authors *authors.miningco.com*
Children's Book Council Authors and Illustrators Page *www.cbcbooks.com/navigation/author.html*
Painted Rock Writers and Readers Colony *ww.paintedrock.com/authors/*
Romance Novels and Women's Fiction: Authors *www.writepage.com/romance.htm*
Romance Writers of America *www.rwanational.com/linkaut.htm*
Science Fiction Authors *sflovers.rutgers.edu/Web/SFRG/sfrgfa.htm*
SFF Net *www.sff.net/people/index.htp*
Useful Links for Romance Writers and Readers: Authors *www.inficad.com/~jacreding/links/auth.html*
Webrings for Authors *www.webring.org/cgi-bin/ringworld/arts/hum.html*
 Search for author Web rings by keyword, such as "author" or "writer."

A Woman's Writing Retreat: Authors (male) *www.prairieden.com/links/men.html*
A Woman's Writing Retreat: Authors (female) *www.prairieden.com/links/women.html*
WritersNet *www.writers.net*
Writepage *www.writepage.com*
Yahoo! *dir.yahoo.com/Arts/Humanities/Literature/Genres/*
Check under your preferred genre for the "Authors" category, and submit your listing.

Amazon.com Programs for Writers

Amazon.com *www.amazon.com*
- "Advantage" program—for small presses, self-publishers, and authors who distribute their own titles: *www.amazon.com/exec/obidos/subst/partners/direct/direct-application.html*
- "Associates" program—offering a commission for selling books (including your own) from your Web site: *www.amazon.com/exec/obidos/subst/partners/associates/associates.html*
- "Catalog Guide"—describing how to include supporting material (such as chapter excerpts, reviews, etc.) on your book's "detail" page: *www.amazon.com/exec/obidos/subst/partners/publishers/catalog-guide.html*

Online Bookstores

Amazon.com (Germany) *www.amazon.de*
Amazon.com (United Kingdom) *www.amazon.co.uk*
Barnes & Noble *www.barnesandnoble.com*
Books.com *www.books.com*
This online bookstore offers interviews with authors. Contact them at *books@books.com* for more information.
Books OnQ *www.onq.org/Welcome.htm*
An online bookstore exclusively for self-published titles. Offers a variety of book promotion resources for authors.
BookZone *bookzone.com/profile/*
Offers links to small and independent publishers, plus many other resources.
Borders *www.borders.com*
WordsWorth *www.wordsworth.com/authinfo/*
A bookstore that allows you to "embed" your own promotional author Web site onsite.

Book-Search Sites

AddAll Book Searching and Price Comparison *www.addall.com*
Searches thirty-four bookstores for titles and price comparisons.
BookFinder.com *www.bookfinder.com*
This site will search bookseller databases online (including electronic bookstores and databases provided by "real-world" bookstores) to locate your title and provide a comparison of prices and shipping information.

Other Promotional Resources

Book Marketing Update *www.bookmarket.com/index.html*
Although the primary focus of this site is to promote a newsletter and other products, it offers a variety of free reports and other materials of use to self-published authors or authors seeking to promote their own books.
E-mail Newsletters: A Growing Market for Freelancers *www.contentious.com/articles/1-10/editorial1-10.html*
An article on how to write for e-mail newsletters.
Newsletter Access *www.newsletteraccess.com/directory.html*
A searchable database of more than five thousand newsletters (online and print).

Newsletter News *Gach98@aol.com*

A free e-mail newsletter listing "article needs" of various newsletters and e-zines. Most are non-paying, but may offer promotional opportunities. To subscribe, send an e-mail saying "subscribe" to the address above.

⑪

Publishing Online:
E-books and E-zines

Rumors that the Internet would replace print books and magazines have proven premature, to say the least. Nevertheless, two forms of electronic publishing are emerging to parallel traditional print venues. One is the electronic magazine, or "e-zine" (and its humbler twin, the electronic newsletter). The second is the electronic book, or "e-book."[1]

These media are based on the notion that anything that can be done in print can also be done without print. Because electronic publishing is far cheaper than any corresponding form of print publishing (if not virtually cost-free), just about anyone can start a magazine or publish a book. Unfortunately, this also means that anyone can e-publish—including would-be writers and nonwriters—regardless of whether they have the writing, editing, production, or other skills necessary to do so effectively. Consequently, the Internet is glutted with some truly dreadful material.

The question is whether such a free-for-all environment is also a viable forum for experienced authors. Will electronic publishing truly bring your work before the desired audience? Will it advance your writing career? The answer is, as usual, "It depends."

---

[1] The term "e-book" is used primarily to refer to a book that has been published in an electronic format. Books that are published primarily in print may have "electronic editions" (such as a "Rocket Edition" for the RocketBook E-reader), but are not generally referred to as "e-books." Similarly, electronic versions of previously published materials (such as scholarly works, classics and literary works now in the public domain, public documents, ancient texts, etc.) are generally referred to as "e-texts" rather than "e-books."

Paperless Periodicals

In the print world, the cost of launching one's own magazine, or even a newsletter, has always been prohibitive. Online, however, cost is an almost nonexistent factor, and starting a magazine of one's own is a real possibility.

The number of e-zines and newsletters on the Web increases almost daily. When Debbie Ridpath Ohi of Inkspot first launched the newsletter *Inklings* in 1995, for example, it was one of a scant handful of electronic publications for writers. Today, writers can turn to more than a dozen online publications, with more on the way. This is both good news and bad news for the writer who wants to become a publisher. While it indicates a growing audience for e-zines, it also means that you should check the market first to make sure no one else has already launched the e-zine of your dreams.

An electronic publication can be a way to add to the content of your Web site, reach a wider audience, and contribute to your professional promotional efforts. For example, if your goal is to establish or promote your expertise in a particular field, an electronic publication can help you do so by educating people on your topic and expanding your list of contacts at the same time. Creating such a publication, however, involves a number of important decisions. Before you launch, consider the following questions:

- **What is your publication about?** Most successful "Weblications" have a well-defined focus that attracts a specific audience. Is your publication fiction or nonfiction? If nonfiction, is the subject sufficiently broad to sustain a series of articles, or will you use up most of your important topics in a month or two? If fiction, what type of material do you wish to present? A publication that tries to be all things to all readers, offering "a little of this and a little of that," may have trouble attracting a steady audience.

- **Who is your audience?** Define the types of readers most likely to be interested in your subject. Where will you find them? How will you attract them? Have you found newsgroups or sites where such readers gather and where you can announce your publication or exchange links? Are there other e-zines or newsletters on similar topics where you could place an ad for your publication?

- **Who will write for your publication?** Do you intend to do all the writing yourself or edit material from other writers? Be cautious about putting out an "all you, all the time" "*me-zine.*" Many Net citizens regard this sort of thing as grandstanding.

- **What type of content will you include?** Long articles or short? News items or timeless features? Most e-mail newsletters incorporate some form of news into their content. For example, writing newsletters offer market listings, contest announcements, news about writers or of interest to writers, etc. How will you find varied content for your publication?

- **How often will you produce your publication?** E-zines are often updated monthly, or even bimonthly. Newsletters, on the other hand, are more likely to come out weekly or biweekly. The less frequent the news-letter, the longer it is likely to be; a monthly newsletter, for example, would typically be longer than a weekly one.

- **How much time do you plan to spend?** A regular publication takes more time than you might imagine, even if you're not writing all the articles yourself. Your estimated schedule should include planning time, design and/or format, administration, correspondence (with your read-ers, writers, sponsors, and sources), promotions, research, surfing, troubleshooting, and the ever-present "miscellaneous tasks." Be sure you can balance this effort with the demands of your regular writing.
- **Will you handle nonwriting tasks?** If you're considering an e-zine, do you want an outside designer to handle the format of your publication, or do you plan to design and update it yourself? If you're gathering market reports, job listings, news updates, or articles, do you plan to search for that information yourself or hire a "contributing editor" to help you?
- **Will you offer the publication for free or charge for subscriptions?** Although there are exceptions, the vast majority of Weblications are offered free to subscribers or visitors. Those that don't charge often at-tempt to break even through the sale of advertising, banner space, or classifieds.
- **If you hire outside help, how will you pay for it?** Even if you do sell subscriptions or advertising space, you're unlikely to see a huge profit in the early stages of your endeavor (if at all). The good news is that people who write for online publications often don't expect a high pay rate. For example, the going rate for an e-mail newsletter ranges from $10 to $50 for a five-hundred- to one-thousand-word article. Even that can add up quickly, however, and other costs, such as design fees, can add even more to your expenditures.
- **How will you promote your publication?** "Build it and they will come" generally doesn't work on the Web. A more accurate phrase reads, "Pro-mote it and they may trickle in if you're lucky." Once you've defined your readership, you'll need to take active steps to bring it in.

The final decision you will need to make is whether to create an e-zine or a newsletter. Each has its advantages and disadvantages, including format considerations that will influence your choice of content and design.

Building an E-zine

An e-zine resides on a Web site. In fact, the only significant difference be-tween an e-zine and an ordinary Web site is that an e-zine is regularly up-dated, offering a new issue at specific intervals. Older issues can be archived on the same site.

An e-zine offers tremendous flexibility in terms of design and presentation options. You could, for example, design your magazine to look much like a print publication, with columns, sidebars, and graphics. You can also go beyond print by incorporating multimedia elements such as animation, audio, and video clips. For example, if you feature an interview with a famous author, you could include an audio clip of the interview, so that readers could hear the author's words in her own voice. Finally, you can add links to material outside your e-zine for more information.

E-zines also enable you to present material in a nonlinear fashion, through hyperlinks that let the reader choose which elements to read, in which order. Don't fall into the design trap of artificially breaking articles into separate pages, however. This practice arose from the desire to track visitors to find out whether they actually read the entire article, but only adds frustration to the reading process. Clicking on a "continue" button and waiting for a new page to download is nothing like flipping a magazine page! If an article is naturally linear, put it on a single "page," unless it is exceptionally long (more than 50 K) and would take excessive time to download.

Be cautious about adding too many bells and whistles to your publication just to attract readers with a snazzy design. Remember that many people still use older equipment that doesn't respond well (or quickly) to a host of Java applets, giant images, complicated wallpaper, and animated features. Assess your audience profile: Is this a high-tech group, or a set of folks who just want easy access to solid information?

Some e-zines open with a cover image that operates like the front cover of a magazine. While this can be attractive, be aware that it also adds an extra level of "noninformation" that a visitor must get past before finding your content. Don't require visitors to download a mega-GIF to view your cover before they can find out what your e-zine is about and how to enter. Be sure to provide clear "enter here" instructions on your cover.

Other e-zines open directly to a table of contents. This will serve as your primary navigation tool, so make sure it is clear and easy to access. Beware of frames that don't allow the reader to return easily to the contents section. Cute titles are fine, but be sure your subtitles give readers an idea of what your publication is about. This page should also point the reader to instructions on how to subscribe (if necessary), how to contact you, and how to find back issues. It should also include (or point to) your copyright notice. You may wish to add a contents bar to each page or article, so that readers can navigate within your site without returning to the table of contents.

Each issue of your e-zine should be clearly dated. Once an issue has expired, you'll need to archive it and provide a contents entry for back issues. One way to create an archive is to simply retitle current pages and move them into an archive file, without changing the pages themselves. Another is to strip pages of their multimedia trimmings and simply archive the text files. Either way, you may wish to discuss archival rights as part of any contract with your writers and artists (see chapter 4).

Creating an E-mail Newsletter

E-mail newsletters are generally easier to produce than e-zines, as you don't have to deal with design issues. Simply dump your information into a text file, then transmit that file as an e-mail.

"No design issues" also means no frills, however. An e-mail newsletter is devoid of graphics, hyperlinks, and multimedia extras. Articles are linear and usually short (up to one thousand words), though some newsletters do run longer features. Debbie Ridpath Ohi, editor of *Inklings*, recommends limiting your newsletter as a whole to thirty or forty thousand.

Like any other e-mail, certain formatting requirements apply to newsletters. Be sure you use "text only," with no curly quotes, special symbols, formatting (such as italics or underlining), long line lengths, or lines that won't wrap. Turn off any features of your e-mail program that automatically format messages into HTML or transmit them as attachments. If your newsletter is longer than thirty thousand words, consider breaking it into more than one section. Many e-mail programs break long incoming messages into sections anyway, so by doing so yourself, you can ensure that the break comes at an appropriate location.

Make sure each issue of your newsletter includes the title and any introductory information, such as a masthead that lists the name of the publisher or publishing organization. If you have a corresponding Web site where readers can find back issues or subscription information, include its URL in your masthead. Be sure to provide full contact and subscription information. Also include a copyright statement with each newsletter, which includes your ISSN (if any), your "all rights reserved" statement, and any related information. If you don't mind subscribers forwarding the newsletter to others, state this in your copyright section. Be sure to advise subscribers to forward the entire newsletter, rather than excerpts. Otherwise, such forwarding could create copyright problems. Also, decide whether you are willing to have subscribers post your newsletter to mailing lists or newsgroups.

Many people launch their newsletters manually (handling all subscription information by hand). Once your subscriber list begins to grow, however, you'll probably want to move it to an automated service that will handle subscribe/unsubscribe requests and, as well, will broadcast the newsletter to that list. A number of services offer free list management in exchange for the placement of a "small ad" in your newsletter; others charge a small fee (around $5).

An automated list manager will provide a unique subscription address, but don't expect everyone to use it. Even when you use an automated service, you'll still receive plenty of subscription requests at your contact address, including address change requests. You'll also receive bounce-backs—newsletters that were undeliverable and are bounced back to your personal box.

Building a List, Promoting It Twice

Regardless of the type of publication you develop, the primary challenge is attracting readers or subscribers. If you sell advertising, your rates will be based on your subscriber base, so tracking subscriptions is important. This can be difficult for an e-zine. Unless you sell subscriptions, your only tracking method is your hit counter, which doesn't tell you which visitors stayed to browse (or what they read), or whether you have repeat visitors from month to month. (It's a good idea to include a counter on each page or article, so that you can determine what percentage of your visitors actually went inside to read your material and which features attracted the most attention.) One way to increase feedback is to offer a guestbook or forum.

Most of the recommendations on promoting your Web site (chapter 9) also apply to promoting your publication. Some other possibilities include:

- Listing your publication in a database of e-zines
- Submitting your publication to review sources
- Exchanging reciprocal links with related Web sites
- Offering a "site of the week" (or month) award to relevant Web sites (consider creating an award GIF that links back to your site)
- Posting information about your publication on your regular Web site
- Including the URL of the publication (or subscription address) in your e-mail signature block
- Developing a business card that includes the address of your publication, so that you can promote it offline as well as online

Several sites, including Chip Rowe's **So, You Want to Start an E-zine?** e-zine development site, offer other tips on building and promoting an e-zine.

While e-zines and newsletters run the gamut from distinguished to downright weird, even the most bizarre have attained an aura of respectability. E-zines are considered valid entities on the Web, often comparable or even superior to corresponding print publications. While creating an effective e-zine can involve considerable effort, it can also enhance your online image and bring your name (and work) before a wide audience.

Electronic Books: "In Print" without Paper

Electronic publishing (or "e-publishing") is a venue in which books are produced, stored, and transmitted electronically rather than in print. E-books are produced in a variety of formats—for example, online, on a disk, or on CD-ROM—as a file that can be downloaded or transmitted as an e-mail attachment, or as a file that can be downloaded to a hand-held electronic reader ("e-reader") or similar device. Most e-publishers offer books in a variety of formats. In some cases, e-books can also be produced in a "print-on-demand" format, which enables the publisher to print a single book at a time when ordered by a customer.

The prices of e-books vary widely. Commercial fiction titles typically range from $5 to $10, averaging around $7 (comparable to a fiction paperback). Shorter works may cost less. Dreams Unlimited, for example, offers novelettes for as little as $2. Subsidy-published books, however, often cost more, and are sometimes priced according to page count, while self-published titles often range between $10 and $30 or more.

E-Publishing: Three Choices

The consumer e-publishing industry (as opposed to scholarly, scientific, or technical e-publishing) is divided into three basic categories: commercial publishers, subsidy publishers, and self-publishers.

Commercial

Commercial e-publishers operate much like commercial print publishers, accepting books on the basis of quality and marketability. Books go through a similar process of review, editing, and proofreading before publication. Most commercial e-publishers accept fewer than 10 percent of submissions. Hard Shell Word Factory, for example, accepted only 6 percent of the 1,200 submissions it received in 1998. Writers receive royalties on all sales.

Such e-books are generally sold through the publisher's Web site and via online bookstores such as Amazon.com and Barnes & Noble. Some e-publishers are also making their books available as "Rocket Editions," which can be downloaded to a RocketBook E-reader through Barnes & Noble. E-books can also be ordered by ISBN through ordinary bookstores, but are rarely found on traditional bookstore shelves.

Subsidy

Subsidy e-publishers, like their print counterparts, produce and distribute books for a fee (which ranges from $200 to $500 per manuscript). Authors receive a royalty, which is usually comparable to that offered by commercial e-publishers.

Unlike commercial e-publishers, however, subsidy e-publishers provide few (if any) editorial services. Books are posted "as is," often without so much as a proofreading. Subsidy e-publishers provide little or no quality screening, except to screen for offensive content (such as pornography or hate material). Subsidy-published books are also available through online bookstores, but are less likely to be available in Rocket Editions.

Self-publishing

While some subsidy publishers describe their services as "self-publishing," this is inaccurate. Self-publishing is a process in which the author is entirely responsible for the development and production of the book, as well as its marketing and distribution. Most often, a self-published book is marketed through the author's own site. Rather than paying a fee to another "publisher" to handle expenses, the author is directly responsible for all publishing expenses. Perhaps the most important criteria to distinguish self-publishing from subsidy publishing, however, is that the author receives all sales revenues, rather than a percentage of revenues in the form of royalties.

Advantages of E-Publishing

Commercial e-publishers (and authors) cite several advantages to this form of publishing:

- **Better chances of acceptance**. "E-publishing is opening the doors for a lot of new authors," says Mary Wolf of Hard Shell Word Factory (HSWF). "It is also a home for those great stories that fall between the cracks with New York publishers for various reasons: don't fit the length requirements; wrong type of hero/heroine; wrong career, era, or setting; etc. We are free to push the envelope, resulting in fresh new voices. . . . At the same time, stories still need to be well-written!"

- **Issues such as length are far less important.** E-novels may be considerably longer than "traditional" novels, or considerably shorter. This is the primary reason best-selling author Diana Gabaldon offered her story, *Hellfire* (previously anthologized in Britain) to Dreams Unlimited: "Care to guess how many paying markets there are for 11,000-word historical mystery stories? Yes, exactly."

- **More control over the process**. "Writers have greater freedom with characters and plot, more 'say' in revisions, and more input in cover art and sales blurbs," says Wolf. While e-publishing editors may make suggestions for revisions in a manuscript, authors note that there is considerably more room for discussion and negotiation.

- **Higher royalties.** Because the costs of e-publishing are significantly (if not monumentally) lower than those of print publishing, authors receive a far higher percentage of revenues. Royalties range between 20 and 40 percent, with 30 percent being fairly typical. Most e-publishers also pay royalties more frequently than print publishers, offering quarterly statements rather than annual or semi-annual payments. Some publishers also provide a breakdown of sales by format, e.g., how many titles were sold on disk, by download or e-mail, or by e-reader download.

- **Author-friendly contracts.** Most e-publishers ask only for electronic rights, leaving the author free to market print rights and subsidiary rights elsewhere. In addition, most e-publishing contracts are renewable rather than indefinite. Thus, instead of tying up an author's work until it "goes out of print" (a meaningless term in e-publishing!), either party usually has the option to renew or terminate the contract at the end of a specified time (usually a year). Most reputable e-publishers also post their complete contracts online, so that an author can review the terms before submitting.

- **Shorter response times.** Most e-publishers attempt to respond to submissions within two to four months. Response times are lengthening, however, as the number of submissions increases. "We used to have a four-to-six-week turnaround time," says Marilyn Nesbitt of DiskUs Publishing, "but we get so many submissions now that this is changing. Still, we try to keep a manuscript no longer than four months."
- **Faster publication.** "It takes a book almost two years to go to print with a traditional publisher," says Bonnee Pierson of Dreams Unlimited. "We can do it in a matter of weeks." In reality, Pierson and other e-publishers tend to stretch out publication time to between three and six months after acceptance to allow time to generate advance reviews and publicity for a book. And while some publishers produce a book within months, others have a backlog of accepted titles and are scheduling release dates well into 2001.
- **Multimedia and format options.** An electronic book—whether online or on CD-ROM—can include a variety of multimedia elements to "add to the experience," notes Siobhan McNally of Domhan Books. Such elements might include music, graphics, animation, audio, or "interactivity-clickable features." McNally also points out that downloadable formats for hand readers often include different fonts, a highlighter, post-it notes, a clickable table of contents, and bookmarking capabilities. This allows the option of providing different formats for different customers. "My publisher [DiskUs] has reached out to the aged and those with visual difficulties, because the medium in which we publish allows readers to set the font size or type, which aids in their reading pleasure," says author Leta Nolan Childers.
- **International availability.** "Readers in Australia can buy the book the same day it's released to a buyer in the U.S.," says Pierson. "They don't have to wait for export or foreign rights negotiations. This is a terrific advantage for families who are stationed overseas. . . . Vacationing in Europe and running out of reading material? Plug into the Net and buy a new book! It's immediately accessible to everyone, everywhere." (Authors should note that this international accessibility may affect one's future ability to sell international rights to another publisher.)
- **Longer "shelf life."** Since it costs very little to keep an e-book "in stock," a book does not have to sell thousands of copies to remain "in print." As long as sales remain "good" (by e-book standards), most e-publishers are willing to keep a title in their inventory, rather than dropping it for a more profitable title.

Disadvantages of E-publishing

- **Lower sales.** "No, I'm not satisfied with sales—if I were to compare them to a traditional author's sales," admits Karen Wiesner, author of *Restless as Rain, Leather and Lace,* and *Falling Star* (Hard Shell Word Factory). "I am satisfied by the fact that each royalty period, my earnings at least double. I'm gaining a following slowly, and with e-publishing being so new, I admit that I'm not expecting to become a bestseller for at least five years." As other authors point out, however, few print publishers would give a title five years to become a "success." According to Mary Wolf of HSWF, sales of five hundred are considered good.

Publishers and authors agree that for an e-book to be successful, the author must devote considerable effort to its promotion. "Don't sit back like your job is over and expect the cash to roll in," warns Wiesner. "In a field this new, you have to do one hundred times more marketing than a traditional author. Don't allow opportunities to pass you by." Authors often promote their books through Web sites, online chats, book signings, interviews, and similar opportunities.

- **Lack of availability in bookstores.** Though e-books are available through many online bookstores such as Amazon.com and Barnes & Noble, they are hard to find in traditional bookstores. Though all e-books can be ordered by their ISBN, this isn't the same as being "on the shelf." When traditional bookstores do accept e-books, it is usually due to the promotional efforts of a local author.
- **No advance.** Besides the obvious financial disadvantage, the lack of an advance can create other problems for authors. Several genre organizations consider a book "commercially published" only if an advance is paid, which means e-books may not qualify as part of an author's membership prerequisites or for certain industry awards.
- **Fewer reviews.** While some publications (especially online) review e-books, many traditional book review sources have been slow to accept e-books. "They're still under the impression that we're not selling 'real' books," says Pierson. Karen Wiesner agrees: "I doubt too many metropolitan newspapers would consider e-books at this time." Nor are e-books likely to be reviewed in major book and library trade publications, such as *Kirkus Reviews* or *Editor and Publisher.*
- **Limited formats.** Some publishers offer only Windows-compatible formats, and some offer disks only for Windows. Although such publishers point out that users with a PowerMac should be able to read these disks, not all potential consumers have the latest technology.
- **Lack of security.** Concerns about piracy deter many authors from considering e-publishing, and indeed, there is little to prevent someone from buying an e-book and making and distributing an unlimited number of copies. E-publishers claim that piracy is not a serious threat, however. Since the market for e-books is still limited to begin with, little is to be gained by pirating copies!
- **Consumer reluctance to read "online."** While the popularity of e-books is growing steadily, many consumers are still reluctant to read a novel onscreen—or to add the cost of printing a book on one's own paper and with one's own toner to the cost of the book itself.

"The comment I've heard most often from consumers is surprise that anyone would want to read a whole book at the computer," says author Cheryl Harrington. "While some of us are most comfortable with our feet up on our desks, one hand on the mouse and the other cradling a hot cup of tea, others associate their computers with 'work' and paper books with 'relaxation.'" Michele Johnson of Petals of Life notes that portability is another issue: It's difficult to read an e-book "in the car, in bed, or in the tub." She notes, however, that "with the new readers coming on the market, this is making e-books more portable, and of course if one has a laptop, one already has a way to take a book with one." Still, many consumers are not ready to pay $300–$500 for a special machine just to read electronic books.

What to Look for in a Commercial E-Publisher

E-publishers offer the following pointers for selecting a publisher:
- Does the publisher have a good Web site?
- Did you learn about the publisher from publicity from outside sources or stumble across the site by chance?
- Did someone recommend the publisher to you?
- Does the contract look fair?
- Is the publisher asking for money up-front?
- Does the publisher publish the sort of books you write?
- Does the publisher offer the kinds of books you like to read?
- Does the publisher have a plan to move with the times, offering new and varied formats (such as print-on-demand or Palm Reader)?
- Does the publisher have staying power? "Because of the prejudice many people have against e-books, it is a slow but steady process—so avoid a publisher with a 'get rich quick' mentality," says Siobhan McNally.
- Where are titles reviewed?
- What is the experience of the publisher's editors?
- Where does the publisher place advertising?
- What steps will the publisher take to promote your book?
- Have the publisher's books (or site) won any awards or achieved particularly favorable reviews or publicity?
- Is the publisher a member of the **Association of Electronic Publishers** (AEP) or the **Electronically Published Internet Connection** (EPIC)?
- Can the publisher provide a list of references of authors?
- Does the publisher offer advance review copies to professional reviewers and review publications?
- How many free copies will you receive, and what is your author discount on disks or downloads?
- Can you communicate with the publisher? Do they answer your questions? Do you feel that the publisher is being honest with you about your book's potential in this medium?
- Will you feel proud of the finished product?

Subsidy E-Publishing: Another Alternative

While many authors and publishers advise against any form of subsidy pub-lishing, many writers choose this route for a variety of reasons. Subsidy pub-lishing can, for example, provide many of the advantages of self-publishing, including complete control of the product, for less hassle and at a compa-rable cost. Subsidy e-publishers offer some of the same (or similar) advan-tages as commercial publishers, including:

- **High acceptance rates.** Many subsidy publishers will accept any manu-script, as long as it does not contain offensive material. In many cases, therefore, "acceptance" is virtually guaranteed.
- **Higher royalties.** A reputable subsidy publisher will offer similar royal-ties to a commercial publisher—usually 40–60 percent.
- **Fast turnaround.** A manuscript may be accepted within one to two weeks of submission and go online in as little as a month.
- **Author-friendly contracts.** Reputable subsidy publishers demand few, if any, rights to your work. Some may request a limited grant of elec-tronic rights; others leave copyright entirely in the hands of the author. As with commercial publishers, subsidy publishing contracts can be re-newed (or terminated) by either party after a specific time.
- **Availability.** Like any e-book, subsidy-published books are available worldwide, both from the publisher's Web site and through online book-stores. Nor are subsidized books dropped from inventory for lack of sales. It is usually the author's choice to keep a book "in stock" or to withdraw it.

These advantages, however, come with corresponding disadvantages, including:

- **Lack of quality control.** Since subsidy publishers accept nearly any manuscript, such sites offer little or no quality screening. Consequently, while your book may be of high quality, it may be sharing "Web space" with other books of much lower quality. Consumers who buy an infe-rior product are less likely to take a risk on another book from the same publisher. Thus, the presence of low-quality books on your publisher's site can actively detract from your own sales.
- **Lack of editing.** Subsidy-published e-books rarely receive any editing—a fact which many sites declare up-front. This means that not only will you not receive any editorial feedback on your material, but that your book will not be copyedited or proofread; it will be posted "as is." Be sure you know how to use a spellchecker! (Some subsidy publishers of-fer editorial services for an extra fee, or you can choose to hire your own freelance editor.)
- **Lack of promotion.** Most subsidy publishers offer few promotional ser-vices; they do not place ads for books in trade magazines or send out

advance copies for reviews. The responsibility for promoting and marketing a book usually rests entirely with the author.

- **Lack of respect.** Subsidized e-books are held in extremely poor regard
by the majority of the publishing industry (including genre organizations). Most organizations (including EPIC) will not consider a subsidized book as a qualification for membership or for industry awards.
Many consumers have also learned to avoid subsidized books, due to
the lack of quality control.
- **Cost.** Subsidy publishing costs money—usually from $300 to $500 to
have your book posted on the site, plus (in some cases) annual mainte-
nance fees. If a site offers editorial services, these come at a cost as well—
either an up-front fee or a portion of royalties. In addition, the author
must still assume the full cost (in both time and money) of promoting
and marketing the book.

Warning Signs of Scams and Rip-offs

While most subsidy publishers are reputable, this aspect of the business also
lends itself to abuses. If you're considering this form of publishing, watch out
for the following telltale signs of rip-off:

- **Excessive up-front cost.** The standard "registration" rates for subsidy
e-publishers range between $300 and $500 per title. Be extremely cautious if a publisher asks for a significantly higher fee.
- **Excessive renewal fees.** Some subsidy publishers request annual renewal
fees in addition to the initial "registration" fee (as well as in addition to
the profits that a publisher is earning, theoretically, from the ongoing
sale of your book). These fees may range from $100 to $500 per year.
- **Additional "production" costs.** Your registration fee should cover the
costs of production, including translating your book into the appropriate online format. (Most subsidy publishers insist that a manuscript be
delivered in a specific electronic format, which means that transferring
it into the final "published" form is a very simple matter.) It should also
include the costs of obtaining an ISBN, copyright registration, and a
Library of Congress number. Beware of any publisher who charges an
additional "formatting" fee (usually per page) on top of the basic registration fee.
- **Low royalties.** The standard commercial e-publishing royalty rate is
between 40 and 60 percent. Most reputable subsidy publishers pay similar
rates. Beware of any publisher that offers a lower fee (10 to 20 percent).
Some publishers claim in their contract that a 10 percent royalty is "standard" for the industry, but this is simply not true. While 10 percent is
standard for many parts of the print industry, it is not standard for the
e-publishing industry and makes no sense whatsoever for an e-publisher
who is receiving an up-front fee to produce your book in the first place.

- **An excessively binding (or demanding) contract.** Most commercial e-publishers use time-limited contracts that enable either party to terminate the agreement easily after a period of one or two years. Reputable subsidy publishers do the same. Some publishers, however, impose a considerably longer limit on the contract (e.g., seven years) and may ask an additional fee or share of royalties if the author manages to sell the book to another publisher in the interim. Also, watch out for any contract that asks for a transfer of additional rights, such as print rights, translation rights, audio rights, movie rights, etc. By transferring these rights, you enable a publisher to claim a percentage of any of those rights that *you* happen to sell.
- **An incomplete contract.** Most reputable publishers post their contracts online. Some, however, post a "sample" contract that includes terms "to be negotiated." This prevents an author from determining in advance what those terms (often involving rights or royalties) might be. With so much openness in the industry as a whole, there seems little plausible reason for a publisher to leave authors in the dark.
- **Inflated hype.** Reputable publishers, both commercial and subsidy, are up-front about the difficulties in placing e-books in traditional bookstores. Beware, therefore, of any publisher who claims to offer "bookstore sales" or makes a big deal about getting your book into Amazon.com or Barnes & Noble. Inclusion in the Amazon.com catalog happens automatically as a result of obtaining an ISBN; it is not the result of any special effort on the part of a publisher. As well, be aware that inclusion in online bookstores does not constitute "bookstore distribution."

Should You or Shouldn't You?

Electronic publishing is an industry in its infancy—"in the toddler stage," says Bonnee Pierson—and also an industry that is undergoing rapid change. Technological advances are continually reshaping the industry. For example, no one can yet predict what the impact of hand-held readers will be on print or electronic publishing. Consequently, it is extremely difficult to predict what will happen next or how the industry may change in the next few years.

Many commercial e-publishers are taking active steps to influence these changes and to improve the reputation and acceptance of e-books. E-publishers and authors consider "consumer education" (and industry education) to be a major part of their mission—a task often more important than promoting their own titles or companies. Most are certain that consumer and industry acceptance of e-books will continue to grow, especially, as Mary Wolf says, "with the next generation, who are growing up with computers and taking reading on them for granted."

"I believe it is only a matter of time before e-books are accepted just the same as print books," says Marilyn Nesbitt. "As more and more print authors turn to electronic publishing, this medium will take off. It may be a few years down the road, but electronic publishing is really the wave of the future."

At the same time, it is not difficult to find those who disagree. The articles listed in the "Resources" section present a range of views on electronic publishing and its future—some optimistic, some pessimistic.

One thing is clear: It is a choice to be made carefully, after serious consideration of the potential advantages and disadvantages. It is not a venue to rush into out of desperation or excessive haste to be published. Decide, first and foremost, what you would consider your measures of success as an author—and then decide what form of publishing is most likely to achieve those goals.

Electronic self-publishing can, indeed, be a path to success. It can also be a siren song that leads unwary authors onto some serious rocks. Opportunities for online publication should be assessed not on the basis of ego, desperation ("I'll never be published any other way"), or the ease with which such publication can be accomplished, but on a serious evaluation of the pros and cons. How much effort will you have to expend, for what return? Will your rewards be tangible (more money) or intangible (an enhanced reputation that will lead to a wider audience and more or better assignments)? Knowing exactly what you must invest (time, money, energy, passion) and what you will receive for that investment is the key to making wise Web-publishing choices.

●

R E S O U R C E S

E-zines and E-mail Newsletters

Discussion and Mailing List Promotion *jlunz.databack.com/listpromo.htm*
Links to resources for promoting e-zines and e-mail newsletters.

E-mail Newsletters: A Growing Market for Freelancers *www.contentious.com/articles/1-10/editorial1-10.html*
An article on how to write for e-mail newsletters.

Guidelines for Publishing and Promoting an E-mail Newsletter *www.trafficplan.com/newsltrtips.htm*
Useful articles, plus a free newsletter and e-zine on Web promotion tips.

How to Start an Online Newsletter *www.inkspot.com/craft/newsletterinfo.html*
An article by Debbie Ridpath Ohi, editor and publisher of *Inklings*.

So, You Want to Start an E-Zine? *www.zinebook.com/roll.html*
Loads of information and resources for e-zine producers.

Use Email Newsletters to Market Your Small Business on the Internet *www.arrowweb.com/graphics/news/aug98o.html*
Contains tips that will be useful to e-zine publishers.

VirtualPROMOTE *virtualpromote.com*
Offers tools and techniques for Web site promotion, plus a free newsletter (the *VirtualPROMOTE Gazette*). Though aimed at commercial sites, many tips also apply to promoting a newsletter or e-zine.

Writing for Webzines: Brave New Markets, Same Old Problems *www.nwu.org/aw/97wint/online.htm*

E-zine Directories and Resources

Directory of Electronic Journals and Newsletters *www.coalliance.org*
E•Journal *www.edoc.com/ejournal/*
E-mail Newsletters and E-zines that Accept Advertising and Sponsorships *www.copywriter.com/lists/ezines.htm*
Etext Archive *www.etext.org/services.shtml*
Ezine Adsource *home.earthlink.net/~blitop3/*
E-zines and newsletters that accept advertising.

eZINE Search *www.site-city.com/members/e-zine-master/*
A searchable list of more than three thousand e-zines.

John Labovitz's E-Zine List *www.meer.net/~johnl/e-zine-list*
One of the largest and most comprehensive e-zine directories.

New Ezine Directory *foxcities.com/webpromote*
NewJour: New Journals and Newsletters on the Internet *gort.ucsd.edu/newjour/NewJour/*
Newsletter Access *www.newsletteraccess.com*
The Sideroad *www.sideroad.com/openroad/contents.html*
Reviews of e-zines, plus tips on e-zine development and marketing.

WWW Virtual Library Electronic Journals List *www.edoc.com/ejournal/*
Zine-World *www.oblivion.net/zineworld/*

Services That Host Newsletters and Mailing Lists

eGroups *www.egroups.com*
ListBot *www.listbot.com*
OakNet Publishing *Oaknetpub.com*
ONEList *onelist.com*

Commercial Electronic Publishers

The following publishers are members of the Association of Electronic Publishers (AEP).
Awe-Struck E-Books *www.awe-struck.net*
Boson Books *www.cmonline/boson/*

DiskUs Publishing *www.diskuspublishing.com*
Domhan Books *www.domhanbooks.com*
Dreams Unlimited *www.dreams-unlimited.com*
The Fiction Works *www.fictionworks.com*
GLB Publishers *www.glbpubs.com*
Hard Shell Word Factory *www.hardshell.com*
Indigo Publishing *www.booktrain.com/index/*
MountainView Publishing *www.whidbey.com/mountainview*
New Concepts Publishing *www.newconceptspublishing.com*
Petals of Life Publishing *www.petalsoflife.com*

For additional links to electronic publishers, see:
Association of Electronic Publishers *welcome.to/AEP*
Electronically Published Internet Connection (EPIC) *www.eclectics.com/epic/*
A clearinghouse for electronically published authors and information on electronic publishing.
Lida Quillen's List of Epublishers *www.sff.net/people/Lida.Quillen/epub.html*
Mary Wolf's Guide to Electronic Publishers *www.coredcs.com/~mermaid/epub.html*
Yahoo's Guide to Electronic Publishers *dir.yahoo.com/Business_and_Economy/Companies/Publishing/Electronic_Publishing/*

Other E-Publishers

1stBooks *www.1stbooks.com*
Electric Works Publishing *www.electricpublishing.com/textindex.htm*
HyperBooks *www.hyperbooks.com/submit.html*
OmniMedia Digital Publishing *www.awa.com/library/omnimedia/aboutus.html*
Tara Publishing *www.tarapublishing.com/publish/authpubinfo.mhtml*
Offers subsidy and commercial publishing.
Xlibris *www.xlibris.com/html/publishing_your_book.html*
Offers both electronic and "books on demand" formats.

Articles on Electronic Publishing

Brave New World: Romance Authors on the Cutting Edge of Publishing *www.booksquare.com/subversion/parlor/exp001.cfm*
Contract Issues: Books Published Online *www.nwu.org/docs/online-p.htm*
The National Writers Union's views on rights and electronic publishing.
E-Publisher Interview [with Lori Soard] *writerexchange.miningco.com/library/weekly/aa070598.htm*
A New Marketing Opportunity: Electronic Publishing *www.paintedrock.com/memvis/rockmag/files/rock99-03.txt*
Preditors and Editors Readers Poll *www.sfwa.org/prededitors/perpoll.htm*
Readers' selections of best electronically published books and short stories in various speculative fiction categories.
Rising Stars on the Electronic Horizon *www.paintedrock.com/memvis/rockmag/files/99-10.txt*
A series of interviews with e-published authors.
Why Sell Your Book to an Electronic Publisher? *www.eclectics.com/articles/ebooks2.htm*
Writer Beware: Epublishers *www.sfwa.org/Beware/epublishers.html*
Warnings on the perils of subsidy e-publishing and unethical e-publishers.

Hand-Held E-Readers

E-books: The End of the Gutenberg Era? *www.pcworld.com/pcwtoday/article/0,1510,7645,00.html*
A discussion of SoftBook and RocketBook e-readers.
Everybook, Inc. *www.everybk.com/aboutus.html*
Manufacturer of the EveryBook Dedicated Reader.
Librius.com *www.librius.com/liccorp8.html*
Manufacturer of the Millennium E-reader

NuvoMedia *www.nuvomedia.com*
>   Manufacturer of the RocketBook E-reader.

SoftBook Press *www.softbooks.com*
>   Manufacturer of the SoftBook reader.

What is the Rocket E-book? *www.barnesandnoble.com/help/rocketbooks.asp*

12

Where
Next?

Trying to make predictions about the future of the Internet is like trying to fish for eels with a wire hanger: The results aren't likely to be what you hoped for, and you're also likely to receive some serious shocks. Perhaps the only prediction that can be made with any degree of safety is that the Internet will change. Moreover, it will change whatever it touches: laws, customs, ideas, commerce, traditions, values, methods of thought.

As this book has shown, the Internet has already profoundly changed the world of writing and the way writers do business. It will surely continue to do so—but in what way? Will those changes continue to be beneficial (as many of the changes have been to date)—or do writers face some shocks along the way? Where is the Internet taking us, and is it somewhere we really want to go? Perhaps most importantly, can we take steps to help shape our own electronic future?

In this chapter, I offer the results of my own "eel fishing," along with the insights of some expert writers and editors who have been watching the Internet trends discussed in this book, including information, markets, rights, communication, book promotion, and online publishing. Here are some tips we've pulled from the murky waters ahead:

The Future of Information

Today, one of the greatest benefits of the Internet is its unprecedented and unparalleled access to free information on just about any imaginable subject.

Perhaps one of the most amazing developments online is the apparent hunger so many people (and organizations) have to share what they know, at no cost. For some, that sharing comes from the desire for self-expression; for others, the desire to make a point; for yet others, the drive is to educate and enlighten. Whatever the motivation, it has been a bounty for information hunters like ourselves. It also seems hard to imagine that such a seemingly infinite well of knowledge could ever run dry.

Yet it might. A war is looming on the electronic horizon, and information is the battleground. Who owns it? Who has the right to control it? Who has the right to use it? Can one person "own" information and charge another for access? If I use your facts, can you sue me?

If certain commercial concerns have their way, the answer could very well be "yes." If it becomes possible to "copyright information" (i.e., by adding copyright protection not simply to the way information is organized and expressed by a writer or database compiler, but to the facts themselves), the well could indeed start to go dry. Once information becomes a commodity that can be "owned" (since copyright is a statement of ownership), it can be controlled, protected, withheld, and bartered.

The peril lies in precedent. Once it becomes clear that certain types of organizations can make a significant profit by restricting and then selling information (rather than giving it away), others will follow. Can we rely on perpetually cash-strapped universities, for example, to continue to hold to the sacred precept of "knowledge shared freely" when it becomes possible to charge every seeker a minimal access fee? The fee doesn't have to be large. Once microtransactions become feasible online, we may find ourselves nickel-and-dimed in a number of unexpected arenas.

And it isn't just nickels and dimes. Résumé databases, for example, once offered their information free to corporations. That has already changed. Most now charge an annual fee—and in one case, that fee rose from $500 to $3,000 within two years. It is not unrealistic to imagine information databases following the same course.

Today, it is still possible to find vast quantities of information online without resorting to those fee-based databases. In the future, we may find less free stuff and more fee stuff as we surf. It is a trend that should be watched with care—and one on which writers should not be silent.

The Future of Markets

One of the big fears about the Internet has been that it would (or will) replace traditional markets for writers, such as (printed) books, magazines, newspapers, and so forth. A related fear has been that the Internet would (or will) change the type of writing we must do, replacing traditional, linear material with multimedia and interactive works.

The problem with so many predictions about "what will happen next" (especially where technology is involved) is the focus on this "replacement" paradigm. Many people view the arrival of anything new as a threat to what already exists. Television, we were told, would replace books. The Internet, we were warned, would also replace books, while e-mail and chat rooms would replace human interaction, and electrons would replace print. One wonders if the first papyrus maker was stoned out of town by the manufacturers of clay tablets: "Papyrus will drive scribes out of business!"

Replacement fears are based on a flawed assumption: namely that two technologies, or two methods of delivering a similar message, cannot coexist. Supporters of such theories often point to the "records versus CDs" or "Beta versus VHS" examples as proof of the replacement paradigm. Those arguments are flawed, however, as records and CDs are simply two methods of delivering the same content, just as papyrus could more effectively deliver the content formerly provided on clay tablets.

Television and books, on the other hand, do not deliver the same content. Television delivers sound and images created by someone else, while a book requires readers to "create" those sounds and images for themselves. Consequently, television has not replaced books, but has evolved alongside them.

Similarly, the Internet is evolving alongside traditional media, rather than replacing those media. Books, e-books, multimedia works, and interactive and hypertext materials are not necessarily delivering the same content. Therefore, one is not replacing another. Instead, each is finding its own niche, its own audience, and its own evolutionary path. Additionally, each may well benefit from advances in the other fields.

As writers, we need not fear the loss of our favorite medium or market to the new electron on the block. Instead, we can look forward to a steady increase in new opportunities, not only in the markets that we already know and love, but in new types of markets that may be the perfect outlet for material we were never able to sell anywhere else. What the Internet is giving us is not *loss* but *choice*—the choice to write traditional works (for both print and electronic markets) or to develop different types of materials incorporating interactive and multimedia elements.

As this market base expands, we should also see an improvement both in the quality of publications online and in the rate of pay. Quality is already improving, because today's publishers are no longer fumbling with a new medium, but learning from the mistakes of their predecessors and benefiting from the expert advice and examples that are now available. Pay should increase, primarily because the Internet is home to a number of highly inventive and determined folks who simply won't tolerate being unable to earn a profit from their efforts. If the avenues attempted so far (advertising and subscriptions) prove unfruitful, these folks will find another way. When they do, writers will benefit.

The Future of Electronic Rights

Perhaps the murkiest part of the forecast involves the issue of electronic rights. This issue affects all writers, online and off, yet there is surprisingly little discussion of the topic. Writers need to be aware that we are in the process of shaping what will become tomorrow's standard practice in this area—and if we don't take an active role in that process, standard practice will be dictated by those who buy writing rather than those who produce and sell it.

We already face an increase in the number of periodicals that demand all-rights or work-for-hire contracts, while offering no extra compensation. Other periodicals have gotten away with lumping electronic rights into the FNASR clause, even though the Tasini decision explicitly precludes such an interpretation (see "The Tasini Decision," chapter 4). We have always faced book publishers who demand all electronic rights "in any medium now known or yet to be discovered, throughout the universe"—effectively precluding writers from making much profit from the reprint markets on Rigel III. Now, as book publishers find opportunities to make lucrative deals for electronic (hand-held) editions that can be sold right alongside print editions, you can be sure they'll want to lock in those electronic rights as quickly and as tightly as possible.

Losses in the arena of electronic rights can take away gains in the area of new markets. When we lose not only our electronic rights, but all future rights to our material, we lose the option to remarket our work to the new markets that are emerging on (or becoming accessible through) online venues. We will lose the ability to offer the same piece (or a similar piece) to a print magazine and an e-zine, or to a U.S. publication and an international publication. In short, we may have more markets at our fingertips, but we could end up with far less to sell.

Writers cannot afford to wait and see how this issue resolves itself through legislation or litigation. Nor can most writers afford to take a wealthy publisher to court over an apparent infringement or inappropriate contract. Our only recourse is to be proactive *today,* securing writers' rights while we still have the opportunity to influence tomorrow's changes.

The Future of Communication

Inklings editor Debbie Ridpath Ohi believes that in the future, "Having online access will become a necessity for writers rather than a luxury." Why? Because the Internet provides prompt, easy access to markets and editors.

In coming years, Ohi believes, more and more editors will want to receive queries and submissions via e-mail. This, she points out, will put any writer who does not use e-mail at a disadvantage, just as many of us were put at a disadvantage a few years ago when publications began demanding manuscripts on disk—and then in specific word-processing formats. Editors will also prefer working with writers who can be reached instantly by e-mail for assignments or revisions.

In addition, announcements of article needs, job openings, and editorial or policy changes are often available only online. This means that writers who rely exclusively on printed sources of information will miss valuable opportunities and, as well, will risk falling behind on industry news. Freelance writer Marla Milling says that this aspect of the Internet has already changed the way she does business:

"Editors will use the Web to put out a call for writers when they have a specific opportunity. Writers won't be sending out as many blind queries; instead, they'll be responding to editors' requests. E-mail makes it possible to work on assignments immediately, which makes writers more productive."

Writer Jim Hillman, who recently sold his first book to a major Christian publisher, is concerned that this type of communication may pose hazards to new writers, online or off. "I see disadvantages in breaking into established markets because of the ease and speed of communication. Editors tend to use writers they know and can rely upon, and I believe they may be less likely to view new writers and material. Of course," he adds, "nothing can ever substitute for good writing."

Hillman's concern points out the need for writers to maintain high professional standards even (or especially) when using newer communication technologies. Editors like to work with established, reliable authors—but they also have a never-ending need for new ideas, which often come from new writers. Those ideas, however, are likely to be shaped by our participation in, and awareness of, the issues and changes we learn about online.

The Future of Promotion

Science fiction/fantasy author Kate Elliott sees a major change in her ability to interact with her audience, thanks to the Internet. "There will be a change in a writer's ability to cheaply and broadly publicize oneself to that audience which has access to the Web. My fan mail volume is much greater via e-mail, I suspect because it seems less daunting than writing regular mail, affixing postage, and sending it off."

Less daunting, and far easier. Locating an author's snail-mail address has always been a challenge, and many readers don't feel comfortable addressing a fan letter "in care of" a publisher. Online, matters are far simpler: Authors who post Web sites often include an e-mail address, and that e-mail address itself functions as an invitation to feedback. The informality of online communication is smoothing the barriers between writer and reader, bringing authors out of their proverbial attics and into the market square, where they can share with and receive from their audience directly.

Communication between writers and readers is no longer one-way only, as with books, articles, radio, or television. It is now two-way, with direct conversations made possible by chat rooms, forums, and e-mail. Authors are no longer obscure, untouchable figures to their audience—and the audience is no longer a sea of dimly glimpsed faces "out there."

Writers will need to keep this level of interaction in mind as they tailor future promotional campaigns. No longer are we simply targeting material *at* readers and hoping it hits. Instead, we can target our material *to* readers and receive immediate feedback as to whether our approach has succeeded or failed. This will enable us to progressively refine our efforts, while reaching a progressively broader market.

The Future of Electronic Books

"I think one of the biggest changes this technology will bring is the ability for almost anyone to become a publisher and a bookseller," says Laura Backes, editor of *Children's Book Insider*. "I don't think e-books will replace old-fashioned paper books, at least for many years, but they could certainly take a chunk out of traditional book sales.

"The ease of creating text for the Internet, and creating Web sites to advertise those books, will make it possible for almost anyone to self-publish and sell their work. However, the danger lies in having too much out there for consumers to wade through. Just as parents are overwhelmed when perusing the shelves of the children's department of Barnes & Noble, they may also feel lost when confronted with so many e-book choices. Most likely, the e-book publishing world will eventually mirror the traditional publishing industry. A few companies with 'brand names' consumers trust will produce the majority of the books. However, smaller publishers will stand on more equal footing with the big guys because of the medium.

"My biggest concern is that we may sacrifice quality for quantity, but that is always a concern with publishing. I believe that after the novelty wears off, the best writers and illustrators will rise to the top of the electronic publishing world, just as they have done on paper."

Victoria Strauss, author of *The Arm of the Stone* and host of the Writer Beware Web site, has a less optimistic view. "From the perspective of a novelist," says Strauss, "I think the Internet will remain a fairly marginal market for fiction writing. I think the rush to develop the hand-held book reader will completely overshadow, if not kill, the nascent online e-book market. E-book readers seem to be where the big publishers are putting their money and attention right now, and I think in ten years or less, this will be a standard method of publishing. My fear is that e-publication will then become the backwater to which new writers and unprofitable midlist writers are relegated, kind of like the mass market today, so that people like me may never see print at all."

Will e-books evolve into a viable form of publication, just as self-published (as opposed to "vanity") books already have? They may. Many e-publishers are taking steps to ensure that their imprints are associated with quality writing, rather than offering a forum to anyone with a manuscript.

It is also possible that the reality may fall somewhere between Backes' and Strauss' views. E-books may continue to evolve as viable outlets for quality authors, both as showcases for their work and as sources of income. At the same time, the bigger traditional houses may move increasingly toward an emphasis on best-selling authors, whose numbers can justify massive print runs. If that happens, newer and less profitable authors may indeed find themselves relegated to electronic publishing outlets—but by their very presence in e-publishing (willing or not), they will bring those outlets the readership that has so far been lacking. Plus, as Backes points out, anyone can become a publisher, which means that even a small e-publisher could stand a chance of bringing out the works of an author like Victoria Strauss—to the benefit (one hopes) of both.

The Future of Creativity

Will the Internet offer expanded opportunities for imagination, vision, and originality? Or will it create its own boundaries, driven by popular tastes and profit margins?

Writer and journalist J. D. Lasica (whose article appears in chapter 3) believes that "filtering" will become increasingly popular as the choices available to readers become overwhelming. "We'll see a torrent of collaborative filtering, as companies such as Amazon.com use customer feedback to suggest books and articles readers find worthwhile. That's all for the good, but readers have to assume an added responsibility in the equation. The most vibrant, personally affecting writings are rarely the ones that win popularity contests."

At the same time, Lasica predicts less filtering from traditional sources: "The Net will increasingly connect writers and readers in direct and vital ways, without the intermediation of publishers, editors, and others who may not know what's important and interesting to you." That is the challenge for readers: "To ferret out those rare, exquisite finds in a sea of mediocrity."

Kate Elliott believes that the Internet "challenges the hierarchy [of publishing] by being a form that encourages many voices rather than few voices. Given the history of literacy and artistic expression, and the ways in which (until the last fifty years) literacy has been confined to the few, I believe the Web opens up a new paradigm in communication"—a paradigm that has little to do with technological issues. And that, she says, "doesn't even begin to cover the shift from the word to the image and the blending of the two, not to mention hypertext as a very early form of some new kind of narration, melding theater, text, film, and so on into something different and perhaps not linear at all, the form of which may not become clear for another hundred years."

Which brings us back to the point made at the beginning of this chapter: The best way to determine what the Internet holds for writers in a year, or ten years, or a hundred years, is not to fish for answers or even to fear the inevitable shocks. It is simply to do the only thing we can do: Wait and see.

And, of course: Keep on writing!

RESOURCES

Appendix A: Online Resources for Writers

CONTENTS

E-Publishers, Commercial and Subsidy
E-Publishing Information
E-Readers, Hand-Held
E-zine Development/Publication
E-zine Directories
Fantasy (under "Science Fiction and Fantasy")
Grammar
Guidelines
Horror
HTML (under "Web Site Development")
International Markets (under "Media, International")
Jobs for Writers
Journalism; Online Journalism
Literary Agents (under "Agents")
Literature Online ("E-texts")
Magazines (under "Media")
Mailing List Services
Media
Media, International
Miscellaneous
Mystery
Names
Newsgroups (under "Discussion Lists/Newsgroups")
Online Instruction Resources
Online Journalism (under "Journalism")
OWLs (Online Writing Labs)
Playwriting (under "Screenwriting and Scriptwriting")
Poetry
Publications for Writers
Research and Search Engine Tips
Research: Directories and Databases
Research: Evaluating Web Sites
Romance
Science Fiction and Fantasy
Screenwriting and Scriptwriting
Search Engines
Search Engines, Meta/Multi
Self-Publishing
Taxes (under "Business")
Technical Writing
Web Guides
Web Site Development: Content
Web Site Development: HTML and Design Tools
Web Site Development: Promotion, Registration, and Site Diagnostic Tools
Westerns
Young Writers' Resources

●

Starting Points: Writers' Resource Sites

(For more information on these listings, see chapter 1.)

Authorlink *www.authorlink.com/*
The Eclectic Writer *www.eclectics.com/writing/writing.html*

Forwriters.com *www.forwriters.com/whatsnew.html*
Inkspot *www.inkspot.com*
Preditors and Editors *www.sfwa.org/prededitors/*
Pure Fiction *www.purefiction.com/menus/writing.htm*
Resources for Writers *www.execpc.com/~dboals/write.html*
SharpWriter.Com *www.sharpwriter.com*
Tips for Writers *www.tipsforwriters.com/*
 Hosted by Moira Allen.
Write Tools: Editors' and Writers' Toolkit *writetools.com*
WriteLinks *www.writelinks.com*
Writers on the Net *www.writers.com*
Writer's Resources *www.webwitch.com/writers/*
Writer's Toolbox: Internet Resources for Writers *www.geocities.com/Athens/6346/*
Writers Write *www.writerswrite.com/*
Zuzu's Petals Literary Resources *www.zuzu.com*

Agents

Agents who Broker Science Fiction and Fantasy Works *members.home.net/wcgrnway/agentlst.html*
Association of Authors' Representatives Inc. *www.bookwire.com/AAR/*
 Information on finding an agent, working with an agent, and what to look for (or look out for) in an
 agent, plus links.
LiteraryAgent.Com *www.literaryagent.com/*
 A searchable list; search by name, state, category, etc. (Hard to assess quality; anyone can "join" the
 list.) Also includes monthly columns on issues of writing and agents.
Literary Agents *mockingbird.creighton.edu/NCW/litag.htm*
 Sponsored by the Nebraska Center for Writers, this site offers links to agent lists and to a variety of
 articles on finding (and using) an agent.
Preditors and Editors: Agent Listings *www.sfwa.org/prededitors/peala.htm*
 This site is a good place to look for warnings against agents who are "not recommended."
Pure Fiction Guide to Literary Agents *www.purefiction.com/pages/usagents.htm*
 "As far as we know, the list that follows contains all of the major U.S. literary agencies that deal with
 fiction." A list of U.K. agents is also provided. The list does not seem to include any distinctions with
 respect to memberships, whether agents charge reading fees, etc.
SFF Net *www.sff.net/sff/agents.htp*
Suggested Agent Checklist for Authors *www.inkspot.com/bt/market/agentlist.html*
 A list of twenty-two questions to ask an agent before "signing."

Articles on Writing

Articles *www.underdown.org/articles.htm*
 A collection of articles with an emphasis on children's literature, compiled by a children's book
 editor.
Articles About Writing *www.sfwa.org/writing/writing.htm*
 Though many of the articles on this site focus primarily on speculative fiction, this extensive list of
 articles offers something for all writers.
Articles for Writers on Everything Imaginable *members.tripod.com/~PetalsofLife/writerslinks.html*
Contracts *www.teleport.com/~until/contract.htm*
 Everything you need to know about understanding and negotiating a book contract, by author Tara
 K. Harper.
E-mail Newsletters: A Growing Market for Freelancers *www.contentious.com/articles/1-10/editorial1-
 10.html*
 How to write for e-mail newsletters, how to find markets, etc.

Fiction Links *www.writerspage.com/write/masterlink/*
"Links to thousands of articles that discuss some aspect of the writing of fiction."

The Fiction Writer's Page *www.capcollege.bc.ca/dept/magic/cmns/fwp.html*
Several good articles by Crawford Kilian on the craft and business of writing fiction (and getting published).

Freelance Writer's Internet FAQ *ourworld.compuserve.com/homepages/MARTINEZ/FAQ.htm*
A lengthy FAQ designed to "introduce ways [writers] can use the Internet to ramp up your writing career." Includes information on writing for the Internet, finding markets online, conducting research, and writing about the Internet.

Inkspot *www.inkspot.com/feature/*
Articles, FAQs, and columns on writing.

Misc.Writing FAQ *www.scalar.com/mw/pages/mwfaq.shtml*
An excellent overview of the writing and marketing process.

Novelists Inc. *www.ninc.com/tips.htm*
Offers several excellent articles by well-known authors on such issues as understanding contracts, taxes, writing, and more.

Query Letter Information *www.accelnet.com/victoria/queries2.html*
A selection of links and articles on writing query letters.

The Slush Pile *www.theslushpile.com*
Articles on a wide range of topics, including cover letters, submissions, formatting, "how to target publishers," and more.

Tips for Writers *www.tipsforwriters.com/*
Articles by Moira Allen on writing and freelancing.

Uncle Orson's Writing Class *www.hatrack.com/writingclass/index.shtml*
It's difficult to categorize the "Hatrack River" site from Orson Scott Card. In addition to chat, forums, links, and other resources, it offers a "writing class" in which Card answers various questions from readers; the result is a series of useful articles on writing fiction.

Writer's Toolbox Article Library *www.geocities.com/Athens/6346/refer.html*
Contains interesting articles on various branches of freelance writing, such as becoming a stringer, developing audiotapes, and writing about local history.

Associations, Organizations, and Groups

American Society of Journalists and Authors (ASJA) *www.asja.org*
Offers articles and support for contract and copyright issues, including the free e-mail newsletter *Contract Watch*, "A free [biweekly] electronic newsletter about the latest terms and negotiations in the world of periodicals, print and electronic."

Associations and Organizations of Interest to Writers *www.poewar.com/articles/associations.htm*
A text listing of associations and groups; few links.

The Author's Guild *www.authorsguild.org/welcome.html*

Copylaw Resources *copylaw.com/res.html*
An extensive list of membership organizations for writers and artists, including a number of copyright resources.

National Writers Union *www.nwu.org*
Dedicated to contract and copyright issues.

Writer's Associations (United States and Canada) *www.inkspot.com/tk/network/assoc.html*

Writers Groups and Organizations *www.forwriters.com/groups.html*
Includes national organizations, local groups, and online workshops.

The Zuzu's Petals Literary Resource: Organizations of Interest to Poets and Writers *www.zuzu.com/wrt-org.htm*

Author Site Lists

(For more information on these listings, see chapter 10.)

Author Web Sites *www.geocities.com/~bookbug/home.html*

Authors *authors.miningco.com*

Children's Book Council: Author and Illustrator Links *www.cbcbooks.org/links/authlink.htm*

Painted Rock Writers and Readers Colony: Author Page and Homepage Links *www.paintedrock.com/authors/romathrs.htm*

The Poetry Resource: Links to Poets *www.pmpoetry.com/linkspb.html*

Romance Novels and Women's Fiction: Authors *www.writepage.com/romance.htm*

Romance Writers of America: Romance Authors *www.rwanational.com/linkaut.htm*

Science Fiction Authors *sflovers.rutgers.edu/Web/SFRG/sfrgfa.htm*

SFF Net *www.sff.net/people/index.htp*

Useful Links for Romance Writers and Readers (Authors) *www.inficad.com/~jacreding/links/auth.html*

Webrings for Writers *www.webring.org/cgi-bin/ringworld/arts/hum.html*
   Search for author Web rings by keywords, such as "authors" or "writing."

A Woman's Writing Retreat: Authors (male) *www.prairieden.com/links/men.html*

A Woman's Writing Retreat: Authors (female) *www.prairieden.com/links/women.html*

WritersNet *www.writers.net*

Writepage *www.writepage.com*

Yahoo! *dir.yahoo.com/Arts/Humanities/Literature/Genres/*
   (Check specific genres for "Author" listings.)

Book Publishers (Lists)

(For more information on these listings, see chapter 3.)

BookWire: Book Publisher Index *www.bookwire.com/index/publishers.html*

WriteLinks: Commercial Book Publishers *www.writelinks.com/resources/pub/pubsbk.htm*

Yahoo! *dir.yahoo.com/Business_and_Economy/Companies/Publishing*

Bookstores, Online

(For more information on these listings, see chapter 10.)

AddAll *www.addall.com*
   A book-search site.

Amazon.com *www.amazon.com*

Amazon.com (Germany) *www.amazon.de*

Amazon.com (United Kingdom) *www.amazon.co.uk*

Barnes & Noble *www.barnesandnoble.com*

Books.com *www.books.com*

BookFinder.com *www.bookfinder.com*
   A book-search site.

Books OnQ *www.onq.org/Welcome.htm*

BookZone *www.bookzone.com*

Borders *www.borders.com*

WordsWorth Author Internet Site *www.wordsworth.com/*

Business and Finance

Canada Post *www.canadapost.ca/CPC2/menu_01.html*
   Canadian postage rates.

Hugh's Mortgage and Financial Calculators *www.interest.com/hugh/calc/*
   A collection of financial tools that can be useful in financial research (or in figuring out how much you're getting paid).

Postal Information *dir.yahoo.com/Reference/Postal_Information*
Links to postal codes, addresses, and rate information from various countries.
Writer's Pocket Tax Guide *foolscap-quill.com/wptg99.html*
A comprehensive overview of handling writing expenses, income, and taxes, by attorney Darlene Cypser.

Character Names—See "Names"

Chats About Writing/Authors

(For more information on these listings, see chapters 6 and 10)
America Online *www.aol.com*
Barnes & Noble: Authors Online *www.barnesandnoble.com/community/commuinity.asp*
Byron's Romance Port *www.geocities.com/Athens/8774*
The Chat Hole *www.geocities.com/SouthBeach/Breakers/5257/Chathole.htm*
Includes the article "Chat Etiquette: The Do's and Don'ts of Online Conversation."
CNN Interactive Interviews *www.cnn.com/chat/*
Compuserve *www.compuserve.com*
Delphi *www.delphi.com*
From the Heart Online *www.delphi.com/FTH*
The *Literary Times* *www.tlt.com/news/itiner.htm*
Provides a place for romance authors to post announcements of events.
The Mining Co. *www.miningco.com*
MSN (Microsoft) Web Communities *communities.msn.com/reading/chat.asp*
Reader's Choice Book Chat *www.thegrid.net/dakaiser/books/chat.htm*
Romance Central *www.romance-central.com*
Romance Club *www.theromanceclub.com*
TalkCity *www.talkcity.com/communities/art_books.htmpl*
Word Museum *www.wordmuseum.com*
WordsWorth *www.wordsworth.com/www/present/interviews/*
The Writer's BBS *www.writers-bbs.com/chat.html*
Writer'sClub.com Chat Schedule *chat.writersclub.com*
Writers Write Chat *www.writerswrite.com*
Your Weekly Kiss *www.mindspring.com/~driordan/kiss*

Chat and Communication Software

(For more information on these listings, see chapter 6.)
AOL Instant Messenger *www.aol.com/aim/promo/73010/aim_download.html*
ICQ *www.icq.com*
Softseek.com *softseek.com/Internet/Chatting_and_IRC/*

Children's Writing

Aaron Shepard's Kidwriter Page *www.aaronshep.com/kidwriter/*
Articles and resources for writers of children's books. See */articles.html* for a variety of articles on the topic.
BookWire Index: Children's Publishers *www.bookwire.com/index/Childrens-Publishers.html*
CANSCAIP *www.interlog.com/~canscaip/*
Canadian Society of Children's Authors, Illustrators, and Performers.
Children's Book Council (CBC) *www.cbcbooks.org/*
Information on writing children's books; membership information; submission guidelines; tips for writers and illustrators; and links to authors' and illustrators' home pages.

Children's Literature Web Guide *www.acs.ucalgary.ca/~dkbrown/index.html*
Resources for children's writers, illustrators, teachers, storytellers, etc.; includes links to children's book publishers, journals, book reviews, recommended books, Newbery and Caldecott awards, and children's literature organizations.
Children's Writers Marketplace *www.inkspot.com/childmkt*
Children's Writing Resource Center *www.write4kids.com/index.html*
Resources and articles, including the *Children's Book Insider* newsletter.
The Purple Crayon *www.users.interport.net/~hdu/*
A site sponsored by a children's book editor, featuring advice for writers and illustrators, links, publishing information, and "visual resources" such as maps and images online.

Citing Internet Sources

How Students Should Reference Online Sources in Bibliographies *www.classroom.com/resource/citingnetresources.asp*
Citing Internet Sources *www.tui.edu/Research/Resources/ResearchHelp/Cites.html*
Evaluating and Citing Internet Sources *www.albion.edu/fac/libr/citing.htm*
A selection of links and resources.
Links to Education Resources on the WWW—Citing Internet Sources *www.umass.edu/education/links/cite.html*
Tracking, Managing, and Citing Resources on the Web *www.wwnorton.com/webworks/ww5.htm*

Classes, Teaching—See "Online Instruction Resources"

Classes, Writing

(For more information on these listings, see chapter 7.)
Explorations Unlimited *www.explorationsu.com*
Freelance Success Institute *www.freelancesuccess.com*
Gotham Writers' Workshop *www.write.org/frame_main.html*
NovelAdvice *www.noveladvice.com/craft/index.html*
Painted Rock Writers and Readers Colony *www.paintedrock.com/conference/confcntr.htm*
UCLA *www.onlinelearning.net/w99*
Word Museum *www.wordmuseum.com*
Writeria: Online Workshops *wkgroup.com/zeugma/writeria/workshops.html*
Writers Club University *www.writersclub.com/wcu/catalog.cfm*
Writers on the Net *www.writers.com/classes.htm*
For individual tutoring, see *www.writers.com/classes/tutors.htm.*
Writer's Village University *4-writers.com*
Writers Write University *www.writerswrite.com*

Conferences and Colonies

Guide to Writers Conferences *www.shawguides.com/index.cgi?s=11*
One of a variety of resources from ShawGuides; searchable by topic, state, or month.
Screenwriters Online Presents: Calendar *screenwriter.com/insider/WritersCalendar.html*
A list of writing conferences of all types, by state; not limited to screenwriting. (Text only; no links.)
Writers' Colonies *mockingbird.creighton.edu/ncw/colonies.htm*
Links to individual colonies and directories of writers' colonies.
Writer's Digest Conference Database *www.writersdigest.com/conferences/*
This site is listed as being "in association with ShawGuides," so it may duplicate much of the information available at the "Guide to Writers Conferences" listed above.

Contests

Inkspot Writers' Classifieds: Contests *www.inkspot.com/classifieds/contests.html*
A wide range of contests for writers.
Inscriptions *come.to/Inscriptions*
Offers an extensive listing of contests for writers; contests are also posted in the weekly newsletter.
Speculative Fiction Contests *www.tipsforwriters.com/contests.shtml*
Writers of the Future *www.authorservicesinc.com/wof_ruls.htm*
L. Ron Hubbard's prestigious contest for amateur science fiction/fantasy writers.
Writing Contest Tips *www.ult-media.com/tips1.htm*
A selection of tips from the publishers of *The Ultimate Book of Writing Contests.*

Copyright

(For more information on these listings, see chapter 4.)
10 Big Myths about Copyright Explained (by Brad Templeton) *www.templetons.com/brad/copymyths.html*
Berne Convention for the Protection of Literary and Artistic Works *www.law.cornell.edu/treaties/berne/overview.html*
Copyright and Fair Use *fairuse.stanford.edu/*
Copyright and Intellectual Property *www.arl.org/info/frn/copy/copytoc.html*
Copyright Code *www.law.cornell.edu/uscode/17/*
Digital Millenium Copyright Act (summary) *www.arl.org/info/frn/copy/band.html*
Digital Millenium Copyright Act (text) *www.gseis.ucla.edu/iclp/dmca1.html*
(Follow the links at the bottom to find the text of the DMCA.)
Giving Credit and Requesting Permission: Guidelines for Using Material Other than Your Own
www.oreilly.com/oreilly/author/permission/
Intellectual Property, Copyright, Patents, Trademarks *www.sil.org/general/copyright.html*
Internet Law Simplified (by Ivan Hoffman) *www.online-magazine.com/copyright.htm*
Journal of Electronic Publishing *www.press.umich.edu:80/jep*
Novice Writer's Guide to Rights *www.writerswrite.com/journal/dec97/cew3.htm*
Publishing Law and Other Articles of Interest *publaw.com/articles.html*
U.S. Copyright Office *lcweb.loc.gov/copyright*

Copyright and Electronic Rights

(For more information on these listings, see chapter 4.)
Authors in the New Information Age: A Working Paper on Electronic Publishing Issues *www.nwu.org/docs/aniabeg.htm#173*
"C" Rights in "E" Mail *www.ivanhoffman.com/rights.html*
Contract Tips for Freelancers *www.asja.org/asjatips.htm*
Copyright Protection in the New World of Electronic Publishing *www.press.umich.edu/jep/works/strong.copyright.html*
Copyright Protection: Understanding Your Options *www.seyboldreport.com/Specials/Copyright.htm*
Derivative Rights and Websites (by Ivan Hoffman) *www.ivanhofman.com/first.html*
Electronic Publishing and the Potential Loss of First Serial Rights (by Ivan Hoffman) *www.ivanhofman.com/derivative.html*
Electronic Publishing: Protecting Your Rights (by Moira Allen) *www.inkspot.com/feature/epublish.html*
Journalist Electronic Rights Negotiation Strategies *www.nwu.org/journ/jstrat.htm*
Myths and Facts about S2291 *www.arl.org/info/frn/copy/myth.html*
Primer on the Proposed WIPO Treaty on Database Extraction Rights *www.essential.org/cpt/ip/cpt-dbcom.html*
Proper Use of a Domain Name for Trademark Protection *www.arvic.com/library/domanuse.asp*
SFWA Statement on Electronic Rights *www.sfwa.org/contracts/ELEC.htm*

UCLA Online Institute for Cyberspace Law and Policy *www.gseis.ucla.edu/iclp/hp.html*
Who Owns the Copyright in Your Web Site? (by Ivan Hoffman) *www.ivanhofman.com/website.html*

Critique Groups and Information

(For more information on these listings, see chapter 7.)
Critters Workshop *brain-of-pooh.tech-soft.com/users/critters/*
Del Rey Online Writing Workshop *www.randomhouse.com/delrey/workshop/*
Hardcore Critique Advice *www.crayne.com/victory/download/casiltip.txt*
How to Critique Fiction *www.crayne.com/victory/howcrit.html*
IRC Undernet Writer's Page *www.getset.com/writers*
Preditors and Editors: Writing Workshops *www.sfwa.org/prededitors/pubwork.htm*
SFNovelist Workshop *www.crayne.com/victory/sfnovel.html*
SFWA: Workshops *www.sfwa.org/links/workshops.htm*
   Links to speculative fiction critique groups and workshops.
Writeria: List of Online Workshops *wkgroup.com/zeugma/writeria/workshops.html*
Writer's Internet Exchange *www.writelinks.com/write/index.html*
Writer's List *web.mit.edu/mbarker/www/writers.html*
Writer Write *www.writerswrite.com/groups.htm*

Dictionaries—See also "Grammar"

AltaVista Translation *babelfish.altavista.com/cgi-bin/translate?*
   A free online translation tool for words and phrases. (Seems to work well with shorter phrases, but use
   caution when attempting to use any automatic "tool" to translate longer materials or documents.)
American-British/British-American Dictionary *www.peak.org/~jeremy/dictionary/dict-toc.html*
   Translates U.S. terms to British and vice versa; also includes acronyms, units of measurement, slang,
   idioms, and explanations of the differences between British English and American English.
Castle Terms *www.castlesontheweb.com/glossary.html*
Cliché Finder *www.westegg.com/cliche/*
   An interesting resource that enables you to search for "clichés" by keyword (e.g., a search on "cat"
   provides such gems as "Busier than a one-eyed cat watching two mouseholes"). Unclear whether
   you're advised to add, or avoid, the results!
A Dictionary of Faeries *faeryland.tamu-commerce.edu/~earendil/faerie/bin/search.cgi*
Glossary of Internet Terms *www.matisse.net/files/glossary.html*
Glossary of Poetic Terms *shoga.wwa.com/~rgs/glossary.html*
   A fascinating collection of terms, from abecedarian to zeugma.
Encyclopedia Mythica *www.pantheon.org/mythica/areas/*
   More than 4,000 entries on various mythological subjects
Encyberpedia: Dictionaries, Glossaries, and Thesauri *www.encyberpedia.com/glossary.htm*
   Links to a wide range of useful dictionaries and glossaries.
The Internet Press: Dictionaries *www.gallery.uunet.be/Internetpress/diction.htm*
   Extensive list of language dictionaries (including a number of non-English to non-English translation
   dictionaries, such as "Berber/French"), plus links to translation software and other language
   resources.
Historical Dictionaries, Slang, and Proverbs *ireland.iol.ie/~mazzold/lang/s-hist.htm*
   Dictionaries of Middle English, rhymes, Bible proverbs, and various types of slang.
One-Look Dictionaries *www.onelook.com*
   Hundreds of links to a wide range of dictionaries and glossaries, including: business, computer/
   Internet, medical, miscellaneous (includes poetry, Shakespeare, military references, literary refer-
   ences), religion, science, sports, technological, acronym, general (including English, Britspeak), slang,
   pronunciation. Offers "look-up" search function.

Origins of Phrases *members.aol.com/MorelandC/Phrases.htm*
Origins and meanings of hundreds of common (and uncommon) phrases.

Phrase Finder *www.shu.ac.uk/web-admin/phrases/*
Search by keyword to find a specific phrase or quote, or search for the meanings and origins of various phrases.

Research-It! *www.iTools.com/research-it/research-it.html*
Searchable dictionary site that includes various English-language dictionaries, thesauri, quotes, biographies, stock quotes, zip codes, and other directories.

Semantic Rhyming Dictionary *www.link.cs.cmu.edu/dougb/rhyme-doc.html*
Look up rhymes by sound, number of syllables, and preferred meaning.

Travlang *www.travlang.com*
Translating dictionaries, foreign language dictionaries, travel information, currency exchange, and other international information.

Web of On-Line Dictionaries *www.facstaff.bucknell.edu/~rbeard/diction.html*
Huge collection of online dictionaries, especially foreign language dictionaries, including language-learning grammars. Each language entry offers several selections, including some downloadable dictionaries. "Artificial" languages (e.g., Klingon, Esperanto) also included.

WordNet 1.6 Vocabulary Helper *www.notredame.ac.jp/cgi-bin/wn*
A useful tool that enables you to look up a word (including uncommon words) to find out its definition, usage, and history.

WorldWideWeb Acronym and Abbreviation Server *www.ucc.ie/info/net/acronyms/acro.html*
An excellent acronym "look-up" site.

WWWebster Dictionary *www.m-w.com/info/info.htm*
Look up words or phrases, or search the thesaurus, vocabulary builder, or other tools on the Merriam-Webster site.

Discussion Lists and Newsgroups

(For more information on these listings, see chapter 6.)

CataList, the Official Catalog of LISTSERV® Lists *www.lsoft.com/lists/listref.html*

DejaNews *www.dejanews.com*

Email Discussion Groups/Lists and Resources *www.webcom.com/impulse/list.html*

E-mail Discussion Lists *www.delphi.com/navnet/faq/mlistsq.html*

Everything E-Mail: Mailing List Discussion Groups/Newsletters *everythingemail.net/e-mail_discussion. html*

Fictech for Novelists' INNER CIRCLE *www.fictioneer.com*
A "writer's club" enabling writers to correspond "one on one" with other writers with similar interests or experience.

ListServe.com: Publicly Accessible Mailing Lists *www.neosoft.com/internet/paml*

Liszt, the Mailing List Directory *www.liszt.com*

Misc. Writing Mailing Lists *www.scalar.com/mw/pages/mwmlist.shtml*

Navigating the Net: E-mail Discussion Lists *www.delphi.com/navnet/faq/listsub.html*

Reference.COM Usenet and Mailing List Archive *www.reference.com*

Tile.Net *tile.net/listserv/*

Vivian's "List of Lists" *www.catalog.com/vivian/interest-group-search.html*

Writers' Groups *www.writers.com/groups.htm*

Editors, Resources for

CopyEditor: Language News for the Publishing Profession *www.copyeditor.com*
Includes an extensive job board for copyeditors.

Editorial Freelancers Association *www.the-efa.org/main.html*
Events, links, articles, and benefits for editorial freelancers.

Editorial Freelancers' Home Page *www.nerc.com/~freelancer/*
Links for editorial freelancers, plus a selection of articles on the "freelancing life."
Tools and Tips for Copy Editors *www.uaa.alaska.edu/jpc/copy.html*
A collection of resources for editors and copyeditors, including grammar sites and useful sites for fact-checking.

Electronic Media, Writing for

Contentious *www.contentious.com*
A web-zine for writers, editors, and others who create content for online media.
Electric Pages: Evolution of Publishing in the Information Age *www.electric-pages.com/artforum/index.htm*
Includes articles and a forum on "writing for interactive media."
Usable Web: Guide to Web Usability Resources *usableweb.com/index.html*
"A collection of 422 links and accompanying information about human factors, user interface issues, and usable design specific to the World Wide Web."
Web Authoring Resources *www.wwwscribe.com/resource.htm*
Links, including domain registration agencies, HTML tools, etc.
Writing for the Web *www.electric-pages.com/articles/wftw1.htm*
Writing for the Web: A New Resource for Writers *www.wwwscribe.com/webwrite.htm*
Overview of web authoring techniques and tools, plus a listing of software.
Writing for Webzines: Brave New Markets, Same Old Problems *www.nwu.org/aw/97wint/online.htm*

Electronic rights—See "Copyright and Electronic Rights"

E-mail

(For more information on these listings, see chapter 5.)
The Basics of Internet E-mail *www.wwwscribe.com/ebasics.htm*
E-Mail Attachments - Your Questions Answered *everythingemail.net/attach_help.html*
E-mail File Attachments *telacommunications.com/nutshell/email.htm*
Everything E-mail *everythingemail.net/index.html*

E-Publishers, Commercial

(The following publishers are members of the Association of
Electronic Publishers. For more information, see chapter 11.)
Awe-Struck E-Books *www.awe-struck.net*
Boson Books *www.cmonline.com/boson*
DiskUs Publishing *www.diskuspublishing.com*
Domhan Books *www.domhanbooks.com*
Dreams Unlimited *www.dreams-unlimited.com*
The Fiction Works *www.fictionworks.com*
GLB Publishers *www.glbpubs.com*
Hard Shell Word Factory *www.hardshell.com*
Indigo Publishing *www.booktrain.com/index/*
MountainView Publishing *www.whidbey.com/mountainview*
New Concepts Publishing *www.newconceptspublishing.com*
Petals of Life Publishing *www.petalsoflife.com*

For additional links, see:
Association of Electronic Publishers *welcome.to/AEP*
Electronically Published Internet Connection (EPIC) *www.eclectics.com/epic/*

Lida Quillen's List of Epublishers *www.sff.net/people/Lida.Quillen/epub.html*
Mary Wolf's Guide to Electronic Publishers *www.coredcs.com/~mermaid/epub.html*
Yahoo!s Guide to Electronic Publishers *dir.yahoo.com/ Business_and_Economy/Companies/Publishing/ Electronic_Publishing/*

E-Publishers, Other

(For more information on these listings, see chapter 11.)
1stBooks *www.1stbooks.com*
Electric Works Publishing *www.electricpublishing.com/textindex.htm*
HyperBooks *www.hyperbooks.com/submit.html*
OmniMedia Digital Publishing *www.awa.com/library/omnimedia/aboutus.html*
Tara Publishing *www.tarapublishing.com/publish/authpubinfo.mhtml*
  Offers subsidy and commercial publishing.
Xlibris *www.xlibris.com/html/publishing_your_book.html*
  Offers both electronic and "books on demand" formats.

E-Publishing Information

(For more information on these listings, see chapter 11.)
Adobe Systems *www.adobe.com*
Brave New World: Romance Authors on the Cutting Edge of Publishing *www.booksquare.com/sub-version/parlor/exp001.cfm*
Contract Issues: Books Published Online *www.nwu.org/docs/online-p.htm*
A New Marketing Opportunity: Electronic Publishing *www.paintedrock.com/memvis/rockmag/files/ rock99-10.txt*
Preditors and Editors Readers Poll *www.sfwa.org/prededitors/perpoll.htm*
Rising Stars on the Electronic Horizon *www.paintedrock.com/memvis/rockmag/files/rock99-10.txt*
Why Sell Your Book to an Electronic Publisher? *www.eclectics.com/articles/ebooks2.htm*
Writer Beware: Epublishers *www.sfwa.org/Beware/epublishers.html*

E-Readers, Hand-Held

(For more information on these listings, see chapter 11.)
E-books: The End of the Gutenberg Era? *www.pcworld.com/pcwtoday/article/0,1510,7645,00.html*
Everybook, Inc. *www.everybk.com/aboutus.html*
  Manufacturer of the EveryBook Dedicated Reader.
Librius.com *www.librius.com/liccorp8.html*
  Manufacturer of the Millennium EBook.
NuvoMedia *www.nuvomedia.com*
  Manufacturer of the RocketBook reader.
SoftBook Press *www.softbooks.com*
  Manufacturer of the SoftBook reader.
What is the Rocket E-book? *www.barnesandnoble.com/help/rocketbooks.asp*

E-zine Development/Publication

(For more information on these listings, see chapter 11.)
Discussion and Mailing List Promotion *jlunz.databack.com/listpromo.htm*
E-Zine Builder *www.zinebook.com/*
Guidelines for Publishing and Promoting an E-mail Newsletter *www.trafficplan.com/newsltrtips.htm*
How to Start an Online Newsletter (by Debbie Ohi, *Inklings*) *www.inkspot.com/bt/craft/newsletterinfo. html*
Newsletter News *Gach98@aol.com*

So, You Want to Start an E-Zine? *www.zinebook.com/roll.html*
Use Email Newsletters to Market Your Small Business on the Internet *www.arrowweb.com/graphics/ news/aug98o.html*
VirtualPROMOTE *virtualpromote.com*

E-zine Directories

(For more information on these listings, see chapter 11.)
Directory of Electronic Journals and Newsletters *www.coalliance.org*
E•Journal *www.edoc.com/ejournal/*
E-mail Newsletters and E-zines that Accept Advertising and Sponsorships *www.copywriter.com/lists/ ezines.htm*
Etext Archive *www.etext.org/services.shtml*
eZINESearch *www.site-city.com/members/e-zine-master/*
John Labovitz's E-Zine List *www.meer.net/~johnl/e-zine-list*
New Ezine Directory *foxcities.com/webpromote*
NewJour: New Journals and Newsletters on the Internet *gort.ucsd.edu/newjour/NewJourWel.html*
Newsletter Access *www.newsletteraccess.com*
The Newsletter Library *www.newsletter-library.com/index.htm*
Newsletters and E-zines *www.copywriter.com/lists/info.html*
The Sideroad *www.sideroad.com/openroad/contents.html*
Zine and E-Zine Resource Guide *www.zinebook.com/resour1.html*
Zine and Noted's Ezine Resource Guide *www.mediacentral.com/Magazines/Folio/Zines/resources.htm*
Zine-World *www.oblivion.net/zineworld/*

Fantasy—See "Science Fiction and Fantasy"

Grammar

The Arrow *www.wport.com/~cawilcox/mainpath/page1.htm*
Bartlett's Quotations *www.columbia.edu/acis/bartleby/bartlett/*
Common Errors in English *www.wsu.edu:8080/~brians/errors/spellcheck.html*
Elements of Style *www.columbia.edu/acis/bartleby/strunk/*
Garbl's Writing Resources On Line *pw1.netcom.com/~garbl1/index.html*
Gender-Neutral Pronoun FAQ *www.lumina.net/gnp/*
Grammar and Style Notes *www.english.upenn.edu/~jlynch/grammar.html*
Grammar Hotline Directory *www.tc.cc.va.us/writcent/gh/hotlinol.htm*
The Grammar Lady *www.grammarlady.com*
Guide to Grammar and Writing/Ask Grammar *webster.commnet.edu/HP/pages/darling/original.htm*
Interactive Grammar Quizzes *webster.commnet.edu/HP/pages/darling/grammar/quiz_list.html-ssi*
The King's English *www.columbia.edu/acis/bartleby/fowler/*
The Linguistic Fun Page *www.ojohaven.com/fun/*
On Line English Grammar *www.edunet.com/english/grammar/index.cfm*
Research-It! *www.iTools.com/research-it/research-it.html*
UVic Writer's Guide *webserver.maclab.comp.uvic.ca/writersguide/*

Guidelines

(For more information on these listings, see chapter 3.)
Guide to Online Guidelines *www.snafu.de/~gadfly/*
The Market List *www.marketlist.com*
Writer's Digest *www.writersdigest.com*
Writer's Guidelines (*The Write Markets Report*) *www.writersmarkets.com/index-guidelines.htm*

Writers' Guidelines Database *mav.net/guidelines/*
The Writer's Place *www.awoc.com/AWOC-Home.cfm*

Horror

Horror Writers Association *www.horror.org*
Market List *www.marketlist.com*
A market listing for writers of science fiction, fantasy, and horror.
Overbooked *www.overbooked.org/bklink.html*
A site dedicated to genre resources, including book links, author links, writing links, and more.

HTML—See "Web Site Development"

International Markets—See "Media, International"

Jobs for Writers

AJR Newslink JobLink for Journalists *ajr.newslink.org/newjoblink.html*
Avalanche of Jobs for Writers, Editors, and Copywriters *www.sunoasis.com*
CyberSearch Writer's Guide to Finding Jobs Online *home.earthlink.net/~cuvelier/INK/JOBS/GUIDE/tutorial.html*
A tutorial on how to locate a writing job via the Internet.
Freelance Online *www.FreelanceOnline.com/faqs.html*
Includes job listings, a directory of freelancers, forums and BBS, and other resources.
How to Find an Online Journalism Job on the Web *www.careermag.com/newsarts/jobsearch/1042.html*
Jobs in Journalism *eb.journ.latech.edu/jobs-o.html*
A listing of journalism-related job openings, sponsored by the Louisiana Tech University Journalism Department.
Monster.com *www.monsterboard.com*
A general career board; search on various writing keywords such as "writer," "editor," etc.
Telecommuting Jobs for Writers *www.tjobs.com/*

Journalism; Online Journalism—See also "Media"

(For sites that offer lists of newspaper and other media links, see "Media".)
The Alpha Complete News Index *www.select-ware.com/news/*
A compendium of free news sources from around the world.
American Journalism Review (AJR) Newslink *ajr.newslink.org/news.html*
Links to more than 4925 newspapers in the United States and abroad, including alternative and campus newspapers; plus job listings, writing resources, and links to journalism resources online.
CIO Web Central: Guide to Electronic and Print Resources for Journalists *www.cio.com/central/journalism.html*
Networking, "New Media," news sites and services, references and research, freelance resources, job listings, Internet information, and writing links.
Documents Center Web Site Directory *www.lib.umich.edu/libhome/Documents.center/webdirec.html*
An interesting collection of online "background" resources on various topics. For example, the topic "Abdullah Ocalan" offers links to the Kurdish Information Network; various news reports from the BBC, USIA, and State Department; and the Turkish Ministry of Foreign Affairs.
Editor and Publisher Interactive *www.mediainfo.com/emedia/*
European Journalism Page *www.demon.co.uk/eurojournalism/general.html*
"Sites and resources of interest to journalists working in or covering Europe."
How to Find an Online Journalism Job on the Web *www.careermag.com/newsarts/jobsearch/1042.html*

International Communication *www.moorhead.msus.edu/~gunarat/ijr/ic.html*
A range of information sources on international topics, including a number of international news publications and sources.

Journalism Resources *www.moorhead.msus.edu/~gunarat/ijr/journalism.html*
A selection of information sources for journalists and researchers.

Journalism Resources - Outside Canada *www.synapse.net/~radio/jour-oth.htm*
As the name implies, this site is designed primarily for Canadian journalists, but offers a number of non-Canadian as well as Canadian journalism resources.

Journalism UK *www.journalismUK.co.uk*
Aimed at "print journalists writing for U.K. magazines or based in the U.K.," this site offers a host of links to information sources, media, jobs, and other useful sites.

National Press Club *npc.press.org*
A variety of resources, including extensive links at "The Eric Friedheim Library and News Information Center" (*/library/reporter.htm*).

Newshare *newshare.com/Newshare/Common/News/news.html*
Links to news and topical directories, search services, newspaper Web sites, business news, media, newsgroups, and research sources.

Newswise Guide to Journalism Grants and Fellowships 1998–2000 *www.newswise.com/grants.htm*

Online Journalist *www.online-journalist.com*
Doug Millison's site, which includes a useful FAQ (*/faq.html*) and an extensive "Kiosk" (*/resources2.html*) of publications, journalist Web sites, online versions of print newspapers and magazines, and other resources for journalists.

Websites for Journalists *www.toad.net.com/~arandrew/majors.html*
Big city newspapers, international newspapers, broadcast sites, magazines, online newspapers, and other journalism sites.

Websites with a Newspaper Connection *MindyMcAdams.com/jacess/*
Links to journalism Web sites, journalism organizations, publications about online journalism, and journalism education sites.

Literary Agents—See "Agents"

Literature Online ("E-texts")

British and Irish Authors on the Web *lang.nagoya-u.ac.jp/~matsuoka/UK-authors.html*
Chronological listing of U.K. texts and author sites online, from 600 A.D. to present.

Links to Electronic Book and Text Sites *www.awa.com/library/omnimedia/links.html*
Links to sites that distribute electronic books and texts, including Project Gutenberg.

Master Works of Western Civilization *www.eskimo.com/~masonw/gwwc.htm*
"A hypertext-annotated compilation of lists of major [recommended] works," with links to those that are available online.

The On-Line Books Page *www.cs.cmu.edu/books.html*
An attempt to list all books currently posted online, including e-text of public domain books, nonfiction materials, and "electronic books." Currently lists more than 8,000 fiction and nonfiction books, plus 25,000 songs; an interesting source of research material.

Project Gutenberg *promo.net/pg/index.html*
Thousands of downloadable texts of copyright-free literature, including classic novels, children's books, nonfiction texts, etc.

Savetz's Unofficial Internet Public Domain Index *www.savetz.com/pd/*
Lists of indices of public-domain materials, including literature, technical works, software, art and images, government works, and audio works.

Magazines—See "Media"

Mailing List Services

eGroups *www.egroups.com*
ListBot *www.listbot.com*
OakNet Publishing *Oaknetpub.com*
ONEList *onelist.com*

Media

(For more information on these listings, see chapter 3.)
1500+ U.S. Newspapers and Their Links *www.acclaimed.com/helpful/new-add.htm*
AJR NewsLink *ajr.newslink.org/mag.html*
Christian Periodical Publishers *www.colc.com/pubbook/key.htm*
Electronic Newsstand (Enews) *www.enews.com*
Markets for Writers *www.chebucto.ns.ca/Culture/WFNS/markets.html*
Editor and Publisher Interactive *www.mediainfo.com/emedia/*
Media List *www.webcom.com/~leavitt/medialist.html*
Michigan Electronic Library: News, Media, and Periodicals *mel.lib.mi.us/news/News-Journal.html*
NewsDirectory.com *www.newsdirectory.com*
Newsletter Access *www.newsletteraccess.com/directory.html*
Newspapers.com *www.newspapers.com*
PPPP.Net: The Ultimate Collection of News Links *pppp.net/links/*
Working List of Speculative Fiction Markets *www.bayarea.net/~stef/sf-markets.txt*
Yahoo!: Magazines *search.yahoo.com/bin/search?p=magazines*

Media, International

(For more information on these listings, see chapter 3.)
Canadian Magazine Publisher's Association: Magazine Index *www.cmpa.ca/magindex.html*
EuroWEB *www.gok.de/int/the-e.html*
Journalism.Net *www.journalismnet.com/papers.htm*
Magazines of Europe *www.travelconnections.com/Magazines/Europeindex.htm*
Media and News Resources Around the Globe *www.uct.ac.za/depts/politics/intnew.htm*
Media UK *www.mediauk.com/directory/*
Newsdirectory.com: Worldwide Magazines *www.newsdirectory.com/news/magazine/world*
PPPP.Net: Ultimate Collection of Newslinks *pppp.net/links/news/*

Miscellaneous

555-1212.com *www.infospace.com/info.go555/*
A collection of directories, including yellow pages, white pages, country codes, area codes, businesses, government departments, international directories, and more. Use this directory to look up types of businesses in a specific area—e.g., every magazine published in California, or every book publisher located in Ohio.
AltaVista Photo Finder *image.altavista.com/cgi-bin/avncgi*
Search for images on the Web; excellent research tool!
AwardWeb: Collections of Literary Award Information *www.dpsinfo.com/awardweb/*
Links to award sites and information for the major literary awards in various genres, including science fiction/fantasy, mysteries, children's literature, and international literary awards.
Fiction Writer's Character Chart *www.eclectics.com/articles/character.html*
An interesting "fill in the blanks" guide to sketching out the background, interests, and characteristics of your characters.

Historic Events and Birth-Dates *www.scopesys.com/today/*

Find out what happened and who was born on any day of the year; fascinating historical "date" research source.

Proper Manuscript Format *www.shunn.net/format.html*

A guide to manuscript format, with examples.

Publishing: Statistics and Research *publishing.miningco.com/msub21.htm*

Links to articles, surveys, and statistics on various aspects of the book and magazine publishing industry.

The River: Resources *www.theriver.com/writers/contents.html*

An interesting collection of research resources for writers, with an emphasis on image-heavy locational materials (e.g., museums, archaeological digs, travel guides, castle sites, etc.).

Scam Alert *www.thewindjammer.com/smfs/newsletter/html/scam_alert.html*

A column on various scams targeting writers.

Soliloquoy *soliloquoy.silkthreads.com*

A "writer's exchange" that offers an online showcase for writers (to display their work), classifieds for writers and publishers, and an interactive "help desk" where writers can submit questions.

Time Converter *www.vtourist.com/cgi-bin/tconverter.cgi?lang=0*

Find out what time it is in any part of the world, relative to any other part of the world. (Useful if you're trying to call your editor in Ankara while you're in New York.)

Writer Beware *www.sfwa.org/Beware/*

Victoria Strauss's excellent compilation of tips and warnings about a wide variety of hazards to writers.

Mystery

BookWire Index: Mystery Publishers *www.bookwire.com/index/Mystery-Publishers.html*

ClueLass *www.cluelass.com*

Links to a variety of mystery writing resources, including articles, books, FAQ, groups, awards, events, and "opportunities" (publishers seeking writers, contests, support groups, and research help). Under "Britology," for example, find out the differences between the old and new U.K. monetary system, the British academic calendar, and the British police force rank structure.

Crimewriters.com *www.hollywoodnetwork.com/Crime/*

Links to sites, resources, writers, and experts on crime and crime-writing. Includes "desks" for information (e.g., cult desk, gang desk) that are available to members only, a Crimewriter's Consultants Center, and a "Bullet-In Board."

Crime Writers of Canada Links Page *www.swifty.com/cwc/links/mystery.htm*

Links to authors, publications, and mystery-writing resources.

Criminology and Policing (glossary) *criminology.nelson.com/glossaryab.html*

A glossary of terms used in criminology, law, and police work.

Forensic Science Web Pages *users.aol.com/murrk/index.htm*

Provides a good introduction to forensic science, including articles on firearms and toolmark identification, forensic psychiatry, forgeries, forensic photography, crime scene processing, and more.

Guide to Lock Picking *www.lysator.liu.se/mit-guide/mit-guide.html*

Exactly what it says it is! Includes tools, exercises, models, and a chapter on "advanced lock picking."

HollywoodNetwork.com *hollywoodnet.com/ic.html*

This site offers a host of resources for crime and mystery writers. It's geared primarily toward screenwriters, and many of the resources are available only to members, but the free resources are worth checking.

The Mysterious Home Page *www.webfic.com/mysthome/*

Links to authors, magazines, media, games, electronic texts, newsgroups, articles on characters and themes, organizations, awards, and a variety of other topics of interest to mystery readers and writers.

Mystery Connections *emporium.turnpike.net/~mystery/crime_pursuits.html*

Links to bookstores, authors, interactive murder mysteries, conventions, and "mysteryzines."

Mystery Writers of America *www.mysterynet.com/mwa/*
Mystery Writers' Resources *www.zott.com/mysforum/default.html*
> Links to resources on "agents, copyrights and legal, organizations, resources, publishers, forensics, law, guns, poisons, police, mafia, and misc. security."

Overbooked *www.overbooked.org/bklink.html*
> A site dedicated to genre resources, including book links, author links, writing links, and more.

Zeno's Forensic Page *users.bart.nl/~geradts/forensic.html*
> Huge list of links to resources on forensic science, medicine, and psychiatry. Includes links to forums, journals, laboratories, associations, universities, employment opportunities, discussion lists, and lots more.

Names

Ayperi's Name Site *www.geocities.com/Athens/Forum/3495/*
> Interesting collections of names under a variety of categories (e.g., "mystical," "nature," etc.) Unfortunately not alphabetized or listed under culture, and no references provided as to the source of the "meanings."

BabyCenter: Baby Name Search *www.babycenter.com/babyname/index.html*
> Database of "names for babies," searchable by name, type of name, country, or meaning. (Slow.)

Babynamefinder *www2.parentsoup.com/babynames/*
> Locate a name based on your own criteria, search for meanings of names, or look up "famous names."

Eponym *student-www.uchicago.edu/users/smhawkin/names/*
> First stop for links to various name and name-definition sites, including specific ethnic name sites (esp. British, Irish), baby name sites, etc.

Etymology of First Names *www.pacificcoast.net/~muck/etym.html*
> Alphabetical list of names and definitions.

John Kasab's Ars Magica Names Database *www.cae.wisc.edu/~kasab/arm/names*
> A collection of names from various countries linked to a specific "gaming" time period; contains many unusual names from less-studied regions; Hungarian section offers definitions. Also links to genealogical information on several fourteenth-century Anglo-Norman families.

Medieval Naming Guides *www.panix.com/~mittle/names/*
> Excellent lists of names from a variety of cultures (not just English/British Isles); well-researched and definitive. Also offers links to other name sites and lists.

Random Vocabularies or Name Generation Page *www.ruf.rice.edu/~pound/*
> Generate names or words, or invent a language.

Scottish Names Resources *www.abdn.ac.uk/~his016/scotnames/index.html*
What's in Your Name? *www.kabalarians.com/gkh/your.htm*
> Offers extensive listings of names and variations; sponsored by the Kabalarians Society, which offers to give you a "personality profile" based on the letter combinations in your name. Excellent source of character name ideas.

Newsgroups—See "Discussion Lists and Newsgroups"

Online Instruction Resources

(For more information on these resources, see chapter 3.)
Conferencing Systems *www.hypernews.org/HyperNews/get/www/collab/conferencing.html*
Diversity University *www.du.org/duSvcs/teachers.htm*
On-Line Lectures *www.idbsu.edu/resource/lectures.htm*
Resources for Writing Instructors *www.devry-phx.edu/lrnresrc/dowsc/instres.htm*
World Lecture Hall: English, Writing, and Rhetoric *www.utexas.edu/world/lecture/e/*

Online Journalism—See "Journalism"

OWLs (Online Writing Labs)

(For more information on these listings, see chapter 7.)

National Writing Centers Association (directory) *departments.colgate.edu/diw/NWCAOWLs.html*

Writing Labs and Writing Centers on the Web *owl.english.purdue.edu/owls/writing-labs.html*

Playwriting—See "Screenwriting and Scriptwriting"

Poetry

Academy of American Poets *www.he.net/~susannah/academy.htm*

A membership site for poets, including contests, publicity, and advertising.

Advice on How to Sell Poetry *www.sff.net/people/neile/how.to.sell.poetry.htp*

Excellent article by Neile Graham on how to prepare and format poetry, locate markets, submit manuscripts, and more.

AlienFlower *www.sonic.net/web/albany/workshop*

A source of poetry workshops, exercises, classes, and resources.

Glossary of Poetic Terms *shoga.wwa.com/~rgs/glossary.html*

A fascinating collection of terms, from abecedarian to zeugma.

Links to Poets *home.earthlink.net/~pjmartin/linksp.html*

Modern and Contemporary American Poetry *www.english.upenn.edu/~afilreis/88/home.html*

National Poetry Association *www.slip.net/~gamuse*

Palindromes *www.rdg.ac.uk/~sssbownj/jnwobsss~/ku.ca.gdr.www//:ptth*

If you're not sure what a palindrome is, just check the URL!

Poetry Markets: Current Calls for Manuscripts *newark.rutgers.edu/~lcrew/markets/index.html*

The Poetry Resource *www.pmpoetry.com*

Links to poets, poems, and other resources.

Rutgers Newark's NJ High School Poetry Contest *newark.rutgers.edu/~lcrew/contest*

Don't be fooled by the title; this is a rich resource of links to poetry references, collections, contests, and other sources online.

Semantic Rhyming Dictionary *www.link.cs.cmu.edu/dougb/rhyme-doc.html*

Find rhymes by matching syllables, sounds, consonants, meanings, and definitions.

Shiki Internet Haiku Salon *mikan.cc.matsuyama-u.ac.jp/~shiki*

A discussion and description of various forms of haiku, plus a contest and links.

Publications for Writers

(For more information on some of these listings, see chapter 1.)

ASJA Contract Watch *www.asja.org/cwpage.htm*

A free [biweekly] electronic newsletter about the latest terms and negotiations in the world of periodicals, print and electronic."

Electronic Publications for Writers *www.inkspot.com/bt/craft/pubwritezines.html*

Global Writers' Ink *www.inskpot.com/global/*

A biweekly e-mail newsletter for writers interested in international markets.

Inklings *www.inkspot.com/inklings/*

Inscriptions *come.to/Inscriptions*

Internet Writing Journal *www.writerswrite.com/journal/*

The Literary Times *www.tlt.com*

(See "Romance" for more information.)

National Writer's Monthly *www.writersmarkets.com*
NovelAdvice *www.noveladvice.com/*
RestStop Writers' Newsletter *www.geocities.com/SoHo/Village/2115/index.html*
The Sideroad *www.sideroad.com*
   Offers a weekly writing article.
Write Markets Report *www.writersmarkets.com*
Writer On Line *www.novalearn.com/wol/*
Writer's Block *www.niva.com/original/writblok/index.htm*
   Though apparently aimed more at academic writers than at freelancers, this newsletter contains a number of useful articles.
Writers on the Net *www.writers.com*
Writing for DOLLARS! *www.awoc.com*

Research and Search Engine Tips

(For more information on these listings, see chapter 2.)
Finding Information on the Internet: A Tutorial *www.lib.berkeley.edu/TeachingLib/Guides/Internet/Findinfo.html*
   Includes "Beyond General WWW Searching" (*/BeyondWeb.html*), "Meta-Search Engines" (*/MetaSearch.html*), and "Searching the World Wide Web: Strategies, Analyzing Your Topic, Choosing Search Tools" (*/Strategies.html*).
Finding that Needle in a Haystack: Internet Search Engines *www.editors-service.com/articlearchive/search.html*
Internet Tools for the Advanced Searcher *www.philb.com/adint.htm*
   Includes "Multi-Search Engines: A Comparison" (*/msengine.htm*) and "Search Engines Comparison" (*/compare.htm*).
The Major Search Engines *searchenginewatch.internet.com/facts/major.html*
THOR: The Online Resource *thorplus.lib.purdue.edu/vlibrary/inet_resources*
Using the Internet for Research (FAQ) *www.purefiction.com/pages/res1.htm*
Web Search Tools *www.moorhead.msus.edu/~gunarat/ijr/tools.html*

Research: Directories and Databases

(For more information on these listings, see chapter 2.)
All-in-One Search Page *www.allonesearch.com*
Argus Clearinghouse *www.clearinghouse.net/searchbrowse.html*
Calculators On-Line Center *www-sci.lib.uci.edu/HSG/RefCalculators.html*
Direct Search *gwis2.circ.gwu.edu/~gprice/direct.htm*
Handilinks *www.handilinks.com*
Historic Events and Birth-Dates *www.scopesys.com/today/*
History/Social Studies Web Site for K–12 Teachers *www.execpc.com/~dboals/*
Internet Sleuth *www.isleuth.com*
Librarians' Index to the Internet *sunsite.berkeley.edu/InternetIndex/*
Library of Congress *www.loc.gov*
LibrarySpot *www.libraryspot.com/*
Multnomah County Library Electronic Resources *www.multnomah.lib.or.us/lib/ref/quick.html*
My Virtual Reference Desk *www.refdesk.com*
Needle in a CyberStack: The InfoFinder *home.revealed.net/albee/*
Pitsco's Ask an Expert *www.askanexpert.com*
ProfNet *www.profnet.com/profsearchguide.html*
Search.com *www.search.com*
Sources and Experts *metalab.unc.edu/slanews/internet/experts.html*
SunSITE Collection Index *www.sunsite.unc.edu/collection/*
Union Institute Research Engine *www.tui.edu/Research/Research.html*

Research: Evaluating Web Sites

Evaluating Information Found on the Internet *milton.mse.jhu.edu:8001/research/education/net.html*
Evaluating Web Sites *servercc.oakton.edu/~wittman/find/eval.htm*

Romance

The Costume Site *milieux.com/costume/costume1.html*
Links to sites covering costumes and costuming from all periods and locations.
HeartRealm *www.heartrealm.com*
Author pages, contests, articles, chat room, critique groups, publisher listings, book reviews, newsletter.
The History of Costume *www.siue.edu/COSTUMES/TEXT_INDEX.HTML*
A useful site for authors seeking to research authentic period costumes.
The Literary Times *www.tlt.com/news/itiner.htm*
Online edition of "A Journal for Lovers of Romantic Fiction," featuring reviews, author profiles, research and reference links, and a place for writers to post upcoming events at no charge.
Overbooked *www.overbooked.org/bklink.html*
A site dedicated to genre resources, including book links, author links, writing links, and more.
The Regency Fashion Page *locutus.ucr.edu/~cathy/reg3.html*
The Romance Authors Page *www.nettrends.com/romanceauthors/*
Links, articles, and an excellent "research index" that offers links to sites on various historical periods common to romance novels.
Romance Medley's Favorite Links to the Past *members.aol.com/_ht_a/MedPub232/index3.html*
Links to timelines, primary sources, and a wealth of historical sites.
Romance Novel Database *www-personal.sl.umich.edu/~sooty/romance/*
Links and lists of Romance novels and authors.
Romance Novels and Women's Fiction: Authors *www.writepage.com/romance.htm*
Romance Novels and Women's Fiction: Publishers *www.sff.net/people/ValerieTaylor/publishers.html*
Romance Writers Exchange RoundTable *gopher://gopher.genie.com:70/00/magazines/romex/about*
A gopher site offers a romance discussion list and newsletter (archived online at *gopher.genie.com/ 11/magazines/romex*)
Romance Writers Homepage *www.simegen.com/out-t/romance/index.html*
Links, writers' Web pages, book reviews, bulletin boards, chat, and promotional opportunities for writers who'd like to host a chat.
Romance Writers of America *www.rwanational.com*
Romancing the Web *www.romanceweb.com/toc.html*
Links, information on upcoming romance events (e.g., chats, book signings, seminars), a newsletter, page hosting services, and an excellent research section.
Useful Links for Romance Writers and Readers *www.inficad.com/~jacreding/inks/index.html*
Includes extensive author links.

Science Fiction and Fantasy

(For more critique groups and workshops, see "Critique.")
Index to Science Fiction Anthologies and Collections *www.best.com/~contento/*
Database of SF short stories, searchable by author, title, magazine, date.
Internet Fantasy Writer's List *www.fantasytoday.com*
A discussion list and critique group for writers of speculative fiction.
Market List *www.marketlist.com/index.htp*
A market listing for writers of science fiction, fantasy, and horror
Overbooked *www.overbooked.org/bklink.html*
A site dedicated to genre resources, including book links, author links, writing links, and more.
Paradox Concepts: Writer's Support Page *members.home.net/wcgrnway/writmain.html*
Loads of useful information, articles, and links specifically focused on writing speculative fiction.

Ralan Conley's SpecFic Webstravaganza *members.xoom.com/_XOOM/RalanConley/sf_pro2.htm*
Detailed listings of speculative fiction markets, divided into pro, semi-pro, and other categories based on payment rates.

Resources for Fantasy Writers *www.tipsforwriters.com/fantasy.shtml*
Hosted by Moira Allen.

Science Fiction and Fantasy Writers of America (SFWA) *www.sfwa.org/site_index.htp*

Science Fiction Publishers (BookWire Index) *www.bookwire.com/index/SciFict-Publishers.html*

Science Fiction Resource Guide *sf.www.lysator.liu.se/sf_archive/sf-texts/SF_resource_guide/*
Loads of links to anything and everything science fiction–related. (If you have difficulty reaching the page directly, go to *www.lysator.liu.se* and click on the SF Resource Guide link.)

Science Fiction Round Table (SFRT) *www.sfrt.com/sfrt2.htm*
Offers a variety of speculative fiction resources, including events, conventions and conferences, publishers' links, media information, research and writing links, and an extensive list of author sites.

Sci-Fi and Fantasy Authors List *www.onelist.com/subscribe/Sci-FiAndFantasyAuth*
A discussion list offering "self help and guidance for aspiring and successful writers."

SF Site *www.sfsite.com*
News, reviews, interviews with science fiction authors, and links to related sites. Among other useful resources, this site offers the Internet Speculative Fiction Database (*/www.sfsite.com/isfdb/*), a database of speculative fiction ovels and short stories that can be searched by author, title, year, award, and other criteria.

Speculative Vision *speculativevision.com*
Described as "The Science Fiction and Fantasy Resource Network," this site includes a gallery of sf/fantasy art, a "music conservatory," an interactive story, discussion forums, and links to other speculative fiction resources.

The Ultimate Science Fiction Web Guide *www.magicdragon.com/UltimateSF/SF-Index.html*
Links to authors, book titles, conventions, information on international science fiction/fantasy writing, games, magazines and newsletters, movies, poetry, publishers, TV shows and more.

Working List of Speculative Fiction Markets *www.bayarea.net/~stef/sf-markets.txt*

Screenwriting and Scriptwriting

Essays on the Craft of Dramatic Writing *www.teleport.com/~bjscript/*
"Explores the craft of writing dramatic stories" for books, plays, or screenplays.

From FADE IN through FADE OUT *members.aol.com/anniraff/contents.htm*
The complete text of a book on screenwriting, available free.

Hollywood Writers' Network (HollywoodNet) *hollywoodnetwork.com/dindex.html*
Information on publishing, producing, scripts, screenwriting, crime-writing, acting, directing, and lots more, including chat rooms, movie databases, profiles, and columns. Some resources require membership; others are free.

How to Write a Screenplay *www.visualwriter.com/descript.htm*
A free downloadable e-book discussing how to write a screenplay "from planning an idea through developing a plot to finishing the play." For Windows only.

Inside Film Magazine **Online: Screenwriting** *www.insidefilm.com/screenwriting.html*
A list of conferences and other events for screenwriters.

The Online Communicator *www.communicator.com/writvid.html*
Links to a variety of screenwriting resources.

The Playwriting Seminars *www.vcu.edu/artweb/playwriting/seminar.html*
Free "seminars" on the content, structure, craft, format, and business of writing plays, plus links to plays and contests.

Screenwriters and Playwrights Home Page *www.teleport.com/~cdeemer/scrwriter.html*
Resources for screenwriters and playwrights, including chat, FAQ, links, and topical articles (such as "dramatic structure").

Screenwriter's Master Chart *members.aol.com/maryjs/scrnrite.htm*
"What's Supposed to Happen—When? A Summary of Various Script Breakdowns and Systems."

This interesting chart lets you know that in a 120-page script, "Point of No Return" should occur by page 60.

Screenwriters Utopia *www.screenwritersutopia.com*

Links to contests, agents, advice from "pros," classes, "Hollywood Internet," software, and magazines.

Screenwriting *screenwriting.miningco.com*

Links, articles, chat, script templates, contacts, dialogue sound files, legal issues, supplies, and research resources.

Screenwriting Resources *home.netvigator.com/~lwgray/writers/links/one.htm*

Sponsored by the Hong Kong Writer's Circle, this offers a variety of interesting links and references.

SCRNWRiT *www.panam.edu/scrnwrit*

This site is a "companion" to the SCRNWRiT mailing list, and offers a range of information on screenwriting, including an extensive FAQ, a list of contests and fellowships (may be outdated), links, and a glossary.

The World Wide Web Virtual Library: Theatre and Drama *www.vl-theatre.com/index.htm*

Links to free plays online, theatre books, articles, and other drama resources.

Writers Guild of America *www.wga.org*

"The official website of the WGA, with valuable advice and information on the art and craft of professional screenwriting for film, television, and interactive projects." The site includes many resources for nonmembers, including interviews, profiles, research sources, and a free newsletter.

Search Engines

AltaVista *www.altavista.com, altavista.digital.com*

Excite *www.excite.com*

HotBot *www.hotbot.com*

InfoSeek *www.infoseek.com*

Looksmart *www.looksmart.com*

Lycos *www.lycos.com*

Reference.COM *www.reference.com/pn/help-1.0/email-access.html*

An e-mail-based search engine.

SearchUK *www.searchuk.com*

WebCrawler *www.webcrawler.com*

Yahoo! *www.yahoo.com*

Search Engines, Meta/Multi

Dogpile *www.dogpile.com*

Easysearcher *www.easysearcher.com*

HuskySearch *huskysearch.cs.washington.edu*

Inference Find *www.infind.com/infind/*

MetaCrawler *www.metacrawler.com*

Metafind *www.metafind.com*

OneSeek *www.oneseek.com*

SavvySearch *savvy.cs.colostate.edu*

Self-Publishing

Book Marketing Update *www.bookmarket.com/index.html*

Though designed primarily to promote products and publications, this site offers a number of free reports and services for the self-publisher or writers attempting to promote their own books.

Books onQ *www.onq.org/Welcome.htm*

A "bookstore" site entirely dedicated to self-published books.

BookWire *www.bookwire.com*
  Describes itself as "the book industry's most comprehensive and thorough online information source."
  Offers extensive links to book-related sites, including publishers, publicists, online bookstores, etc.
BookZone *www.bookzone.com*
  Offers a range of resources for self-publishers, links to independent publisher sites, and a bookstore
  of books by small presses or self-publishers.
CyberInk Press Resource Center *www.cyberinkpress.com/link1.htm*
  Various references and resources for the self-publisher.
How to Publish Yourself *www.devce.demon.co.uk/h2pub.htm*
  An article from the United Kingdom that effectively summarizes the steps that must be taken for
  self-publishing.
Publisher's Marketing Association (PMA) *www.pma-online.org*
  Organization for self-publishers and small presses.
SPAN *www.SPANnet.org*
  An organization for self-publishers and small presses, organized by Tom and Marilyn Ross, authors
  of *The Complete Guide to Self-Publishing.*

Taxes—See "Business and Finance"

Technical Writing

Business and Technical Communication *www.cohums.ohio-state.edu/english/areas/bizcom.htm*
  Links to business and technical communications journals, organizations, discussion lists, and related
  pages.
Internet Links for Technical Communication *www.muohio.edu/~mtsccwis/techcommlinks.html*
John December Technical Communications Information Sources *www.december.com/john/study/*
  techcomm/info.html
Resources for Tech/Scientific Writers *www.inkspot.com/genres/tech.html*
Society for Technical Communication *www.stctoronto.org*
  Articles, links, and membership resources.
Technical Writing *techwriting.miningco.com/*
  Gary Conroy's extensive coverage of business and technical writing.

Web Guides

(For more information on these listings, see chapter 3.)
FutureFantastic.net *www.marketing4technology.com/futurefantastic/*
The Mining Co. (also knows as **About.com**) *beaguide.miningco.com*
Suite101 *www.suite101.com*

Web Site Development: Content

(For more information on these listings, see chapter 8.)
Be Succinct! (Writing for the Web) *www.useit.com/alertbox/9703b.html*
Building a Writer's Website *www.sff.net/people/victoriastrauss/victoria%2ostrauss%2owhywebsite.html*
Concise, Scannable, and Objective: How to Write for the Web *www.useit.com/papers/webwriting/*
  writing.html
How Users Read the Web *www.useit.com/alertbox/9710a.html*
Resources for New Web Authors *darkwing.uoregon.edu/~lincicum/resource.html*
Usable Web: Guide to Web Usability Resources *usableweb.com/index.html*
Web Authoring Resources *www.wwwscribe.com/resource.htm*
Writing for the Web: A New Resource for Writers *www.wwwscribe.com/webwrite.htm*

Web Site Development: HTML and Design Tools

(For more information on these listings, see chapter 9.)

The Bare Bones Guide to HTML *werbach.com/barebones/*

Beginner's Guide to HTML *www.ncsa.uiuc.edu/General/Internet/WWW/HTMLPrimer.html*

Color Specifier *www.users.interport.net/~giant/COLOR/1ColorSpecifier.html*

GIF Wizard *uswest.gifwizard.com*

HTML Goodies *www.htmlgoodies.com*

Matt's Script Archive *worldwidemart.com/scripts/*

META Tags *northernwebs.com/set/*

Miscellaneous Web Tools *www.lib.msu.edu/harris23/general/webtools.htm*

Robin's Nest: Web Site Development *www2.netdoor.com/~smslady/websitedevelop.html*

TableMaker *www.bagism.com/tablemaker/*

Top Ten Mistakes in Web Design *www.useit.com/alertbox/9605.html*

Webmaster's Guide to Search Engines *searchenginewatch.internet.com/webmasters/*
Includes "Checking Your URL" (*/checkurl.html*), "How Search Engines Work" (*/work.html*), "How to Use META Tags" (*/meta.html*), "Search Engines and Frames" (*/frames.html*), and "Search Engines Features Chart" (*/features.html*).

Web Style Guide *info.med.yale.edu/caim/manual/contents.html*

Web Wonk: Tips for Writers and Designers *www.dsiegel.com/tips/index.html*

Willcam's Comprehensive HTML Cross Reference *www.willcam.com/cmat/html/*

Web Site Development: Promotion, Registration, and Site Diagnostic Tools

(For more information on these listings, see chapter 9.)

1 2 3 Add-It! *www.123add-it.com*

Auto Submit *www.autosubmit.com/promote.html*

Bobby *www.cast.org/bobby/*

Cozy Cabin *www.cozycabin.com/add.html*

did-it.com/did-it detective *www.did-it.com*

Go Net-Wide *www.gonetwide.com/gopublic.html*

Internet Promotions MEGALIST *www.2020tech.com/submit.html*

Meta Medic *www.northernwebs.com/set/setsimjr.html*

Register-It! *www.liquidimaging.com/submit/*

Site Inspector *siteinspector.linkexchange.com*

Virtual Promote *www.virtualpromote.com/promotea.html*

Westerns

Overbooked *www.overbooked.org/bklink.html*
A site dedicated to genre resources, including book links, author links, writing links, and more.

Western Writers of America *www.imt.net/~gedison/wwahome.html*

Young Writers' Resources

A+ Research and Writing *www.ipl.org/teen/aplus/*
An excellent site on writing essays and research papers, with detailed step-by-step writing and research tips.

Aaron Shepard's Young Author Page *www.aaronshep.com/youngauthor/index.html*
Articles and links for young authors.

Creative Writing for Kids *kidswriting.miningco.com*
Links to writing tips, publishing resources, chats, and fun sites.

infogranny.com *www.infogranny.com*
Links to reading, topics, research, writing, and publishing resources for young writers.

Inkspot: For Young Writers *www.inkspot.com/young/*

FAQs (from a number of authors), articles, links, markets for young authors, classifieds.

Katharsis *www.katharsis.org*

Described as "The place for young writers to gather on the Web," this site offers contests, chat, a "showcase" for young writers, and interesting writing exercises to stimulate ideas and stories.

Scriptito's Place *members.aol.com/vangarnews/scriptito.html*

Places for young writers to publish/post their work, plus information on writing skills, contests, resources, illustration information, workshops, etc.

Stone Soup *www.stonesoup.com*

"The beautiful magazine by young writers and artists!"

Things You Should Never Do to a Young Writer *www.geocities.com/Athens/8506/never.html*

Good advice for parents and teachers—and perhaps a good resource for young writers who would like adults to understand them better.

WebTopics *www.dimensional.com/~janf/wtwriting.html*

Links to a variety of resources and fun sites for young writers.

Young Writers Club *www.cs.bilkent.edu.tr/~david/derya/about.htm*

Writing resources for young writers, plus a place to post/publish material, a magazine for contributions (*Global Wave*), etc.

Young Writers' Clubhouse *www.realkids.com/club.shtml*

How to get started, FAQs, chat, contests, critique group, and more for young writers.

Appendix B: Alphabetical List of Resources

1 2 3 Add It! *www.123add-it.com*
10 Big Myths About Copyright Explained (by Brad Templeton) *www.templetons.com/brad/copymyths.html*
1500+ U.S. Newspapers and Their Links *www.acclaimed.com/helpful/new-add.htm*
1stBooks *www.1stbooks.com*
555-1212.com *www.infospace.com/info.go555/*
A+ Research and Writing *www.ipl.org/teen/aplus/*
Aaron Shepard's Kidwriter Page *www.aaronshep.com/kidwriter/*
Aaron Shepard's Young Author Page *www.aaronshep.com/youngauthor/index.html*
Academy of American Poets *www.he.net/~susannah/academy.htm*
AddAll *www.addall.com*
Adobe Systems *www.adobe.com*
Advice on How to Sell Poetry *www.sff.net/people/neile/how.to.sell.poetry.htp*
Agents who Broker Science Fiction and Fantasy Works *members.home.net/wcgrnway/agentlst.html*
AlienFlower *www.sonic.net/web/albany/workshop*
All-in-One Search Page *www.allonesearch.com*
Alpha Complete News Index, The *www.select-ware.com/news/*
AltaVista *www.altavista.com, altavista.digital.com*
AltaVista Photo Finder *image.altavista.com/cgi-bin/avncgi*
AltaVista Translation *babelfish.altavista.com/cgi-bin/translate?*
Amazon.com *www.amazon.com*
Amazon.com (Germany) *www.amazon.de*
Amazon.com (UK) *www.amazon.co.uk*
America Online *www.aol.com*
American Journalism Review (AJR) NewsLink (AJR NewsLink, JobLink for Journalists) *ajr.newslink.org*
American Society of Journalists and Authors (ASJA) *www.asja.org*
American-British/British-American Dictionary *www.peak.org/~jeremy/dictionary/dict-toc.html*
AOL Instant Messenger *www.aol.com/aim/promo/73010/aim_download.html*
Argus Clearinghouse *www.clearinghouse.net/searchbrowse.html*
Arrow, The *www.wport.com/~cawilcox/mainpath/page1.htm*
Articles *www.underdown.org/articles.htm*

Articles About Writing *www.sfwa.org/writing/writing.htm*

Articles for Writers on Everything Imaginable *members.tripod.com/~PetalsofLife/writerslinks.html*

ASJA Contract Watch *www.asja.org/cwpage.htm*

Ask Grammar (See "Guide to Grammar and Writing").

Association of Authors' Representatives Inc. *www.bookwire.com/AAR/*

Association of Electronic Publishers *welcome.to/AEP*

Association of Research Libraries *www.arl.org*

Associations and Organizations of Interest to Writers *www.poewar.com/articles/associations.html*

Author Web Sites *www.geocities.com/~bookbug/home.html*

Authorlink *www.authorlink.com/*

Authors *authors.miningco.com*

Author's Guild, The *www.authorsguild.org/welcome.html*

Authors in the New Information Age: A Working Paper on Electronic Publishing Issues *www.nwu.org/docs/aniabeg.htm#173*

Auto Submit *www.autosubmit.com/promote.html*

Avalanche of Jobs for Writers, Editors, and Copywriters *www.sunoasis.com*

AwardWeb: Collections of Literary Award Information *www.dpsinfo.com/awardweb/*

Awe-Struck E-Books *www.awe-struck.net*

Ayperi's Name Site *www.geocities.com/Athens/Forum/3495/*

BabyCenter: Baby Name Search *www.babycenter.com/babyname/index.html*

Babynamefinder *www2.parentsoup.com/babynames/*

Bare Bones Guide to HTML *werbach.com/barebones/*

Barnes & Noble *www.barnesandnoble.com*

Barnes & Noble: Authors Online *www.barnesandnoble.com/community/archive/authors/*

Bartlett's Quotations *www.columbia.edu/acis/bartleby/bartlett/*

Basics of Internet E-mail *www.wwwscribe.com/ebasics.htm*

Be Succinct! (Writing for the Web) *www.useit.com/alertbox/9703b.html*

A Beginner's Guide to HTML *www.ncsa.uiuc.edu/General/Internet/WWW/HTMLPrimer.html*

Berne Convention for the Protection of Literary and Artistic Works *www.law.cornell.edu/treaties/berne/overview.html*

Bobby *www.cast.org/bobby/*

Book Marketing Update *www.bookmarket.com/index.html*

BookFinder.com *www.bookfinder.com*

Books onQ *www.onq.org/Welcome.htm*

Books.com *www.books.com*

BookWire: Book Publisher Index *www.bookwire.com/index/publishers.html*

BookZone *www.bookzone.com*

Borders *www.borders.com*

Boson books *www.cmonline.com/boson/*

Brave New World: Romance Authors on the Cutting Edge of Publishing *www.booksquare.com/sub-version/parlor/exp001.cfm*

British and Irish Authors on the Web *lang.nagoya-u.ac.jp/~matsuoka/UK-authors.html*

Building a Writer's Website *www.sff.net/people/victoriastrauss/victoria%20strauss%20whywebsite.html*

Business and Technical Communication *www.cohums.ohio-state.edu/english/areas/bizcom.htm*

Byron's Romance Port *www.geocities.com/Athens/8774*

"C" Rights in "E" Mail *www.ivanhoffman.com/rights.html*

Calculators On-Line Center *www-sci.lib.uci.edu/HSG/RefCalculators.html*

Canada Post *www.canadapost.ca/CPC2/menu_01.html*

Canadian Magazine Publisher's Association: Magazine Index *www.cmpa.ca/magindex.html*

CANSCAIP *www.interlog.com/~canscaip/*

Castle Terms *www.castlesontheweb.com/glossary.html*

CataList, the Official Catalog of LISTSERV® Lists *www.lsoft.com/lists/listref.html*

Chat Hole, The *www.geocities.com/SouthBeach/Breakers/5257/Chathole.htm*

Children's Book Council (CBC) (including "Author and Illustrator Links") *www.cbcbooks.org/*

Children's Literature Web Guide *www.acs.ucalgary.ca/~dkbrown/index.html*
Children's Writers Marketplace *www.inkspot.com/childmkt*
Children's Writing Resource Center *www.write4kids.com/index.html*
Christian Periodical Publishers *www.colc.com/pubbook/key.htm*
CIO Web Central: Guide to Electronic and Print Resources for Journalists *www.cio.com/central/ journalism.html*
Citing Internet Sources *www.tui.edu/Research/Resources/ResearchHelp/Cites.html*
Clearing Rights for Multimedia Works *www.ut.system.edu/ogc/intellectual property/*
Cliché Finder *www.westegg.com/cliche/*
ClueLass *www.cluelass.com*
CNN Interactive Interviews *www.cnn.com/chat/*
Color Specifier *www.users.interport.net/~giant/COLOR/1 ColorSpecifier.html*
Commercial Book Publishers (WriteLinks) *www.writelinks.com/resources/pub/pubsbk.htm*
Common Errors in English *www.wsu.edu:8080/~brians/errors/spellcheck.html*
Compuserve *www.compuserve.com*
Concise, Scannable, and Objective: How to Write for the Web *www.useit.com/papers/webwriting/ writing.html*
Conferencing Systems *www.hypernews.org/HyperNews/get/www/collab/conferencing.html*
Contentious *www.contentious.com*
Contract Issues: Books Published Online *www.nwu.org/docs/online-p.htm*
Contract Tips for Freelancers *www.asja.org/asjatips.htm*
Contracts *www.teleport.com/~until/contract.htm*
CopyEditor: Language News for the Publishing Profession *www.copyeditor.com*
Copylaw Resources *copylaw.com/res.html*
Copyright and Fair Use *fairuse.stanford.edu/*
Copyright and Intellectual Property *www.arl.org/info/frn/copy/copytoc.html*
Copyright Code *www.law.cornell.edu/uscode/17/*
Copyright for Computer Authors *www.FPLC.edu/tfield/copysof.htm*
Copyright Protection in the New World of Electronic Publishing *www.press.umich.edu/jep/works/ strong.copyright.html*
Copyright Protection: Understanding Your Options *www.seyboldreport.com/Specials/Copyright.htm*
Costume Site, The *milieux.com/costume/costume1.html*
Cozy Cabin *www.cozycabin.com/add.html*
Creative Writing for Kids *kidswriting.miningco.com*
Crime Writers of Canada Links Page *www.swifty.com/cwc/links/mystery.htm*
Crimewriters.com *www.hollywoodnetwork.com/Crime/*
Criminology and Policing (glossary) *criminology.nelson.com/glossaryab.html*
Critters Workshop *brain-of-pooh.tech-soft.com/users/critters/*
CyberInk Press Resource Center *www.cyberinkpress.com/link1.htm*
CyberSearch Writer's Guide to Finding Jobs Online *home.earthlink.net/~cuvelier/INK/JOBS/GUIDE/ tutorial.html*
DejaNews *www.dejanews.com*
Del Rey Online Writing Workshop *www.randomhouse.com/delrey/workshop/*
Delphi *www.delphi.com*
Derivative Rights and Websites *www.ivanhoffman.com/derivative.html*
Dictionary of Faeries *faeryland.tamu-commerce.edu/~earendil/faerie/bin/search.cgi*
did-it.com/did-it detective *www.did-it.com*
The Digital Millenium Copyright Act (summary) *www.arl.org/info/frn/copy/band.html*
The Digital Millenium Copyright Act (text) *www.gseis.ucla.edu/iclp/dmca1.html*
Direct Search *gwis2.circ.gwu.edu/~gprice/direct.htm*
Directory of Electronic Journals and Newsletters *www.coalliance.org/ejournal/*
Discussion and Mailing List Promotion *jlunz.databack.com/listpromo.htm*
DiskUs Publishing *www.diskuspublishing.com*
Diversity University *www.du.org/duSvcs/teachers.htm*

Findinfo.html
Finding that Needle in a Haystack: Internet Search Engines *www.editors-service.com/articlearchive/search.html*
Forensic Science Web Pages *users.aol.com/murrk/index.htm*
Forwriters.com *www.forwriters.com/*
Free HTML Validator *www.iaehv.ni/users/fpieters/validate.htm/*
Freelance Online *www.FreelanceOnline.com/faqs.html*
Freelance Success Institute *www.freelancesuccess.com*
Freelance Writer's Internet FAQ *ourworld.compuserve.com/homepages/MARTINEZ/FAQ.htm*
From FADE IN through FADE OUT *members.aol.com/anniraff/contents.htm*
From the Heart Online *www.delphi.com/FTH*
FutureFantastic.net *www.marketing4technology.com/futurefantastic/*
Garbl's Writing Resources On Line *pw1.netcom.com/~garbl1/index.html*
The Gender-Neutral Pronoun FAQ *www.lumina.net/gnp*
GIF Wizard *uswest.gifwizard.com/*
Giving Credit and Requesting Permission: Guidelines for Using Material Other than Your Own *www.oreilly.com/oreilly/author/permission/*
Glossary of Internet Terms *www.matisse.net/files/glossary.html*
GLB Publishers *www.glbpubs.com*
Global Writers' Ink *www.inskpot.com/global/*
Glossary of Poetic Terms *shoga.wwa.com/~rgs/glossary.html*
Go Net-Wide *www.gonetwide.com/gopublic.html*
Gotham Writers' Workshop *www.write.org/frame_main.html*
Grammar and Style Notes *andromeda.rutgers.edu/~jlynch/writing/*
Grammar Hotline Directory *www.tc.cc.va.us/writcent/gh/hotlinol.htm*
Grammar Lady, The *www.grammarlady.com*
Guide to Grammar and Writing *webster.commnet.edu/HP/pages/darling/original.htm*
Guide to Lock Picking *www.lysator.liu.se/mit-guide/mit-guide.html*
Guide to Online Guidelines *www.snafu.de/~gadfly/*
Guide to Writers Conferences *www.shawguides.com/index.cgi?s=11*
Guidelines for Publishing and Promoting an E-mail Newsletter *www.trafficplan.com/newsltrtips.htm*
Handilinks *www.handilinks.com*
Hard Shell Word Factory *www.hardshell.com*
Hardcore Critique Advice *www.crayne.com/victory/download/casiltip.txt*
HeartRealm *www.heartrealm.com*
Historic Events and Birth-Dates *www.scopesys.com/today/*
Historical Dictionaries, Slang, and Proverbs *ireland.iol.ie/~mazzold/lang/s-hist.htm*
History of Costume, The *www.siue.edu/COSTUMES/TEXT_INDEX.HTML*
History/Social Studies Web Site for K–12 Teachers *www.execpc.com/~dboals/*
Hollywood Writers' Network (HollywoodNet) *hollywoodnetwork.com/dindex.html*
HollywoodNetwork.com *hollywoodnet.com/ic.html*
Horror Writers Association *www.horror.org*
HotBot *www.hotbot.com*
How Students Should Reference Online Sources in Bibliographies *www.classroom.com/resource/citingnetresources.asp*
How to Critique Fiction *www.crayne.com/victory/howcrit.html*
How to Find an Online Journalism Job on the Web *www.careermag.com/newsarts/jobsearch/1042.html*
How to Publish Yourself *www.device.demon.co.uk/h2pub.htm*
How to Start an Online Newsletter (by Debbie Ohi, *Inklings*) *www.inkspot.com/craft/newsletterinfo.html*
How to Write a Screenplay *www.visualwriter.com/descript.htm*
How Users Read the Web *www.useit.com/alertbox/9710a.html*
HTML Goodies *www.htmlgoodies.com*
Hugh's Mortgage and Financial Calculators *www.interest.com/hugh/calc/*
HuskySearch *huskysearch.cs.washington.edu*

HyperBooks *www.hyperbooks.com/submit.html*
ICQ *www.icq.com*
Index to Science Fiction Anthologies and Collections *www.best.com/~contento/*
Inference Find *www.infind.com/infind*
infogranny.com *www.infogranny.com*
InfoSeek *www.infoseek.com*
Inklings *www.inkspot.com/inklings/*
Inkspot *www.inkspot.com*
Inscriptions *come.to/Inscriptions*
Inside Film Magazine **Online: Screenwriting** *www.insidefilm.com/screenwriting.html*
Intellectual Property, Copyright, Patents, Trademarks *www.sil.org/general/copyright.html*
Interactive Grammar Quizzes *webster.commnet.edu/HP/pages/darling/grammar/quiz_list.html-ssi*
International Communication *www.moorhead.msus.edu/~gunarat/ijr/ic.html*
Internet Fantasy Writer's List *www.fantasytoday.com*
Internet Law Simplified *www.online-magazine.com/copyright.htm*
Internet Links for Technical Communication *www.muohio.edu/~mtsccwis/techcommlinks.html*
Internet Press: Dictionaries, The *www.gallery.uunet.be/Internetpress/diction.htm*
Internet Promotions MEGALIST *www.2020tech.com/submit.html*
Internet Sleuth *www.isleuth.com*
Internet Tools for the Advanced Searcher *www.philb.com/adint.htm*
Internet Writing Journal *www.writerswrite.com/journal/*
IRC Undernet Writers Page *www.getset.com/writers*
Jakob Nielsen's Alertbox *www.useit.com/alertbox/*
Jobs in Journalism *eb.journ.latech.edu/jobs-o.html*
John December Technical Communications Information Sources *www.december.com/john/study/*
   techcomm/info.html
John Hewitt's Technical Writing Center *www.azstarnet.com/~poewar/writer/pg/tech.html*
John Kasab's Ars Magica Names Database *www.cae.wisc.edu/~kasab/arm/names*
John Labovitz's E-Zine List *www.meer.net/~johnl/e-zine-list*
Journal of Electronic Publishing *www.press.umich.edu:80/jep/works*
Journalism Resources *www.moorhead.msus.edu/~gunarat/ijr/journalism.html*
Journalism Resources—Outside Canada *www.synapse.net/~radio/jour-oth.htm*
Journalism UK *www.journalismuk.co.uk*
Journalism.Net *www.journalismnet.com/papers.htm*
Journalist Electronic Rights Negotiation Strategies *www.nwu.org/journ/jstrat.htm*
Katharsis *www.katharsis.org*
King's English, The *www.columbia.edu/acis/bartleby/fowler/*
Librarians' Index to the Internet *sunsite.berkeley.edu/InternetIndex/*
Library of Congress *www.loc.gov*
LibrarySpot *www.libraryspot.com/*
Librius.com (Millenium E-reader) *www.librius.com/*
Lida Quillen's List of Epublishers *www.sff.net/people/Lida.Quillen/epub.html*
Linguistic Fun Page, The *www.ojohaven.com/fun/*
Links to Education Resources on the WWW—Citing Internet Sources *www.umass.edu/education/*
   links/cite.html
Links to Electronic Book and Text Sites *www.awa.com/library/omnimedia/links.html*
ListBot *www.listbot.com*
ListServe.com: Publicly Accessible Mailing Lists *www.neosoft.com/internet/paml*
Liszt, the Mailing List Directory *www.liszt.com*
Literary Agents *mockingbird.creighton.edu/NCW/litag.htm*
Literary Agents, Pure Fiction Guide to *www.purefiction.com/pages/usagents.htm*
Literary Times, The *www.tlt.com*
LiteraryAgent.Com *www.literaryagent.com/*
Looksmart *www.looksmart.com*

Lycos *www.lycos.com*
Magazines of Europe *www.travelconnections.com/Magazines/Europeindex.htm*
The Major Search Engines *searchenginewatch.internet.com/facts/major.html*
Market List *www.marketlist.com*
Markets for Writers *www.chebucto.ns.ca/Culture/WFNS/markets.html*
Mary Wolf's Guide to Electronic Publishers *www.coredcs.com/~mermaid/epub.html*
Master Works of Western Civilization *www.eskimo.com/~masonw/gwwc.htm*
Matt's Script Archive *worldwidemart.com/scripts/*
Media and News Resources Around the Globe *www.uct.ac.za/depts/politics/intnew.htm*
Media List *www.webcom.com/~leavitt/medialist.html*
Media UK *www.mediauk.com/directory/*
Medieval Naming Guides *www.panix.com/~mittle/names/*
Meta Medic *www.northernwebs.com/set/setsimjr.html*
META Tags *northernwebs.com/set/*
MetaCrawler *www.metacrawler.com*
Metafind *www.metafind.com*
Michigan Electronic Library: News, Media, and Periodicals *mel.lib.mi.us/news/News-Journal.html*
Mining Co., The *www.miningco.com*
Miscellaneous Writing *www.scalar.com/mw/pages/*
Miscellaneous Web Tools *www.lib.msu.edu/harris23/general/webtools.htm*
Modern and Contemporary American Poetry *www.english.upenn.edu/~afilreis/88/home.html*
Monster.com *www.monsterboard.com*
MountainView Publishing *www.whidbey.com/mountainview*
MSN (Microsoft) Web Communities *communities.msn.com/reading/chat.asp*
Multnomah County Library Electronic Resources *www.multnomah.lib.or.us/lib/ref/quick.html*
My Virtual Reference Desk *www.refdesk.com*
Mysterious Home Page, The *www.webfic.com/mysthome/*
Mystery Connections *emporium.turnpike.net/~mystery/crime_pursuits.html*
Mystery Writers of America *www.mysterynet.com/mwa/*
Mystery Writers' Resources *www.zott.com/mysforum/default.html*
Myths and Facts about S2291 *www.arl.org/info/frn/copy/myth.html*
National Poetry Association *www.slip.net/~gamuse*
National Press Club *npc.press.org*
National Writer's Monthly *www.writersmarkets.com*
National Writers Union *www.nwu.org*
National Writing Centers Association (directory) *departments.colgate.edu/diw/NWCAOWLs.html*
Navigating the Net: E-mail Discussion Lists *www.delphi.com/navnet/faq/listsub.html*
Needle in a CyberStack: The InfoFinder *home.revealed.net/albee/*
New Concepts Publishing *www.newconceptspublishing.com*
New Ezine Directory *foxcities.com/webpromote*
New Marketing Opportunity: Electronic Publishing *www.paintedrock.com/memvis/rockmag/files/rock99-03.txt*
NewJour: New Journals and Newsletters on the Internet *gort.ucsd.edu/newjour/NewJourWel.html*
NewsDirectory.com *www.newsdirectory.com*
Newsdirectory.com: Worldwide Magazines *www.newsdirectory.com/news/magazine/world*
Newshare *newshare.com/Newshare/Common/News/news.html*
Newsletter Access Directory *www.newsletteraccess.com/directory.html*
Newsletter Access *www.newsletteraccess.com*
Newsletter Library, The *www.newsletter-library.com/index.htm*
Newsletter News *Gach98@aol.com*
Newsletters and E-zines *www.copywriter.com/lists/info.html*
Newspapers.com *www.newspapers.com*
Newswise Guide to Journalism Grants and Fellowships 1998-2000 *www.newswise.com/grants.htm*
NovelAdvice *www.noveladvice.com/craft/index.html*

Novelists Inc. *www.ninc.com/tips.htm*
Novice Writer's Guide to Rights *www.writerswrite.com/journal/dec97/cew3.htm*
NuvoMedia (RocketBook E-reader) *www.nuvomedia.com*
OakNet Publishing *Oaknetpub.com*
OmniMedia Digital Publishing *www.awa.com/library/omnimedia/aboutus.html*
On Line English Grammar *www.edunet.com/english/grammar/index.cfm*
ONEList *onelist.com*
One-Look Dictionaries *www.onelook.com*
OneSeek *www.oneseek.com*
On-Line Books Page, The *www.cs.cmu.edu/books.html*
Online Communicator, The *www.communicator.com/writvid.html*
Online Journalist *www.online-journalist.com*
On-Line Lectures *www.idbsu.edu/resource/lectures.htm*
Origins of Phrases *members.aol.com/MorelandC/Phrases.htm*
Overbooked *www.overbooked.org/bklink.html*
Painted Rock Writers and Readers Colony *www.paintedrock.com/conference/confcntr.htm*
Palindromes *www.rdg.ac.uk/~sssbownj/jnwobsss~/ku.ca.gdr.www//:ptth*
Paradox Concepts: Writer's Support Page *members.home.net/wcgrnway/writmain.html*
Petals of Life Publishing *www.petalsoflife.com*
Phrase Finder *www.shu.ac.uk/web-admin/phrases/*
Pitsco's Ask an Expert *www.askanexpert.com*
Playwriting Seminars, The *www.vcu.edu/artweb/playwriting/seminar.html*
Poetry Markets: Current Calls for Manuscripts *newark.rutgers.edu/~lcrew/markets/index.html*
Poetry Resource *www.pmpoetry.com*
Postal Information *dir.yahoo.com/Reference/Postal_Information*
PPPP.Net: Ultimate Collection of Newslinks *pppp.net/links/news/*
Preditors and Editors *www.sfwa.org/prededitors/*
Primer on the Proposed WIPO Treaty on Database Extraction Rights *www.essential.org/cpt/ip/cpt-dbcom.html*
ProfNet *www.profnet.com/profsearchguide.html*
Project Gutenberg *promo.net/pg/index.html*
Proper Manuscript Format *www.shunn.net/format.html*
Proper Use of a Domain Name for Trademark Protection *www.arvic.com/library/domanuse.asp*
Publisher's Marketing Association (PMA) *www.pma-online.org*
Publishing Law and Other Articles of Interest *publaw.com/articles.html*
Publishing: Statistics and Research *publishing.miningco.com/msub21.htm*
Pure Fiction *www.purefiction.com/menus/writing.htm*
Purple Crayon, The *www.users.interport.net/~hdu/*
Query Letter Information *www.accelnet.com/victoria/queries2.html*
Ralan Conley's SpecFic Webstravaganza *members.xoom.com/_XOOM/RalanConley/sf_pro2.htm*
Random Vocabularies or Name Generation Page *www.ruf.rice.edu/~pound/*
Reader's Choice Book Chat *www.thegrid.net/dakaiser/books/chat.htm*
Reference.COM *www.reference.com*
Regency Fashion Page, The *locutus.ucr.edu/~cathy/reg3.html*
Register-It! *www.liquidimaging.com/submit/*
Research-It! *www.iTools.com/research-it/research-it.html*
Resources for Fantasy Writers *www.tipsforwriters.com/fantasy.shtml*
Resources for New Web Authors *darkwing.uoregon.edu/~lincicum/resource.html*
Resources for Tech/Scientific Writers *www.inkspot.com/genres/tech.html*
Resources for Writers *www.execpc.com/~dboals/write.html*
Resources for Writing Instructors *www.devry-phx.edu/lrnresrc/dowsc/instres.htm*
RestStop Writers' Newsletter *www.geocities.com/SoHo/Village/2115/index.html*
Rising Stars on the Electronic Horizon *www.paintedrock.com/memvis/rockmag/files/rock99-10.txt*
River: Resources, The *www.theriver.com/writers/contents.html*

Robin's Nest: Web Site Development *www2.netdoor.com/~smslady/websitedevelop.html*
Romance Authors Page, The *www.nettrends.com/romanceauthors/*
Romance Central *www.romance-central.com*
The Romance Club *www.theromanceclub.com*
Romance Medley's Favorite Links to the Past *members.aol.com/_ht_a/MedPub232/index3.html*
Romance Novel Database *www-personal.sl.umich.edu/~sooty/romance/*
Romance Novels and Women's Fiction: Authors *www.writepage.com/romance.htm*
Romance Writers Exchange RoundTable *gopher://gopher.genie.com:70/00/magazines/romex/about*
Romance Writers Homepage *www.simegen.com/out-t/romance/index.html*
Romance Writers of America *www.rwanational.com*
Romancing the Web *www.romanceweb.com/toc.html*
Rutgers Newark's NJ High School Poetry Contest *newark.rutgers.edu/~lcrew/contest*
Savetz's Unofficial Internet Public Domain Index *www.savetz.com/pd/*
SavvySearch *savvy.cs.colostate.edu*
Scam Alert *www.thewindjammer.com/smfs/newsletter/html/scam_alert.html*
Science Fiction and Fantasy Writers of America (SFWA) *www.sfwa.org/site_index.htp*
Science Fiction Authors *sflovers.rutgers.edu/Web/SFRG/sfrgfa.htm*
Science Fiction Publishers (BookWire Index) *www.bookwire.com/index/SciFict-Publishers.html*
Science Fiction Resource Guide *sf.www.lysator.liu.se/sf_archive/sf-texts/SF_resource_guide/*
Science Fiction Round Table (SFRT) *www.sfrt.com/sfrt2.htm*
Sci-Fi and Fantasy Authors List *www.onelist.com/subscribe/Sci-FiAndFantasyAuth*
Scottish Names Resources *www.abdn.ac.uk/~his016/scotnames/index.html*
Screenwriters and Playwrights Home Page *www.teleport.com/~cdeemer/scrwriter.html*
Screenwriter's Master Chart *members.aol.com/maryjs/scrnrite.htm*
Screenwriters Online Presents: Calendar *screenwriter.com/insider/WritersCalendar.html*
Screenwriters Utopia *www.screenwritersutopia.com*
Screenwriting Resources *home.netvigator.com/~lwgray/writers/links/one.htm*
Screenwriting *screenwriting.miningco.com*
Scriptito's Place *members.aol.com/vangarnews/scriptito.html*
SCRNWRiT *www.panam.edu/scrnwrit*
Search Engine Watch *searchenginewatch.internet.com/facts/major.html*
Search.com *www.search.com*
SearchUK *www.searchuk.com*
Semantic Rhyming Dictionary *www.link.cs.cmu.edu/dougb/rhyme-doc.html*
SF Site *www.sfsite.com*
SFF Net *www.sff.net/*
SFNovelist Workshop *www.crayne.com/victory/sfnovel.html*
SFWA: Statement on Electronic Rights *www.sfwa.org/contracts/ELEC.htm*
SFWA: Workshops *www.sfwa.org/links/workshops.htm*
SharpWriter.Com *www.sharpwriter.com*
Shiki Internet Haiku Salon *milkan.cc.matsuyama-u.ac.jp/~shiki*
Sideroad, The *www.sideroad.com*
Site Inspector *siteinspector.linkexchange.com*
Slush Pile, The *www.theslushpile.com*
So, You Want to Start an E-Zine? *www.zinebook.com/roll.html*
Society for Technical Communication *www.stc-toronto.org*
SoftBook Press *www.softbooks.com*
Softseek.com *soliloquoy.silkthreats.com*
Soliloquoy *members.xoom.com/ellipsis/*
Sources and Experts *metalab.unc.edu/slanews/internet/experts.html*
SPAN *www.SPANnet.org*
Speculative Fiction Contests *www.tipsforwriters.com/contests.shtml*
Speculative Vision *speculativevision.com*
Stone Soup *www.stonesoup.com*

Suggested Agent Checklist for Authors *www.inkspot.com/bt/market/agentlist.html*
Suite101 *www.suite101.com*
SunSITE Collection Index *www.sunsite.unc.edu/collection/*
TableMaker *www.bagism.com/tablemaker/*
TalkCity *www.talkcity.com/communities/art_books.htmpl*
Tara Publishing *www.tarapublishing.com/publish/authpubinfo.mhtml*
Technical Writing *techwriting.miningco.com/*
Telecommuting Jobs for Writers *www.tjobs.com/*
Things You Should Never Do to a Young Writer *www.geocities.com/Athens/8506/never.html*
THOR: The Online Resource *thorplus.lib.purdue.edu/vlibrary/inet_resources*
Tile.Net *tile.net/listserv/*
Time Converter *www.vtourist.com/cgi-bin/tconverter.cgi?lang=0*
Tips for Writers *www.tipsforwriters.com/*
Tools and Tips for Copy Editors *www.uaa.alaska.edu/jpc/copy.html*
Top Ten Mistakes in Web Design *www.useit.com/alertbox/9605.html*
Tracking, Managing, and Citing Resources on the Web *www.wwnorton.com/webworks/ww5.htm*
Travlang *www.travlang.com*
U.S. Copyright Office *lcweb.loc.gov/copyright*
UCLA Online Institute for Cyberspace Law and Policy *www.gseis.ucla.edu/iclp/hp.html*
UCLA *www.onlinelearning.net/w99*
Ultimate Science Fiction Web Guide, The *www.magicdragon.com/UltimateSF/SF-Index.html*
Uncle Orson's Writing Class *www.hatrack.com/writingclass/index.shtml*
Union Institute Research Engine *www.tui.edu/Research/Research.html*
Usable Web: Guide to Web Usability Resources *usableweb.com/index.html*
Use Email Newsletters to Market Your Small Business on the Internet *www.arrowweb.com/graphics/ news/aug98o.html*
Useful Links for Romance Writers and Readers *www.inficad.com/~jacreding/links/index.html*
Usenet and Mailing List Archive *www.reference.com*
Using the Internet for Research (FAQ) *www.purefiction.com/pages/res1.htm*
UVic Writer's Guide *webserver.maclab.comp.uvic.ca/writersguide/*
Virtual Promote *www.virtualpromote.com/*
Vivian's "List of Lists" *www.catalog.com/vivian/interest-group-search.html*
Web Authoring Resources *www.wwscribe.com/resource.htm*
Web of On-Line Dictionaries *www.facstaff.bucknell.edu/~rbeard/diction.html*
Web Search Tools *www.moorhead.msus.edu/~gunarat/ijr/tools.html*
Web Style Guide *info.med.yale.edu/caim/manual/contents.html*
Web Wonk: Tips for Writers and Designers *www.dsiegel.com/tips/index.html*
WebCrawler *www.webcrawler.com*
Webmaster's Guide to Search Engines *searchenginewatch.internet.com/webmasters/*
Webrings for Writers *www.webring.org/cgi-bin/ringworld/arts/hum.html*
Websites for Journalists *www.toad.net/~arandrew/majors.html*
Websites with a Newspaper Connection *MindyMcAdams.com/jaccess/*
WebTopics *www.dimensional.com/~janf/wtwriting.html*
Western Writers of America *www.imt.net/~gedison/wwahome.html*
What is the Rocket E-book? *www.barnesandnoble.com/help/rocketbooks.asp*
What's in Your Name? *www.kabalarians.com/gkh/your.htm*
Who Owns the Copyright in Your Web Site? *www.ivanhoffmann.com/website.html*
Why Sell Your Book to an Electronic Publisher? *www.eclectics.com/articles/ebooks2.htm*
Willcam's Comprehensive HTML Cross Reference *www.willcam.com/cmat/html/*
Woman's Writing Retreat: Authors (female) *www.prairieden.com/links/women.html*
Woman's Writing Retreat: Authors (male) *www.prairieden.com/links/men.html*
Word Museum *www.wordmuseum.com*
WordNet 1.6 Vocabulary Helper *www.notredame.ac.jp/cgi-bin/wn*
WordsWorth Author Internet Site *www.wordsworth.com/*

Working List of Speculative Fiction Markets *www.bayarea.net/~stef/sf-markets.txt*

World Lecture Hall: English, Writing, and Rhetoric *www.utexas.edu/world/lecture/e/*

World Wide Web Virtual Library: Theatre and Drama *www.vl-theatre.com/index.htm*

WorldWideWeb Acronym and Abbreviation Server *www.ucc.ie/info/net/acronyms/acro.html*

The Write Markets Report *www.writersmarkets.com*

Write Tools: Editors' and Writers' Toolkit *writetools.com*

WriteLinks *www.writelinks.com*

Writepage *www.writepage.com*

Writer Beware *www.sfwa.org/Beware/*

Writer On Line *www.novalearn.com/wol/*

Writeria: Online Workshops *wkgroup.com/zeugma/writeria/workshops.html*

Writer's Associations (U.S. and Canada) *www.inkspot.com/network/assoc.html*

The Writer's BBS, The *www.writers-bbs.com/chat.html*

Writer's Block *www.niva.com/writblok*

Writers Club University *www.writersclub.com/wcu/catalog.cfm*

Writers' Colonies *mockingbird.creighton.edu/ncw/colonies.htm*

Writer's Digest *www.writersdigest.com*

Writers Groups and Organizations *www.forwriters.com/groups.html*

Writers' Groups *www.writers.com/groups.htm*

Writer's Guidelines (*The Write Markets Report*) *www.writersmarkets.com/index-guidelines.htm*

Writers' Guidelines Database *mav.net/guidelines/*

Writers Guild of America *www.wga.org*

Writer's Internet Exchange *www.writelinks.com/write/index.html*

Writer's List *web.mit.edu/mbarker/www/*

Writers of the Future *www.authorservicesinc.com/wof_ruls.htm*

Writers on the Net *www.writers.com/newsletter.htm*

The Writer's Place, The *www.awoc.com/AWOC-Home.cfm*

Writer's Pocket Tax Guide *www.nyx.net/~dycpser/wptge99.html*

Writer's Toolbox: Internet Resources for Writers *www.geocities.com/Athens/6346/*

Writer's Village University *4-writers.com*

Writers Write *www.writerswrite.com*

Writers Write University *www.writerswrite.com*

Writer'sClub.com Chat Schedule *chat.writersclub.com*

Writing Contest Tips *www.ult-media.com/tips1.htm*

Writing for DOLLARS! *www.awoc.com*

Writing for the Web *www.electric-pages.com/articles/wftw1.htm*

Writing for the Web: A New Resource for Writers *www.wwwscribe.com/webwrite.htm*

Writing for Webzines: Brave New Markets, Same Old Problems *www.nwu.org/aw/97wint/online.htm*

Writing Labs and Writing Centers on the Web *owl.english.purdue.edu/owls/writing-labs.html*

WWWebster Dictionary *www.m-w.com/info/info.htm*

Xlibris *www.xlibris.com/html/publishing_your_book.html*

Yahoo! *www.yahoo.com*

Yahoo!: Magazines *search.yahoo.com/bin/search?p=magazines*

Yahoo!s Guide to Electronic Publishers *dir.yahoo.com/Business_and_Economy/Companies/Publishing/ Electronic_Publishing/*

Young Writers Club *www.cs.bilkent.edu.tr/~david/derya/about.htm*

Young Writers' Clubhouse *www.realkids.com/club.shtml*

Zeno's Forensic Page *users.bart.nl/~geradts/forensic.html*

Zine and E-Zine Resource Guide *www.zinebook.com/resour1.html*

Zine and Noted's Ezine Resource Guide *www.mediacentral.com/Magazines/Folio/Zines/resources.htm*

Zine-World *www.oblivion.net/zineworld/*

Zuzu's Petals Literary Resource: Organizations of Interest to Poets and Writers *www.zuzu.com/wrt-org.htm*

Zuzu's Petals Literary Resources *www.zuzu.com*

Index

Books from Allworth Press

The Internet Research Guide, Revised Edition
by Timothy K. Maloy (softcover, 6 × 9, 208 pages, $18.95)

The Writer's Internet Handbook
by Timothy K. Maloy (softcover, 6 × 9, 192 pages, $18.95)

Writing for Interactive Media: The Complete Guide
by Jon Samsel and Darryl Wimberley (hardcover, 6 × 9, 320 pages, $19.95)

Marketing Strategies for Writers
by Michael Sedge (softcover, 6 × 9, 224 pages, $16.95)

The Writer's Legal Guide, Second Edition
by Tad Crawford and Tony Lyons (hardcover, 6 × 9, 320 pages, $19.95)

Business and Legal Forms for Authors and Self-Publishers, Revised Edition
by Tad Crawford (softcover, includes CD-ROM, 8½ × 11, 192 pages, $22.95)

The Writer's and Photographer's Guide to Global Markets
by Michael Sedge (hardcover, 6 × 9, 288 pages, $19.95)

Photography for Writers: Using Photography to Increase Your Writing Income *by Michael Havelin* (softcover, 6 × 9, 224 pages, $18.95)

This Business of Publishing: An Insider's View of Current Trends and Tactics *by Richard Curtis* (softcover, 6 × 9, 224 pages, $18.95)

How to Write Books That Sell, Second Edition
by L. Perry Wilbur and Jon Samsel (hardcover, 6 × 9, 224 pages, $19.95)

How to Write Articles That Sell, Second Edition
by L. Perry Wilbur and Jon Samsel (hardcover, 6 × 9, 224 pages, $19.95)

The Writer's Guide to Corporate Communications
by Mary Moreno (softcover, 6 × 9, 192 pages, $18.95)

Please write to request our free catalog. To order by credit card, call 1-800-491-2808 or send a check or money order to Allworth Press, 10 East 23rd Street, Suite 210, New York, NY 10010. Include $5 for shipping and handling for the first book ordered and $1 for each additional book. Ten dollars plus $1 for each additional book if ordering from Canada. New York State residents must add sales tax.

To see our complete catalog on the World Wide Web, or to order online, you can find us at *www.allworth.com.*